THE POLITICAL WRITINGS OF
THOMAS JEFFERSON

THE POLITICAL WRITINGS OF
THOMAS JEFFERSON

Edited by
Merrill D. Peterson

THOMAS JEFFERSON MEMORIAL FOUNDATION

Monticello Monograph Series

The Thomas Jefferson Memorial Foundation, Inc.

Supported by a grant from The Pew Charitable Trusts.
This publication is made possible by a gift from Mr. and Mrs. Martin S. Davis.

Copyright © 1993 by Thomas Jefferson Memorial Foundation, Inc.

Designed by Gibson Design Associates.
Printed by GraphTec, Annapolis Junction, Maryland.

H G F E D C
ISBN 1-882886-01-1

NOTE

The selections in this volume are organized, with minor exceptions, chronologically according to date of the writing. Precisely because Jefferson's political thought eludes systematic analysis, any attempt to organize it topically must encounter serious problems. The present arrangement, for all its deficiencies, reflects the fact that Jefferson's thought developed in response to his experience and in the flow of a life engaged in public affairs. The editor has given titles to writings otherwise lacking them. All the texts are derived from standard editions on Jefferson's writings, of which the most inclusive are the following: *The Writings of Thomas Jefferson*, Paul L. Ford, ed., 10 vols. (New York, 1892-99). *The Writings of Thomas Jefferson*, A. A. Lipscomb and A. E. Bergh, eds., 20 vols. (Washington, 1903-04). *The Papers of Thomas Jefferson*, Julian P. Boyd, *et al*, ed., 24 vols. to date (Princeton, 1950-92). See also the present editor's *Thomas Jefferson: Writings* in the Library of America (New York, 1984). The Library of America also should be recognized for granting permission to use the texts included in this work that appear in Jefferson's *Writings*.

CONTENTS

INTRODUCTION

*F*rom the time he took his seat in the Virginia House of Burgesses in 1769, as the twenty-six-year-old delegate from Albemarle County, until his retirement as President of the United States forty years later, Thomas Jefferson was intimately concerned in the affairs of the emerging American nation. Nor did it end then. During seventeen years in retirement the Sage of Monticello remained a servant and a spokesman of American freedom, democracy, enlightenment, and nationhood. His death on July 4th, 1826, the fiftieth anniversary of the Declaration of Independence (which he wrote), was symbolically important. It dramatized the central theme of a life devoted to the principles and ideals—"the self-evident truths"—proclaimed in that manifesto, and made his life a monument to the creed of the American nation born in 1776.

Jefferson thus found his place in history as a philosopher-statesman identified with the revolutionary experiment in America. He was, in truth, somewhat less than a philosopher, at least in any formal sense, and much more than a statesman. In his youth "a hard student," as he said, Jefferson developed a love of books and learning. To this he brought native intelligence, omnivorous curiosity, and relentless industry. He became a prodigy of talents, remembered as the multifaceted "Renaissance man," not only a statesman but a scientist, architect, agriculturalist, geographer, linguist, educator, inventor, and man of letters. Nature had destined him for the arts and sciences, he always said, but swept up in the democratic revolution that defined his age, he gave his talents and his energies to the task of launching the experiment of free government in his new country. He became successively a legislator, a governor, an ambassador, a secretary of state, a vice president, and president; and in these several positions a writer of important state papers, a draftsman of landmark legislation, a political leader, and persuasive advocate.

Jefferson never found the occasion, and probably never felt the desire, to reduce his thoughts about man and nature, or society and government, to a system. He had an aversion to cosmic philosophizing. His intellectual bent was activist, pragmatic, and utilitarian. He distinguished himself in the work of implementing the principles and advancing the goals of the American Revolution through education, laws, and institutions. This was not the work for ivory-towered philosophers but for men of affairs. It was work, moreover, that had to be revised and readjusted to meet the challenge of changing historical forces and events. In meeting these challenges Jefferson sometimes seemed to contradict himself. The most famous instance was his acceptance of the Louisiana Purchase Treaty, in 1803, despite his conviction that it made "blank paper of the Constitution" he had insisted should be strictly construed. But all his other values and goals were promoted by that grand acquisition; and Jefferson's political thought, when viewed in the shifting contexts of history, reveals a pattern of consistency that truly makes hobgoblins of apparent inconsistencies.

The one book that Jefferson wrote, *Notes on the State of Virginia*, first published in Paris in 1785, offers the best introduction to the whole range of his mind. In this book—an intellectual voyage of discovery of his native land—Jefferson freely expressed his opinions on such subjects as the Virginia constitution, religious freedom, slavery, education, the virtues of husbandry, and the vices of cities. For the most part, however, Jefferson's thought must be pieced together, like a mosaic, from numerous observations and reflections in state papers, reports, addresses, memoranda, and, above all, thousands of letters, some of which are brilliant little essays on topics as diverse as the natural aristocracy and "the sovereignty of the living generation." Even in his travel notes Jefferson could not refrain from political observation, as in his advice to Lafayette, written from the south of France in 1787, to "ferret the people out of their hovels as I have done, look into their kettles, eat their bread, loll on their beds under the pretense of resting yourself, but in fact to find if they are soft," all with a view to hereafter applying your knowledge "to the softening of their beds, or the throwing a morsel of meat into the kettle of vegetables."

The principal sources of Jefferson's political thought lay, first, in the history and traditions of English law and government and, second, in the modern philosophy of the Enlightenment. Educated for the law, he made a special study of the English constitution, generally esteemed before 1776 as the freest in the world. With the Whigs in England he traced its best elements back to the primitive Saxons, who had introduced an annual assembly of tribal chiefs—the forerunner of Parliament—fee simple land tenure, trial by jury, and the common law. The polity was prefeudal. It was overthrown by the Norman Conquest, and English history henceforth became a recurring struggle to recover the liberty and self-government of the ancient constitution. Jefferson encountered this Saxon myth in the writings of legal commentators, historians, and belligerently libertarian Whigs like Algernon Sidney and the pamphleteer authors of the "Cato Letters," John Trenchard and Thomas Gordon. The Tory witness against this Whig view was David Hume's celebrated *History of England*, a work that, in Jefferson's opinion, had undermined the free principles of the English constitution, yet exercised such a "seductive influence," even in America, that Jefferson struggled all his life to combat it. The esteemed genius of the English constitution in the eighteenth century lay in its mixture or balance of the three great orders of hierarchical society (royalty, nobility, and populace) as embodied in a government of King, Lords, and Commons. Each order represented a distinctive political principle—monarchy, aristocracy, democracy—the one, the few, and the many—working like some marvelous Newtonian machine of reciprocating attractions and repulsions to maintain order in the state and liberty for the subjects. Jefferson, with other colonial leaders, had admired this theory and looked to the balance of the English constitution to preserve their own liberties. Alas, as Americans came to realize, the machine had broken down: the three orders, instead of checking and balancing each other, combined to make the government an engine of tyranny. In 1774, in his important pamphlet, *A Summary View of the Rights of British America*, Jefferson appealed to the king for protection from a tyrannical parliament. His appeal failed, of course, and in 1776 the same indictment was laid against George III.

The Declaration of Independence put an end to the need Jefferson, with other patriots, previously felt to justify American claims under English law. They were now free to enter the new rational world of political ideas of the Enlightenment. The transition is particularly striking in Jefferson; increasingly, though not all at once and never completely, he conformed his ideas to the canons of the Enlightenment. For Jefferson this was a movement from history to theory, from law to nature, from the localism and particularism of the English tradition to the rationalism and universalism of the Enlightenment. The spirit of the Enlightenment was one of criticism of received truths and of untrammeled free inquiry in the pursuit of knowledge. "Knowledge is power," Francis Bacon had said; and Jefferson was never more typically a child of the Enlightenment than in his optimistic conviction that reason and inquiry may lead men away from whatever is false, twisted, or capricious in human affairs toward the truths inherent in the nature of things. Man had been too long alienated from nature. For centuries he had been dominated by dogmatic authority and superstition. Now these false idols were crumbling and man might take control of his destiny by discovering the laws of nature and putting them to the service of the species. Jefferson's heroes were neither statesmen nor warriors but philosophers, in particular Bacon, Newton, and Locke, the trinity upon whom the edifice of the Enlightenment was raised. John Locke was especially important for Jefferson's political thought. The natural rights philosophy of the great preamble of the Declaration of Independence came in considerable part from Locke's *Second Treatise on Civil Government*. From his exposure at college to the English and Scottish rationalists, Jefferson turned to the Continental votaries of the Enlightenment, to Voltaire, Montesquieu, Holbach, Helvetius, Beccaria, and others. And when in the 1780s he took up residence in Paris, the capital of the Enlightenment, he became something of a *philosophe* himself.

Another tradition upon which Jefferson drew was that of ancient literature and philosophy. But he read the classical authors in the context of the modern world view. With other men of the Enlightenment he found in pagan Greece and Rome a basis for a critical perspective on his own age, one that exhibited ideals of learning, beauty, virtue, and furnished a whole armory of weapons for the assault on mystery and authority both civil and ecclesiastical. In his youth, Jefferson thought the moral teachings of Epicurus, Cicero, Seneca, and other ancients superior to those of Jesus, though he later changed this opinion. In his architecture he went back to Roman antiquity for his models; again, however, the spirit of this neoclassicism was innovative and modern. He revived classical architecture because in that, rather than in the vernacular of his own time and place, he found a conception of beauty as universal, chaste, and orderly as the Newtonian laws of motion. Perhaps, too, he felt a neoclassical aesthetic would communicate an ideal of citizenship associated with the Roman republic. But Jefferson had a poor opinion of ancient political philosophy and of ancient governments. For the most part, he thought, they only offered admonitions against what not to do.

The most important themes of Jefferson's political discourse deserve some definition and comment by way of introduction.

Human Rights. Jefferson and his fellow revolutionaries described these as the natural and inalienable rights of man. All men are created equal in the sense that all are equal in the order of nature and none is dependent on the will of another. Governments are instituted to secure the rights of life, liberty, and the pursuit of happiness, and while they may be further defined and regulated, citizens may not be deprived of them. Citizenship itself, in Jefferson's view, was a natural right: a person might freely acquire it or resign it. The individualism of the doctrine assumed the natural sociability of mankind, indeed the fundamental goodness of human nature. Jefferson postulated an innate moral sense in man which leads to virtuous actions and advances the happiness of others. (See, for example, his letter to Thomas Law in 1814.) Locke's phrasing of the inalienable rights was "life, liberty, and property." By substituting for the last of these "the pursuit of happiness," Jefferson altered the hierarchy of human values. At the same time, he withheld the mantle of protection from such unnatural forms of property as slaves. The assertion of the twin principles of equality and natural rights in the presence of African slavery, and by the pen of a Virginia slaveholder, has always seemed an expression of hypocrisy. Although Jefferson was fundamentally opposed to slavery and acted to curb it, its abolition never rose to the top of his political agenda, and his speculation "hazarding" the inferiority of the Negro race stood in blatant contradiction to his belief in the unity of the human species.

Constitutions. The unhappy colonial experience with the unwritten English constitution led the American founders to invent the idea of a written constitution as the means of giving firmness, permanence, and supremacy to the fundamental law. Jefferson was in the vanguard of this development. In the Declaration of Independence he laid down the principle that governments derive their just powers from "the consent of the governed." Just how the people might establish a government over themselves, and over the rulers, was unclear. Political theory was silent on the process to implement the principle. While Jefferson was drafting the Declaration of Independence in Philadelphia, however, Virginians were meeting in convention at Williamsburg to draw up a constitution for the new commonwealth. He eagerly forwarded his own draft, but it arrived too late for serious consideration. Henceforth he was an outspoken critic of that frame of government and sought repeatedly, without success, to replace it. In part, this was because he thought it too conservative in its provisions. His own draft was more liberal in important respects and would have accomplished at one stroke certain reforms, such as disestablishment of the Anglican Church, that were finally accomplished only after years of protracted struggle. No less significantly, Jefferson thought the Virginia constitution flunked the test of republican legitimacy. The convention, so called, had not been properly constituted to form a government, nor had the people consented to its work. Jefferson was not being frivolous; he was groping toward the conception of the sovereign authority of the people embodied in an appropriate convention, and of popular ratification of the constitution thus proposed. He had actually set forth a form of popular ratification in his draft constitution, together with provision for future amendment with the consent of the governed, both unprecedented in the constitution-making of 1776. Jefferson was a strong advocate of periodic amendment and revision of constitutions to see that they advanced "hand in hand with the progress of the human mind." The idea of "the sovereignty of the living generation," first expounded in a letter to James Madison at the onset of the French Revolution, was the most radical expression of this outlook, though it contemplated more than constitutional change. The corollary of ongoing popular consent to the fundamental law was a strict construction of the law in being. This became a political issue, and Jefferson suffered defeat at the hands of Alexander Hamilton and John Marshall with their doctrine of "implied powers."

Bills of Rights. Most of the new state constitutions were accompanied by bills (or declarations) of rights. The aim was to codify the most fundamental human rights and liberties and thereby better secure them against civil authority. Much of Jefferson's thinking on this subject revolved around religious freedom. His Virginia Statute for Religious Freedom, which became the law in 1786, secured the twin principles of freedom of religious conscience and separation of church and state. The statute was also an exultant manifesto of the freedom of the human mind and spirit. Through the efforts of James Madison, his constant collaborator, the same principles were embodied in the "free exercise" clause of the First Amendment of the United States Constitution, becoming, in the words of a Supreme Court justice, "warp and woof of our constitutional tradition." Jefferson's persuasive rhetoric, addressed to Madison from his post in

Paris, helped to convince him that a bill of rights should be added to the Constitution, and it was mainly because of Madison's efforts in the First Congress that this was done. Jefferson's deep concern for the freedom of speech, press, and assembly arose, on the one hand, from the value he placed on freedom of inquiry, whether in science or religion or politics, and on the other hand, from the very nature of a government based upon public opinion.

Federalism. Jefferson held that a free republican government in a country as large as the United States must of necessity be federal. It should rise like a pyramid from a broad foundation in the local communities. During the Revolution he advocated in Virginia the creation of new units of local government, called wards, which among other things would be responsible for the public schools he wanted. Every man should be made to feel that he is a participant in civil affairs, and this must begin at the local level. After the establishment of a new and stronger national government under the Constitution, Jefferson appeared as an advocate of state rights. Whereas before, during the Confederation, the encroachments had come from the states, now the danger came from consolidation in the federal head. "What," he asked, "has destroyed liberty and the rights of man in every government under the sun? The generalizing and concentrating of all cares and power in one body." With an avowed monarchist like Alexander Hamilton in the driver's seat of the new government, Jefferson feared that it would be returned by degrees to the English model. The way to meet the danger, as he wrote in 1791, was not to weaken the central government but to strengthen the state governments that could block encroachments. After the passage of the Alien and Sedition Laws in 1798, during the administration of John Adams, Jefferson drafted the Kentucky Resolutions, adopted by the legislature of that state, to protest the constitutionality of these laws and to rally opposition to them. These resolutions, along with others drafted by Madison in Virginia, were the first authoritative expositions of state rights doctrine under the Constitution.

Democratic Government. Beginning with the proposition that government rested upon the will of the people, questions arose on how that will should be organized and expressed. Who should have the suffrage? How should representation be apportioned? What limits, if any, should be placed upon organized political opposition outside the constituted channels of authority? Jefferson's thought ranged over all these questions. In general, he took a liberal view in advance of the opinion of the time. While he did not propose universal white manhood suffrage in his draft constitution of 1776, he would have achieved that, virtually, by the grant of sufficient landed property to everyone to satisfy the existing freehold requirement. He never ceased agitation against the inequality of representation under the Virginia constitution. He would surely have approved the "one man, one vote" ideal of contemporary democracy. One of the intellectual obstacles the American republicans overcame with difficulty was the traditional association of political representation with different classes or interests in society, for instance, basing the more popular lower house of the legislature on population and the more aristocratic upper house on property. As the problem was overcome, the theory of separation of powers—the functional separation of executive, legislative, and judicial authorities—was disentangled from the older theory of balanced government. Jefferson, of course, championed separation of powers; however, at least in the federal government, he was uncomfortable with the power exercised by the judiciary appointed to life tenure and wholly independent of the will of the people. He was elected president in 1800 as the candidate of an organized political party, the Republican party, standing in opposition to the regnant Federalist party. He called his victory "the revolution of 1800" because it marked the first time an opposition party, organized in the electorate, and competing against the ruling power, won control of the government through the democratic process of free election. Whether or not Jefferson foresaw, or wished for, a regular two-party system such as developed a quarter-century later is uncertain. There can be no doubt, however, that he grew more democratic in his political opinions as the years passed. In his correspondence he actually began to employ the word *democracy* in place of the ubiquitous *republicanism* to describe his favored form of government. Thus in 1816 he told Dupont de Nemours, "We of the United States, you know, are constitutionally and conscientiously democrats," and he wrote John Taylor that the measure of republicanism is "the control of the people over the organs of government."

Education. Jefferson was unusual, even prophetic, in his belief that education of all the citizens was a paramount responsibility of republican government. In 1778 he drafted his Bill for the More General Diffusion of Knowledge, which laid out a complete plan of public education. Eight years later, crushed by the legislature's rejection of the plan, he warned of the political consequences of so shortsighted an act. The preamble of the bill defined two leading objects: first, "to illuminate so far as practicable, the minds of the people at large," as the most effectual agent to secure free government; and second, to ensure "that those persons, whom nature hath endowed with genius and virtue, should be rendered by liberal education worthy to receive, and able to guard … the rights and liberties of their fellow citizens." In Jefferson's mind there was no incompatibility between the two objects: rudimentary education for the mass of citizens and superior cultivation of the "natural aristocracy." Education, like science, was progressive. As it improved and accumulated from generation to generation, it must, Jefferson said, "advance the knowledge and well-being of mankind, not infinitely, as some have said, but indefinitely, and to a term which no man can fix and foresee."

International Order. Jefferson was a student of the law of nations and a proponent of the "new diplomacy" of the Enlightenment, with its emphasis on fairness, peace, and openness in international affairs. Ten years of his life, 1784-1793, were devoted primarily to the foreign affairs of the new nation; his presidency was finally consumed by a crisis with Great Britain. As secretary of state in 1792, after the establishment of the French Republic, he formulated the principle of diplomatic recognition that was consonant with the principle upon which the United States was founded, that is, the will of the nation substantially declared. From the American Revolution forward, he championed freedom of trade both in the national interest and in the interest of international peace and friendship. Great Britain was his principal antagonist. Much of Jefferson's thinking in both foreign and domestic policy, including his support for the French Revolution in Europe, was conditioned by the need, as he saw it, to combat the power and influence of the former mother country. One of his most important ideas was that of "peaceable coercion," wherein he maintained that by the granting or withholding of its commerce the United States could introduce among nations "another umpire than arms." Alas, when finally put to the test by the Embargo Law in the foreign crisis of his presidency, the policy of peaceable coercion failed.

— MERRILL D. PETERSON

Thomas Jefferson
A Brief Chronology

1743	Born April 13 at Shadwell, Goochland (now Albemarle) County, Virginia.
1760–62	Attended the College of William and Mary in the capital, Williamsburg.
1767	Admitted to the bar.
1769	Began building his home, Monticello.
1769–76	Member of the House of Burgesses for Albemarle County.
1772	Married Martha Wayles Skelton, January 1; daughter Martha born September 27.
1774	Drafted proposed Instructions to the Virginia Delegates in the Continental Congress, published as *A Summary View of the Rights of British America*.
1775	Attended Continental Congress, in Philadelphia, as a Virginia delegate.
1776	Drafted a constitution for Virginia, and authored the Declaration of Independence.
1776–79	Member of the Virginia Assembly; appointed to a Committee to Revise the Laws of the Commonwealth, which reported in 1779.
1779–81	Governor of the Commonwealth.
1782	Martha Wayles Jefferson died after birth of sixth child.
1783–84	Attended Continental Congress; drafted plan of government for the western territory.
1784	Appointed minister plenipotentiary to a commission in Paris to negotiate treaties of amity and commerce with European states.
1785	*Notes on the State of Virginia* published in a private edition in Paris.
1785–89	United States Minister to France.

1786	The Statute of Virginia for Religious Freedom, drafted in 1777, enacted into law.
1787	*Notes on the State of Virginia* published by Stackpole in England, and in the first American edition, Philadelphia, the next year.
1790–93	Secretary of State.
1792	Viewed as the leader in the cabinet of an opposition party taking form in Congress.
1794–97	Farmed at Monticello and began to rebuild the mansion.
1797–1801	Vice President of the United States; also president of the American Philosophical Society, to 1814.
1798	Drafted the Kentucky Resolutions in response to the Alien and Sedition Laws.
1801–09	President of the United States.
1803	Made the Louisiana Purchase and launched the Lewis and Clark Expedition.
1807	Signed into law the Embargo Act he recommended.
1809–26	In retirement at Monticello.
1814	Revived plan of public education in Virginia.
1818	Wrote the report of the Rockfish Gap Commission recommending the plan of the University of Virginia, chartered the following year.
1819–26	Rector of the Board of Visitors of the University of Virginia.
1821	Wrote an autobiography for the information of his family.
1826	Died on July 4 at Monticello.

A Summary View of
the Rights of British America (1774)

RESOLVED, that it be an instruction to the said deputies, when assembled in general congress with the deputies from the other states of British America, to propose to the said congress that an humble and dutiful address be presented to his majesty, begging leave to lay before him, as chief magistrate of the British empire, the united complaints of his majesty's subjects in America....

    ... To remind him that our ancestors, before their emigration to America, were the free inhabitants of the British dominions in Europe, and possessed a right which nature has given to all men, of departing from the country in which chance, not choice, has placed them, of going in quest of new habitations, and of there establishing new societies, under such laws and regulations as to them shall seem most likely to promote public happiness. That their Saxon ancestors had, under this universal law, in like manner left their native wilds and woods in the north of Europe, had possessed themselves of the island of Britain, then less charged with inhabitants, and had established there that system of laws which has so long been the glory and protection of that country. Nor was ever any claim of superiority or dependence asserted over them by that mother country from which they had migrated; and were such a claim made, it is believed that his majesty's subjects in Great Britain have too firm a feeling of the rights derived to them from their ancestors, to bow down the sovereignty of their state before such visionary pretensions. And it is thought that no circumstance has occurred to distinguish materially the British from the Saxon emigration. America was conquered, and her settlements made, and firmly established, at the expence of individuals, and not of the British public. Their own blood was spilt in acquiring lands for their settlement, their own fortunes expended in making that settlement effectual; for themselves they fought, for themselves they conquered, and for themselves alone they have right to hold. Not a shilling was ever issued from the public treasures of his majesty, or his ancestors, for their assistance, till of very late times, after the colonies had become established on a firm and permanent footing. That then, indeed, having become valuable to Great Britain for her commercial purposes, his parliament was pleased to lend them assistance against an enemy, who would fain to have drawn to herself the benefits of their commerce, to the great aggrandizement of herself, and danger of Great Britain. Such assistance, and in such circumstances, they had often before given to Portugal, and other allied states, with whom they carry on a commercial intercourse; yet these states never supposed, that by calling in her aid, they thereby submitted themselves to her sovereignty. Had such terms been proposed, they would have rejected them with disdain, and trusted for better to the moderation of their enemies, or to a vigorous exertion of their own force. We do not, however, mean to under-rate those aids, which to us were doubtless valuable, on whatever principles granted; but we would shew that they cannot give a title to that authority which the British parliament would arrogate over us, and that they may amply be repaid by our giving to the inhabitants of Great Britain such exclusive privileges in trade as may be advantageous to them, and at the same time not too restrictive to ourselves. That settlements having been thus effected in the wilds of America, the emigrants thought proper to adopt that system of laws under which they had hitherto lived in the mother country, and to continue their union with her by submitting themselves to the same common sovereign, who was thereby made the central link connecting the several parts of the empire thus newly multiplied....

Open your breast, sire, to liberal and expanded thought. Let not the name of George the third be a blot in the page of history. You are surrounded by British counsellors, but remember that they are parties. You have no ministers for American affairs, because you have none taken from among us, nor amenable to the laws on which they are to give you advice. It behoves you, therefore, to think and to act for yourself and your people. The great principles of right and wrong are legible to every reader; to pursue them requires not the aid of many counsellors. The whole art of government consists in the art of being honest....

The God who gave us life gave us liberty at the same time; the hand of force may destroy, but cannot disjoin them. This, sire, is our last, our determined resolution; and that you will be pleased to interpose with that efficacy which your earnest endeavours may ensure to procure redress of these our great grievances, to quiet the minds of your subjects in British America, against any apprehensions of future encroachment, to establish fraternal love and harmony through the whole empire, and that these may continue to the latest ages of time, is the fervent prayer of all British America!

❦

The Declaration of Independence (1776)*

When in the course of human events it becomes necessary for one people to dissolve the political bands which have connected them with another, and to assume among the powers of the earth the separate & equal station to which the laws of nature and of nature's God entitle them, a decent respect to the opinions of mankind requires that they should declare the causes which impel them to the separation.

We hold these truths to be self-evident: that all men are created equal; that they are endowed by their creator with *inherent and* inalienable rights; that among these are life, liberty, & the pursuit of happiness: that to secure these rights, governments are instituted among men, deriving their just powers from the consent of the governed; that whenever any form of government becomes destructive of these ends, it is the right of the people to alter or abolish it, & to institute new government, laying it's foundation on such principles, & organizing it's powers in such form, as to them shall seem most likely to effect their safety & happiness. Prudence indeed will dictate that governments long established should not be changed for light & transient causes; and accordingly all experience hath shown that mankind are more disposed to suffer while evils are sufferable, than to right themselves by abolishing the forms to which they are accustomed. But when a long train of abuses & usurpations *begun at a distinguished period and* pursuing invariably the same object, evinces a design to reduce them under absolute despotism, it is their right, it is their duty to throw off such government, & to provide new guards for their future security. Such has been the patient sufferance of these colonies; & such is now the necessity which constrains them to *expunge* their former systems of government. The history of the present king of Great Britain is a history of *unremitting* injuries & usurpations, *among which appears no solitary fact to con-*

---

*The Declaration is printed here in the form Jefferson gave it in his Autobiography (1821). The parts struck by Congress from the document reported are in italics; the parts inserted are enclosed in brackets.

tradict the uniform tenor of the rest but all have in direct object the establishment of an absolute tyranny over these states. To prove this let facts be submitted to a candid world *for the truth of which we pledge a faith yet unsullied by falsehood.*

He has refused his assent to laws the most wholesome & necessary for the public good.

He has forbidden his governors to pass laws of immediate & pressing importance, unless suspended in their operation till his assent should be obtained; & when so suspended, he has utterly neglected to attend to them.

He has refused to pass other laws for the accommodation of large districts of people, unless those people would relinquish the right of representation in the legislature, a right inestimable to them, & formidable to tyrants only.

He has called together legislative bodies at places unusual, uncomfortable, and distant from the depository of their public records, for the sole purpose of fatiguing them into compliance with his measures.

He has dissolved representative houses repeatedly *& continually* for opposing with manly firmness his invasions on the rights of the people.

He has refused for a long time after such dissolutions to cause others to be elected, whereby the legislative powers, incapable of annihilation, have returned to the people at large for their exercise, the state remaining in the meantime exposed to all the dangers of invasion from without & convulsions within.

He has endeavored to prevent the population of these states; for that purpose obstructing the laws for naturalization of foreigners, refusing to pass others to encourage their migrations hither, & raising the conditions of new appropriations of lands.

He has *suffered* the administration of justice *totally to cease in some of these states* refusing his assent to laws for establishing judiciary powers.

He has made *our* judges dependant on his will alone, for the tenure of their offices, & the amount & paiment of their salaries.

He has erected a multitude of new offices *by a self assumed power* and sent hither swarms of new officers to harass our people and eat out their substance.

He has kept among us in times of peace standing armies *and ships of war* without the consent of our legislatures.

He has affected to render the military independant of, & superior to the civil power.

He has combined with others to subject us to a jurisdiction foreign to our constitutions & unacknowledged by our laws, giving his assent to their acts of pretended legislation for quartering large bodies of armed troops among us; for protecting them by a mock-trial from punishment for any murders which they should commit on the inhabitants of these states; for cutting off our trade with all parts of the world; for imposing taxes on us without our consent; for depriving us [in many cases] of the benefits of trial by jury; for transporting us beyond seas to be tried for pretended offences; for abolishing the free system of English laws in a neighboring province, establishing therein an arbitrary government, and enlarging it's boundaries, so as to render it at once an example and fit instrument for introducing the same absolute rule into these *states;* for taking away our charters, abolishing our most valuable laws, and altering fundamentally the forms of our governments; for suspending our own legislatures, & declaring themselves invested with power to legislate for us in all cases whatsoever.

He has abdicated government here *withdrawing his governors, and declaring us out of his allegiance & protection.*

He has plundered our seas, ravaged our coasts, burnt our towns, & destroyed the lives of our people.

He is at this time transporting large armies of foreign mercenaries to compleat the works of death, desolation & tyranny already begun with circumstances of cruelty and perfidy [scarcely paralleled in the most barbarous ages, & totally] unworthy the head of a civilized nation.

He has constrained our fellow citizens taken captive on the high seas to bear arms against their country, to become the executioners of their friends & brethren, or to fall themselves by their hands.

He has [excited domestic insurrection among us, & has] endeavored to bring on the inhabitants of our frontiers the merciless Indian savages, whose known rule of warfare is an undistinguished destruction of all ages, sexes, & conditions *of existence.*

He has incited treasonable insurrections of our fellow-citizens, with the allurements of forfeiture & confiscation of our property.

He has waged cruel war against human nature itself, violating it's most sacred rights

of life and liberty in the persons of a distant people who never offended him, captivating &
carrying them into slavery in another hemisphere, or to incur miserable death in their transportation thither. This piratical warfare, the opprobrium of INFIDEL powers, is the warfare
of the CHRISTIAN king of Great Britain. Determined to keep open a market where MEN
should be bought & sold, he has prostituted his negative for suppressing every legislative
attempt to prohibit or to restrain this execrable commerce. And that this assemblage of horrors
might want no fact of distinguished die, he is now exciting those very people to rise in arms
among us, and to purchase that liberty of which he has deprived them, by murdering the people
on whom he also obtruded them: thus paying off former crimes committed against the LIBER-
TIES of one people, with crimes which he urges them to commit against the LIVES of another.

In every stage of these oppressions we have petitioned for redress in the most
humble terms: our repeated petitions have been answered only by repeated injuries.

A prince whose character is thus marked by every act which may define a tyrant
is unfit to be the ruler of a people *who mean to be free. Future ages will scarcely believe that
the hardiness of one men adventured, within the short compass of twelve years only, to lay a
foundation so broad & so undisguised for tyranny over a people fostered & fixed in principles
of freedom.*

Nor have we been wanting in attentions to our British brethren. We have warned
them from time to time of attempts by their legislature to extend *a* jurisdiction over
these our states. We have reminded them of the circumstances of our emigration & settlement here, *no one of which could warrant so strange a pretension: that these were effected at
the expense of our own blood & treasure, unassisted by the wealth or the strength of Great
Britain: that in constituting indeed our several forms of government, we had adopted one
common king, thereby laying a foundation for perpetual league & amity with them: but that
submission to their parliament was no part of our constitution, nor ever in idea, if history
may be credited: and,* we [have] appealed to their native justice and magnanimity *as well
as to* the ties of our common kindred to disavow these usurpations which *were likely to*
interrupt our connection and correspondence. They too have been deaf to the voice of
justice & of consanguinity, *and when occasions have been given them, by the regular course
of their laws, of removing from their councils the disturbers of our harmony, they have, by
their free election, re-established them in power. At this very time too they are permitting
their chief magistrate to send over not only soldiers of our common blood, but Scotch & foreign*

mercenaries to invade & destroy us. These facts have given the last stab to agonizing affection, and manly spirit bids us to renounce forever these unfeeling brethren. We must endeavor to forget our former love for them, and hold them as we hold the rest of mankind, enemies in war, in peace friends. We might have been a free and a great people together; but a communication of grandeur & of freedom it seems is below their dignity. Be it so, since they will have it. The road to happiness & to glory is open to us too. We will tread it apart from them, and acquiesce in the necessity which denounces our *eternal* separation [and hold them as we hold the rest of mankind, enemies in war, in peace friends]!

We therefore the representatives of the United States of America in General Congress assembled do in the name & by authority of the good people of these *states reject & renounce all allegiance & subjection to the kings of Great Britain & all others who may hereafter claim by, through or under them: we utterly dissolve all political connection which may heretofore have subsisted between us & the people or parliament of Great Britain: & finally we do assert & declare these colonies to be free & independent states,* & that as free & independent states, they have full power to levy war, conclude peace, contract alliances, establish commerce, & to do all other acts & things which independent states may of right do.

And for the support of this declaration we mutually pledge to each other our lives, our fortunes, & our sacred honor.

We therefore the representatives of the United States of America in General Congress assembled, appealing to the supreme judge of the world for the rectitude of our intentions, do in the name, & by the authority of the good people of these colonies, solemnly publish & declare that these united colonies are & of right ought to be free & independent states; that they are absolved from all allegiance to the British crown, and that all political connection between them & the state of Great Britain is, & ought to be, totally dissolved; & that as free & independent states they have full power to levy war, conclude peace, contract alliances, establish commerce & to do all other acts & things which independant states may of right do.

And for the support of this declaration, with a firm reliance on the protection of divine providence we mutually pledge to each other our lives, our fortunes, & our sacred honor.

Draft Constitution for Virginia (1776)

... The Legislative, Executive and Judiciary offices shall be kept forever separate; no person exercising the one shall be capable of appointment to the others, or to either of them.

I. Legislative.

Legislation shall be exercised by two separate houses, to wit a house of Representatives, and a house of Senators, which shall be called the General Assembly of Virginia.

The sd house of Representatives shall be composed of persons chosen by the people annually on the [1st day of October] and shall meet in General assembly on the [1st day of November] following and so from time to time on their own adjournments, or at any time when summoned by the Administrator and shall continue sitting so long as they shall think the publick service requires.

Vacancies in the said house by death or disqualification shall be filled by the electors under a warrant from the Speaker of the said house.

All male persons of full age and sane mind having a freehold estate [one fourth of an acre] of land in any town, or in [25] acres of land in the country, and all persons resident in the colony who shall have paid scot and lot to government the last [two years] shall have right to give their vote in the election of their respective representatives. And every person so qualified to elect shall be capable of being elected, provided he shall have given no bribe either directly or indirectly to any elector, and shall take an oath of fidelity to the state and of duty in his office, before he enters on the exercise thereof. During his continuance in the said office he shall hold no public pension nor post of profit, either himself, or by another for his use.

The number of Representatives for each county or borough shall be so proportioned to the numbers of it's qualified electors that the whole number of representatives shall not exceed [300] nor be less than [125.] for the present there shall be one representative for every [ ] qualified electors in each county or borough: but whenever this or any future proportion shall be likely to exceed or fall short of the limits beforementioned, it shall be again adjusted by the house of representatives.

The house of Representatives when met shall be free to act according to their own judgment and conscience.

The Senate shall consist of not less than [15] nor more than [50] members who shall be appointed by the house of Representatives. One third of them shall be removed out of office by lot at the end of the first [three] years and their places be supplied by a new appointment; one other third shall be removed by lot in like manner at the end of the second [three] years and their places be supplied by a new appointment; after which one third shall be removed annually at the end of every [three] years according to seniority. When once removed, they shall be forever incapable of being reappointed to that house. Their qualifications shall be an oath of fidelity to the state, and of duty in their office, the being [31] years of age at the least, and the having given no bribe directly or indirectly to obtain their appointment. While in the senatorial office they shall be incapable of holding any public pension or post of profit either themselves, or by others for their use.

The judges of the General court and of the High court of Chancery shall have session and deliberative voice, but not suffrage in the house of Senators.

The Senate and the house of representatives shall each of them have power to originate and amend bills; save only that bills for levying money [bills]* shall be originated and amended by the representatives only: the assent of both houses shall be requisite to pass a law.

The General assembly shall have no power to pass any law inflicting death for any crime, excepting murder, & [such]* those offences in the military service for which they shall think punishment by death absolutely necessary: and all capital punishments in other cases are hereby abolished. Nor shall they have power to prescribe torture in any case whatever: nor shall there be power anywhere to pardon crimes or to remit fines or punishments: nor shall any law for levying money be in force longer than [ten years] from the time of its commencement.

[Two thirds] of the members of either house shall be a Quorum to proceed to business.

*Word struck by Jefferson. Ed.

II. Executive.

The executive powers shall be exercised in manner following.

One person to be called the [Administrator] shall be annually appointed by the house of Representatives on the second day of their first session, who after having acted [one] year shall be incapable of being again appointed to that office until he shall have been out of the same [three] years.

Under him shall be appointed by the same house and at the same time, a Deputy-Administrator to assist his principal in the discharge of his office, and to succeed, in case of his death before the year shall have expired, to the whole powers thereof during the residue of the year.

The administrator shall possess the power formerly held by the king: save only that, he shall be bound by acts of legislature tho' not expressly named;

he shall have no negative on the bills of the Legislature;

he shall be liable to action, tho' not to personal restraint for private duties or wrongs;

he shall not possess the prerogatives;

of dissolving, proroguing or adjourning either house of Assembly;

of declaring war or concluding peace;

of issuing letters of marque or reprisal;

of raising or introducing armed forces, building armed vessels, forts or strongholds;

of coining monies or regulating their values;

of regulating weights and measures;

of erecting courts, offices, boroughs, corporations, fairs, markets, ports, beacons, lighthouses, seamarks.

of laying embargoes, or prohibiting the exportation of any commodity for a longer space than [40] days.

of retaining or recalling a member of the state but by legal process pro delicto vel contractu.

of making denizens.

of pardoning crimes, or remitting fines or punishments.

of creating dignities or granting rights of precedence.

but these powers shall be exercised by the legislature alone, and excepting also those powers which by these fundamentals are given to others, or abolished.

A Privy council shall be annually appointed by the house of representatives whose duties it shall be to give advice to the Administrator when called on by him. With them the Deputy Administrator shall have session and suffrage.

Delegates to represent this colony in the American Congress shall be appointed when necessary by the house of Representatives. After serving [one] year in that office they shall not be capable of being re-appointed to the same during an interval of [one] year.

A Treasurer shall be appointed by the house of Representatives who shall issue no money but by authority of both houses.

An Attorney general shall be appointed by the house of Representatives

High Sheriffs and Coroners of counties shall be annually elected by those qualified to vote for representatives: and no person who shall have served as high sheriff [one] year shall be capable of being re-elected to the said office in the same county till he shall have been out of office [five] years.

All other Officers civil and military shall be appointed by the Administrator; but such appointment shall be subject to the negative of the Privy council, saving however to the Legislature a power of transferring to any other persons the appointment of such officers or any of them.

III. JUDICIARY.

The Judiciary powers shall be exercised

First, by County courts and other inferior jurisdictions:

Secondly, by a General court & a High court of Chancery:

Thirdly, by a Court of Appeals.

The judges of the county courts and other inferior jurisdictions shall be appointed by the Administrator, subject to the negative of the privy council. They shall not be fewer than [five] in number. Their jurisdictions shall be defined from time to time by the legislature: and they shall be removable for misbehavior by the court of Appeals.

The Judges of the General court and of the High court of Chancery shall be appointed by the Administrator and Privy council. If kept united they shall be [5] in number, if separate, there shall be [5] for the General court & [3] for the High court of

Chancery. The appointment shall be made from the faculty of the law, and of such persons of that faculty as shall have actually exercised the same at the bar of some court or courts of record within this colony for [seven] years. They shall hold their commissions during good behavior, for breach of which they shall be removable by the court of Appeals. Their jurisdiction shall be defined from time to time by the Legislature.

The Court of Appeals shall consist of not less than [7] nor more than [11] members, to be appointed by the house of Representatives: they shall hold their offices during good behavior, for breach of which they shall be removable by an act of the legislature only. Their jurisdiction shall be to determine finally all causes removed before them from the General Court or High Court of Chancery, or of the county courts or other inferior jurisdictions for misbehavior: [to try impeachments against high offenders lodged before them by the house of representatives for such crimes as shall hereafter be precisely defined by the Legislature, and for the punishment of which, the said legislature shall have previously prescribed certain and determinate pains.] In this court the judges of the General court and High court of Chancery shall have session and deliberative voice, but no suffrage.

All facts in causes whether of Chancery, Common, Ecclesiastical, or Marine law, shall be tried by a jury upon evidence given vivâ voce, in open court: but where witnesses are out of the colony or unable to attend through sickness or other invincible necessity, their deposition may be submitted to the credit of the jury.

All Fines or Amercements shall be assessed, & Terms of imprisonment for Contempts & Misdemeanors shall be fixed by the verdict of a Jury.

All Process Original & Judicial shall run in the name of the court from which it issues.

Two thirds of the members of the General court, High court of Chancery, or Court of Appeals shall be a Quorum to proceed to business.

IV. Rights, Private and Public.

Unappropriated or Forfeited lands shall be appropriated by the Administrator with the consent of the Privy council.

Every person of full age neither owning nor having owned [50] acres of land, shall be entitled to an appropriation of [50] acres or to so much as shall make up what he owns or has owned [50] acres in full and absolute dominion. And no other person shall be capable of taking an appropriation.

Lands heretofore holden of the crown in fee simple, and those hereafter to be appropriated shall be holden in full and absolute dominion, of no superior whatever.

No lands shall be appropriated until purchased of the Indian native proprietors; nor shall any purchases be made of them but on behalf of the public, by authority of acts of the General assembly to be passed for every purchase specially.

The territories contained within the charters erecting the colonies of Maryland, Pennsylvania, North and South Carolina, are hereby ceded, released, & forever confirmed to the people of those colonies respectively, with all the rights of property, jurisdiction and government and all other rights whatsoever which might at any time heretofore have been claimed by this colony. The Western and Northern extent of this country shall in all other respects stand as fixed by the charter of *

until by act of the Legislature one or more territories shall be laid off Westward of the Alleghaney mountains for new colonies, which colonies shall be established on the same fundamental laws contained in this instrument, and shall be free and independent of this colony and of all the world.

Descents shall go according to the laws Gavelkind, save only that females shall have equal rights with males.

No person hereafter coming into this county shall be held within the same in slavery under any pretext whatever.

All persons who by their own oath or affirmation, or by other testimony shall give satisfactory proof to any court of record in this colony that they propose to reside in the same [7] years at the least and who shall subscribe the fundamental laws, shall be considered as residents and entitled to all the rights of persons natural born.

All persons shall have full and free liberty of religious opinion; nor shall any be compelled to frequent or maintain any religious institution.

No freeman shall be debarred the use of arms [within his own lands].

There shall be no standing army but in time of actual war.

*Blank spaces are in the original text. Ed.

Printing presses shall be free, except so far as by commission of private injury cause may be given of private action.

All Forfeitures heretofore going to the king, shall go the state; save only such as the legislature may hereafter abolish.

The royal claim to Wrecks, waifs, strays, treasure-trove, royal mines, royal fish, royal birds, are declared to have been usurpations on common right.

No Salaries or Perquisites shall be given to any officer but by some future act of the legislature. No salaries shall be given to the Administrator, members of the legislative houses, judges of the court of Appeals, judges of the County courts, or other inferior jurisdictions, Privy counsellors, or Delegates to the American Congress: but the reasonable expences of the Administrator, members of the house of representatives, judges of the court of Appeals, Privy counsellors, & Delegates for subsistence while acting in the duties of their office, may be borne by the public, if the legislature shall so direct.

No person shall be capable of acting in any office Civil, Military [or Ecclesiastical] who shall have given any bribe to obtain such office, or who shall not previously take an oath of fidelity to the state.

None of these fundamental laws and principles of government shall be repealed or altered, but by the personal consent of the people on summons to meet in their respective counties on one and the same day by an act of Legislature to be passed for every special occasion: and if in such county meetings the people of two thirds of the counties shall give their suffrage for any particular alteration or repeal referred to them by the said act, the same shall be accordingly repealed or altered, and such repeal or alteration shall take it's place among these fundamentals and stand on the same footing with them, in lieu of the article repealed or altered.

The laws heretofore in force in this colony shall remain in force, except so far as they are altered by the foregoing fundamental laws, or so far as they may be hereafter altered by acts of the Legislature.

Suffrage, Senate, and Representation

To Edmund Pendleton, August 26, 1776

Dear Sir—Your's of the 10ᵗʰ inst. came to hand about three days ago, the post having brought no mail with him the last week. You seem to have misapprehended my proposition for the choice of a Senate. I had two things in view: to get the wisest men chosen, & to make them perfectly independent when chosen. I have ever observed that a choice by the people themselves is not generally distinguished for it's wisdom. This first secretion from them is usually crude & heterogeneous. But give to those so chosen by the people a second choice themselves, & they generally will chuse wise men. For this reason it was that I proposed the representatives (& not the people) should chuse the Senate, & thought I had notwithstanding that made the Senators (when chosen) perfectly independant of their electors. However I should have no objection to the mode of election proposed in the printed plan of your committee, to wit, that the people of each county should chuse twelve electors, who should meet those of the other counties in the same district & chuse a senator. I should prefer this too for another reason, that the upper as well as lower house should have an opportunity of superintending & judging of the situation of the whole state & be not all of one neighborhood as our upper house used to be. So much for the wisdom of the Senate. To make them independent, I had proposed that they should hold their places for nine years, & then go out (one third every three years) & be incapable for ever of being re-elected to that house. My idea was that if they might be re-elected, they would be casting their eye forward to the period of election (however distant) & be currying favor with the electors, & consequently dependant on them. My reason for fixing them in office for a term of years rather than for life, was that they might have in idea that they were at a certain period to return into the mass of the people & become the governed instead of the governor which might still keep alive that regard to the public good that otherwise they might perhaps be induced by their independance to forget. Yet I could submit, tho' not so willingly to an appointment for life, or to any thing rather than a mere creation by & dependance on the people. I think the present mode of election objectionable because the larger county will be able to send & will always send a man (less fit perhaps) of their own county to the exclusion of a fitter who may chance to live in a smaller county.—I wish experience may contradict my fears.—That the Senate as well as lower [or shall I speak truth & call it upper] house should hold no office of profit I am clear; but not that they should of necessity possess distinguished property. You have lived longer than I have and perhaps may have formed a different judgment on better grounds; but my observations do not enable me to say I think integrity the characteristic of wealth. In general I beleive the decisions of the people, in a body, will be more honest & more disinterested than those of wealthy men: & I can never doubt an attachment to his country in any man who has his family & peculium in it:—Now as to the representative house which ought to be so constructed as to answer that character truly. I was for extending the right of suffrage (or in other words the rights of a citizen) to all who had a permanent intention of living in the country. Take what circumstances you please as evidence of this, either the having resided a certain time, or having a family, or having property, any or all of them. Whoever intends to live in a country must wish that country well, & has a natural right of assisting in the preservation of it. I think you cannot distinguish between such a person residing in the country & having no fixed property, & one residing in a township whom you say you would admit to a vote.—The other point of equal representation I think capital & fundamental. I am glad you think an alteration may be attempted in that matter.—The fantastical idea of virtue & the public good being a sufficient security to the state against the commission of crimes, which you say you have heard insisted on by some, I assure you was never mine. It is only the sanguinary hue of our penal laws which I meant to object to. Punishments I know are necessary, & I would provide them, strict & inflexible, but proportioned to the crime. Death might be inflicted for murther & perhaps for treason if you would take out of the description of treason all crimes which are not such in their nature. Rape, buggery &c—punish by castration. All other crimes by working on high roads, rivers, gallies &c. a certain time proportioned to the offence. But as this would be no punishment or change of condition to slaves (me miserum!) let them be sent to other countries. By these means we should be freed from the wickedness of the latter, & the former would be living monuments of public vengeance. Laws thus proportionate & mild should never be dispensed with. Let mercy be the character of the lawgiver, but let the judge be a mere machine. The mercies of the law will be dispensed equally

& impartially to every description of men; those of the judge, or of the executive power, will be the eccentric impulses of whimsical, capricious designing man.—I am indebted to you for a topic to deny to the Pensylvania claim to a line 39 complete degrees from the equator. As an advocate I shall certainly insist on it; but I wish they would compromise by an extension of Mason & Dixon's line.—They do not agree to the temporary line proposed by our assembly....

Revision of the Laws (1776–79)
Autobiography (1821)

... I obtained leave to bring in a bill declaring tenants in tail to hold their lands in fee simple. In the earlier times of the colony when lands were to be obtained for little or nothing, some provident individuals procured large grants, and, desirous of founding great families for themselves, settled them on their descendants in fee-tail. The transmission of this property from generation to generation in the same name raised up a distinct set of families who, being privileged by law in the perpetuation of their wealth were thus formed into a Patrician order, distinguished by the splendor and luxury of their establishments. From this order too the king habitually selected his Counsellors of State, the hope of which distinction devoted the whole corps to the interests & will of the crown. To annul this privilege, and instead of an aristocracy of wealth, of more harm and danger, than benefit, to society, to make an opening for the aristocracy of virtue and talent, which nature has wisely provided for the direction of the interests of society, & scattered with equal hand through all it's conditions, was deemed essential to a well ordered republic. To effect it no violence was necessary, no deprivation of natural right, but rather an enlargement of it by a repeal of the law. For this would authorize the present holder to divide the property among his children equally, as his affections were divided; and would place them, by natural generation on the level of their fellow citizens. But this repeal was strongly opposed by Mr. Pendleton, who was zealously attached to ancient establishments; and who, taken all in all, was the ablest man in debate I have ever met with. He had not indeed the poetical fancy of Mr. Henry, his sublime imagination, his lofty and overwhelming diction; but he was cool, smooth and persuasive; his language flowing, chaste & embellished, his conceptions quick, acute and full of resource; never vanquished; for if he lost the main battle, he returned upon you, and regained so much of it as to make it a drawn one, by dexterous manœuvres, skirmishes in detail, and the recovery of small advantages which, little singly, were important altogether. You never knew when you were clear of him, but were harassed by his perseverance until the patience was worn down of all who had less of it than himself. Add to this that he was one of the most virtuous & benevolent of men, the kindest friend, the most amiable & pleasant of companions, which ensured a favorable reception to whatever came from him. Finding that the general principle of entails could not be maintained, he took his stand on an amendment which he proposed, instead of an absolute abolition, to permit the tenant in tail to convey in fee simple, if he chose it: and he was within a few votes of saving so much of the old law. But the bill passed finally for entire abolition....

So far we were proceeding in the details of reformation only; selecting points of legislation prominent in character & principle, urgent, and indicative of the strength of the general pulse of reformation. When I left Congress, in 76. it was in the persuasion that our whole code must be reviewed, adapted to our republican form of government, and, now that we had no negatives of Councils, Governors & Kings to restrain us from doing right, that it should be corrected, in all it's parts, with a single eye to reason, & the good of those for whose government it was framed. Early therefore in the session of 76. to which I returned, I moved and presented a bill for the revision of the laws; which was passed on the 24th. of October, and on the 5th. of November Mr. Pendleton, Mr. Wythe, George Mason, Thomas L. Lee and myself were appointed a committee to execute the work. We agreed to meet at Fredericksburg to settle the plan of operation and to distribute the work. We met there accordingly, on the 13th. of January 1777. The first question was whether we should propose to abolish the whole existing system of laws, and prepare a new and complete Institute, or preserve the general system, and only modify it to the present state of things. Mr. Pendleton, contrary to his usual disposition in favor of antient things, was for the former proposition, in which he was joined by Mr. Lee. To this it was objected that to abrogate our whole system would be a bold measure, and probably far beyond the views of the legislature; that they had been in the practice of revising from time to time the laws of the colony, omitting the expired, the repealed and the obsolete, amending only those retained, and probably meant we should now do the same, only including the British statutes as well as our own: that to compose a new Institute like those of Justinian and Bracton, or that of Blackstone, which was the model proposed by Mr. Pendleton, would be an arduous undertaking, of vast research, of great consideration & judgment; and when reduced to a text, every word of that text, from the imperfection of human language, and it's incompetence to express distinctly every shade of idea, would become a subject of question & chicanery until settled by repeated adjudications; that this would involve us for ages in litigation, and render property uncertain until, like the statutes of old, every word had been tried, and settled by numerous decisions, and by new volumes of reports & commentaries; and that no one of us probably would undertake such a work, which, to be systematical, must be the work of one hand....

The bill on the subject of slaves were a mere digest of the existing laws respecting them, without any intimation of a plan for a future & general emancipation. It was thought better that this should be kept back, and attempted only by way of amendment whenever the bill should be brought on. The principles of the amendment however were agreed on, that is to say, the freedom of all born after a certain day, and deportation at a proper age. But it was found that the public mind would not yet bear the proposition, nor will it bear it even at this day. Yet the day is not distant when it must bear and adopt it, or worse will follow. Nothing is more certainly written in the book of fate than that these people are to be free. Nor it is less certain that the two races, equally free, cannot live in the same government. Nature, habit, opinion has drawn indelible lines of distinction between them. It is still in our power to direct the process of emancipation and deportation peaceably and in such slow degree as that the evil will wear off insensibly, and their place be pari passu filled up by free white laborers. If on the contrary it is left to force itself on, human nature must shudder at the prospect held up. We should in vain look for an example in the Spanish deportation or deletion of the Moors. This precedent would fall far short of our case.

I considered 4 of these bills, passed or reported, as forming a system by which every fibre would be eradicated of antient or future aristocracy; and a foundation laid for a government truly republican. The repeal of the laws of entail would prevent the accumulation and perpetuation of wealth in select families, and preserve the soil of the country from being daily more & more absorbed in Mortmain. The abolition of primogeniture, and equal partition of inheritances removed the feudal and unnatural distinctions which made one member of every family rich, and all the rest poor, substituting equal partition, the best of all Agrarian laws. The restoration of the rights of conscience relieved the people from taxation for the support of a religion not theirs; for the establishment was truly of the religion of the rich, the dissenting sects being entirely composed of the less wealthy people; and these, by the bill for a general education, would be qualified to understand their rights, to maintain them, and to exercise with intelligence their parts in self-government: and all this would be effected without the violation of a single natural right of any one individual citizen. To these too might be added, as a further security, the introduction of the trial by jury, into the Chancery courts, which have already ingulfed and continue to ingulf, so great a proportion of the jurisdiction over our property....

A BILL FOR ESTABLISHING RELIGIOUS FREEDOM (1777)

SECTION I. Well aware that the opinions and belief of men depend not on their own will, but follow involuntarily the evidence proposed to their minds; that Almighty God hath created the mind free, and manifested his supreme will that free it shall remain by making it altogether insusceptible of restraint; that all attempts to influence it by temporal punishments, or burthens, or by civil incapacitations, tend only to beget habits of hypocrisy and meanness, and are a departure from the plan of the holy author of our religion, who being lord both of body and mind, yet chose not to propagate it by coercions on either, as was in his Almighty power to do, but to extend it by its influence on reason alone; that the impious presumption of legislators and rulers, civil as well as ecclesiastical, who, being themselves but fallible and uninspired men, have assumed dominion over the faith of others, setting up their own opinions and modes of thinking as the only true and infallible, and as such endeavoring to impose them on others, hath established and maintained false religions over the greatest part of the world and through all time: That to compel a man to furnish contributions of money for the propagation of opinions which he disbelieves and abhors, is sinful and tyrannical; that even the forcing him to support this or that teacher of his own religious persuasion, is depriving him of the comfortable liberty of giving his contributions to the particular pastor whose morals he would make his pattern, and whose powers he feels most persuasive to righteousness; and is withdrawing from the ministry those temporary rewards, which proceeding from an approbation of their personal conduct, are an additional incitement to earnest and unremitting labours for the instruction of mankind; that our civil rights have no dependance on our religious opinions, any more than our opinions in physics or geometry; that therefore the proscribing any citizen as unworthy the public confidence by laying upon him an incapacity of being called to offices of trust and emolument, unless he profess or renounce this or that religious opinion, is depriving him injuriously of those privileges and advantages to which, in common with his fellow citizens, he has a natural right; that it tends also to corrupt the principles of that very religion it is meant to encourage, by bribing, with a monopoly of worldly honours and emoluments, those who will externally profess and conform to it; that though indeed these are criminal who do not withstand such temptation, yet neither are those innocent who lay the bait in their way; that the opinions of men are not the object of civil government, nor under its jurisdiction; that to suffer the civil magistrate to intrude his powers into the field of opinion and to restrain the profession or propagation of principles on supposition of their ill tendency is a dangerous falacy, which at once destroys all religious liberty, because he being of course judge of that tendency will make his opinions the rule of judgment, and approve or condemn the sentiments of others only as they shall square with or differ from his own; that it is time enough for the rightful purposes of civil government for its officers to interfere when principles break out into overt acts against peace and good order; and finally, that truth is great and will prevail if left to herself; that she is the proper and sufficient antagonist to error, and has nothing to fear from the conflict unless by human interposition disarmed of her natural weapons, free argument and debate; errors ceasing to be dangerous when it is permitted freely to contradict them.

SECT. II. We the General Assembly of Virginia do enact that no man shall be compelled to frequent or support any religious worship, place, or ministry whatsoever, nor shall be enforced, restrained, molested, or burthened in his body or goods, nor shall otherwise suffer, on account of his religious opinions or belief; but that all men shall be free to profess, and by argument to maintain, their opinions in matters of religion, and that the same shall in no wise diminish, enlarge, or affect their civil capacities.

Sect. III. And though we well know that this Assembly, elected by the people for the ordinary purposes of legislation only, have no power to restrain the acts of succeeding Assemblies, constituted with powers equal to our own, and that therefore to declare this act irrevocable would be of no effect in law; yet we are free to declare, and do declare, that the rights hereby asserted are of the natural rights of mankind, and that if any act shall be hereafter passed to repeal the present or to narrow its operation, such act will be an infringement of natural right.

A Bill for the More General Diffusion of Knowledge (1778)

Section I. Whereas it appeareth that however certain forms of government are better calculated than others to protect individuals in the free exercise of their natural rights, and are at the same time themselves better guarded against degeneracy, yet experience hath shewn, that even under the best forms, those entrusted with power have, in time, and by slow operations, perverted it into tyranny; and it is believed that the most effectual means of preventing this would be, to illuminate, as far as practicable, the minds of the people at large, and more especially to give them knowledge of those facts, which history exhibiteth, that, possessed thereby of the experience of other ages and countries, they may be enabled to know ambition under all its shapes, and prompt to exert their natural powers to defeat its purposes; And whereas it is generally true that the people will be happiest whose laws are best, and are best administered, and that laws will be wisely formed, and honestly administered, in proportion as those who form and administer them are wise and honest; whence it becomes expedient for promoting the publick happiness that those persons, whom nature hath endowed with genius and virtue, should be rendered by liberal education worthy to receive, and able to guard the sacred deposit of the rights and liberties of their fellow citizens, and that they should be called to that charge without regard to wealth, birth or other accidental condition or circumstance; but the indigence of the greater number disabling them from so educating, at their own expence, those of their children whom nature hath fitly formed and disposed to become useful instruments for the public, it is better that such should be sought for and educated at the common expence of all, than that the happiness of all should be confided to the weak or wicked:

SECT II. Be it therefore enacted by the General Assembly, that in every county within this commonwealth, there shall be chosen annually, by the electors qualified to vote for Delegates, three of the most honest and able men of their county, to be called the Aldermen of the county; and that the election of the said Aldermen shall be held at the same time and place, before the same persons, and notified and conducted in the same manner as by law is directed for the annual election of Delegates for the county....

SECT. VI. At every of these schools shall be taught reading, writing, and common arithmetick, and the books which shall be used therein for instructing the children to read shall be such as will at the same time make them acquainted with Græcian, Roman, English, and American history. At these schools all the free children, male and female, resident within the respective hundred, shall be intitled to receive tuition gratis, for the term of three years, and as much longer, at their private expence, as their parents, guardians or friends, shall think proper....

SECT. XVI. Every overseer of the hundred schools shall, in the month of September annually, after the most diligent and impartial examination and enquiry, appoint from among the boys who shall have been two years at the least at some one of the schools under his superintendance, and whose parents are too poor to give them farther education, some one of the best and most promising genius and disposition, to proceed to the grammar school of his district; which appointment shall be made in the court-house of the county, on the court day for that month, if fair, and if not, then on the next fair day, excluding Sunday, in the presence of the Aldermen, or two of them at the least, assembled on the bench for that purpose, the said overseer being previously sworn by them to make such appointment, without favor or affection, according to the best of his skill and judgment, and being interrogated by the said Aldermen, either on their own motion, or on suggestions from the parents, guardians, friends, or teachers of the children, competitors for such appointment; which teachers shall attend for the information of the Aldermen. On which interrogatories the said Aldermen, if they be not satisfied with the appointment proposed, shall have right to negative it; whereupon the said visiter may proceed to make a new appointment, and the said Aldermen again to interrogate and negative, and so toties quoties until an appointment be approved....

Sect. XIX. The visiters for the districts which, or any part of which, be southward and westward of James river, as known by that name, or by the names of Fluvanna and Jackson's river, in every other year, to wit, at the probation meetings held in the years, distinguished in the Christian computation by odd numbers, and the visiters for all the other districts at their said meetings to be held in those years, distinguished by even numbers, after diligent examination and enquiry as before directed, shall chuse one among the said seniors, of the best learning and most hopeful genius and disposition, who shall be authorised by them to proceed to William and Mary College, there to be educated, boarded, and clothed, three years; the expence of which annually shall be paid by the Treasurer on warrant from the Auditors....

A Bill Declaring Who Shall Be Deemed Citizens of this Commonwealth (1779)

Section I. Be it enacted by the General Assembly, that all white persons born within the territory of this commonwealth and all who have resided therein two years next before the passing of this act, and all who shall hereafter migrate into the same; and shall before any court of record give satisfactory proof by their own oath or affirmation, that they intend to reside therein, and moreover shall give assurance of fidelity to the commonwealth; and all infants wheresoever born, whose father, if living, or otherwise, whose mother was, a citizen at the time of their birth, or who migrate hither, their father, if living, or otherwise their mother becoming a citizen, or who migrate hither without father or mother, shall be deemed citizens of this commonwealth, until they relinquish that character in manner as herein after expressed: And all others not being citizens of any the United States of America, shall be deemed aliens. The clerk of the court shall enter such oath of record, and give the person taking the same a certificate thereof, for which he shall receive the fee of one dollar. And in order to preserve to the citizens of this commonwealth, that natural right, which all men have of relinquishing the country, in which birth, or other accident may have thrown them, and, seeking subsistance and happiness wheresoever they may be able, or may hope to find them: And to declare unequivocally what circumstances shall be deemed evidence of an intention in any citizen to exercise that right, it is enacted and declared, that whensoever any citizen of this commonwealth, shall by word of mouth in the presence of the court of the county, wherein he resides, or of the General Court, or by deed in writing, under his hand and seal, executed in the presence of three witnesses, and by them proved in either of the said courts, openly declare to the same court, that he relinquishes the character of a citizen, and shall depart the commonwealth; or whensoever he shall without such declaration depart the commonwealth and enter into the service of any other state, not in enmity with this, or any other of the United States of America, or do any act whereby he shall become a subject or citizen of such state, such person shall be considered as having exercised his natural right of expatriating himself, and shall be deemed no citizen of this commonwealth from the time of his departure. The free white inhabitants of every of the states, parties to the American confederation, paupers, vagabonds and fugitives from justice excepted, shall be intitled to all rights, privileges, and immunities of free citizens in this commonwealth, and shall have free egress, and regress, to and from the same, and shall enjoy therein, all the privileges of trade, and commerce, subject to the same duties, impositions and restrictions as the citizens of this commonwealth. And if any person guilty of, or charged with treason, felony, or other high misdemeanor, in any of the said states, shall flee from justice and be found in this commonwealth, he shall, upon demand of the Governor, or Executive power of the state, from which he fled, be delivered up to be removed to the state having jurisdiction of his offence. Where any person holding property, within this commonwealth, shall be attainted within any of the said states, parties to the said confederation, of any of those crimes, which by the laws of this commonwealth shall be punishable by forfeiture of such property, the said property shall be disposed of in the same manner as it would have been if the owner thereof had been attainted of the like crime in this commonwealth.

Limits of Public Duty

To James Monroe, May 20, 1782

... Before I ventured to declare to my countrymen my determination to retire from public employment, I examined well my heart to know whether it were thoroughly cured of every principle of political ambition, whether no lurking particle remained which might leave me uneasy when reduced within the limits of mere private life. I became satisfied that every fibre of that passion was thoroughly eradicated. I examined also in other views my right to withdraw. I considered that I had been thirteen years engaged in public service, that during that time I had so totally abandoned all attention to my private affairs as to permit them to run into great disorder and ruin, that I had now a family advanced to years which require my attention & instruction, that to these were added the hopeful offspring of a deceased friend whose memory must be forever dear to me who have no other reliance for being rendered useful to themselves & their country, that by a constant sacrifice of time, labour, loss, parental & family duties, I had been so far from gaining the affection of my countrymen, which was the only reward I ever asked or could have felt, that I had even lost the small estimation I before possessed.... If we are made in some degree for others, yet in a greater are we made for ourselves. It were contrary to feeling & indeed ridiculous to suppose that a man had less right in himself than one of his neighbors or indeed all of them put together. This would be slavery & not that liberty which the bill of rights has made inviolable and for the preservation of which our government has been charged. Nothing could so completely divest us of that liberty as the establishment of the opinion that the state has a *perpetual* right to the services of all it's members. This to men of certain ways of thinking would be to annihilate the blessing of existence; to contradict the giver of life who gave it for happiness & not for wretchedness; and certainly to such it were better that they had never been born. However with these I may think public service & private misery inseparably linked together, I have not the vanity to count myself among those whom the state would think worth oppressing with perpetual service. I have received a sufficient memento to the contrary. I am persuaded that having hitherto dedicated to them the whole of the active & useful part of my life I shall be permitted to pass the rest in mental quiet. I hope too that I did not mistake the modes any more than the matter of right when I preferred a simple act of renunciation to the taking sanctuary under those disqualifications provided by the law for other purposes indeed, but which afford asylum also for rest to the wearied. I dare say you did not expect by the few words you dropped on the right of renunciation to expose yourself to the fatigue of so long a letter, but I wished you to see that if I had done wrong I had been betrayed by a semblance of right at least....

DRAFT OF A CONSTITUTION FOR VIRGINIA (1783):
Selected Articles

... During the progress of that war, through which we had to labour for the establishment of our rights, the legislature of the commonwealth of Virginia found it necessary to make a temporary organization of government for preventing anarchy, and pointing our efforts to the two important objects of war against our invaders, and peace and happiness among ourselves. But this, like all other their acts of legislation, being subject to change by subsequent legislatures, possessing equal powers with themselves, it has been thought expedient, that it should receive those amendments which time and trial have suggested, and be rendered permanent by a power superior to that of the ordinary legislature. The general assembly therefore of this state recommend it to the good people thereof, to chuse delegates to meet in general convention, with powers to form a constitution of government for them, and to declare those fundamentals to which all our laws present and future shall be subordinate: and, in compliance with this recommendation, they have thought proper to make choice of us, and to vest us with powers for this purpose....

The powers of government shall be divided into three distinct departments, each of them to be confided to a separate body of magistracy; to wit, those which are legislative to one, those which are judiciary to another, and those which are executive to another. No person, or collection of persons, being of one of these departments, shall exercise any power properly belonging to either of the others, except in the instances hereinafter expressly permitted....

... The general assembly shall not have power to infringe this constitution; to abridge the civil rights of any person on account of his religious belief; to restrain him from professing and supporting that belief, or to compel him to contributions, other than those he shall have personally stipulated, for the support of that or any other; to ordain death for any crime but treason or murder, or military offences; to pardon, or give a power of pardoning persons duly convicted of treason or felony, but instead thereof they may substitute one or two new trials, and no more; to pass laws for punishing actions done before the existence of such laws; to pass any bill of attainder of treason or felony; to prescribe torture in any case whatever; nor to permit the introduction of any more slaves to reside in this state, or the continuance of slavery beyond the generation which shall be living on the thirty-first day of December, one thousand eight hundred: all persons born after that day being hereby declared free.

The general assembly shall have power to sever from this state all or any part of its territory westward of the Ohio....

II. EXECUTIVE. GOVERNOR.

The executive powers shall be exercised by a *governor,* who shall be chosen by joint ballot of both houses of assembly, and when chosen shall remain in office five years, and be ineligible a second time. During his term he shall hold no other office or emolument under this state, or any other state or power whatsoever. By executive powers, we mean no reference to those powers exercised under our former government by the crown as of its prerogative, nor that these shall be the standard of what may or may not be deemed the rightful powers of the governor. We give him those powers only, which are necessary to execute the laws (and administer the government) and which are not in their nature either legislative or judiciary....

CONVENTION.

Any two of the three branches of government concurring in opinion, each by the voices of two thirds of their whole existing number, that a convention is necessary for altering this constitution, or correcting breaches of it, they shall be authorized to issue writs to every county for the election of so many delegates as they are authorized to send to the General Assembly, which elections shall be held, and writs returned, as the laws shall have provided in the case of elections of Delegates to assembly, mutatis mutandis, and the said Delegates shall meet at the usual place of holding assemblies, three months after the date of such writs, and shall be acknowledged to have equal powers with this present convention. The said writs shall be signed by all the members approving the same....

❧

"Notes on the State of Virginia" (1785):
Virginia Constitution

... This constitution was formed when we were new and unexperienced in the science of government. It was the first too which was formed in the whole United States. No wonder then that time and trial have discovered very capital defects in it.

1. The majority of the men in the state, who pay and fight for its support, are unrepresented in the legislature, the roll of freeholders intitled to vote, not including generally the half of those on the roll of the militia, or of the tax-gatherers.

2. Among those who are the representation, the shares are very unequal. Thus the county of Warwick, with only one hundred fighting men, has an equal representation with the county of Loudon, which has 1746. So that every man in Warwick has as much influence in the government as 17 men in Loudon. But lest it should be thought that an equal interspersion of small among large counties, through the whole state, may prevent any danger of injury to particular parts of it, we will divide it into districts, and shew the proportions of land, of fighting men, and of representation in each....

3. The senate is, by its constitution, too homogeneous with the house of delegates. Being chosen by the same electors, at the same time, and out of the same subjects, the choice falls of course on men of the same description. The purpose of establishing different houses of legislation is to introduce the influence of different interests or different principles. Thus in Great-Britain it is said their constitution relies on the house of commons for honesty, and the lords for wisdom; which would be a rational reliance if honesty were to be bought with money, and if wisdom were hereditary. In some of the American states the delegates and senators are so chosen, as that the first represent

the persons, and the second the property of the state. But with us, wealth and wisdom have equal chance for admission into both houses. We do not therefore derive from the separation of our legislature into two houses, those benefits which a proper complication of principles is capable of producing, and those which alone can compensate the evils which may be produced by their dissensions.

4. All the powers of government, legislative, executive, and judiciary, result to the legislative body. The concentrating these in the same hands is precisely the definition of despotic government. It will be no alleviation that these powers will be exercised by a plurality of hands, and not by a single one. 173 despots would surely be as oppressive as one. Let those who doubt it turn their eyes on the republic of Venice. As little will it avail us that they are chosen by ourselves. An *elective despotism* was not the government we fought for; but one which should not only be founded on free principles, but in which the powers of government should be so divided and balanced among several bodies of magistracy, as that no one could transcend their legal limits, without being effectually checked and restrained by the others....

5. That the ordinary legislature may alter the constitution itself. On the discontinuance of assemblies, it became necessary to substitute in their place some other body, competent to the ordinary business of government, and to the calling forth the powers of the state for the maintenance of our opposition to Great-Britain. Conventions were therefore introduced, consisting of two delegates from each county, meeting together and forming one house, on the plan of the former house of Burgesses, to whose places they succeeded. These were at first chosen anew for every particular session. But in March 1775, they recommended to the people to chuse a convention, which should continue in office a year. This was done accordingly in April 1775, and in the July following that convention passed an ordinance for the election of delegates in the month of April annually. It is well known, that in July 1775, a separation from Great-Britain and establishment of Republican government had never yet entered into any person's mind. A convention therefore, chosen under that ordinance, cannot be said to have been chosen for purposes which certainly did not exist in the minds of those who passed it. Under this ordinance, at the annual election in April 1776, a convention for the year was chosen. Independance, and the establishment of a new form of government, were not even yet the objects of the people at large. One extract from the pamphlet called

Common Sense had appeared in the Virginia papers in February, and copies of the pamphlet itself had got into a few hands. But the idea had not been opened to the mass of the people in April, much less can it be said that they had made up their minds in its favor. So that the electors of April 1776, no more than the legislators of July 1775, not thinking of independance and a permanent republic, could not mean to vest in these delegates powers of establishing them, or any authorities other than those of the ordinary legislature. So far as a temporary organization of government was necessary to render our opposition energetic, so far their organization was valid. But they received in their creation no powers but what were given to every legislature before and since. They could not therefore pass an act transcendant to the powers of other legislatures. If the present assembly pass any act, and declare it shall be irrevocable by subsequent assemblies, the declaration is merely void, and the act repealable, as other acts are. So far, and no farther authorized, they organized the government by the ordinance entitled a Constitution or Form of government. It pretends to no higher authority than the other ordinances of the same session; it does not say, that it shall be perpetual; that it shall be unalterable by other legislatures; that it shall be transcendant above the powers of those, who they knew would have equal power with themselves. Not only the silence of the instrument is a proof they thought it would be alterable, but their own practice also: for this very convention, meeting as a House of Delegates in General Assembly with the new Senate in the autumn of that year, passed acts of assembly in contradiction to their ordinance of government; and every assembly from that time to this has done the same. I am safe therefore in the position, that the constitution itself is alterable by the ordinary legislature. Though this opinion seems founded on the first elements of common sense, yet is the contrary maintained by some persons. 1. Because, say they, the conventions were vested with every power necessary to make effectual opposition to Great-Britain. But to complete this argument, they must go on, and say further, that effectual opposition could not be made to Great-Britain, without establishing a form of government perpetual and unalterable by the legislature; which is not true. An opposition which at some time or other was to come to an end, could not need a perpetual institution to carry it on: and a government, amendable as its defects should be discovered, was as likely to make effectual resistance, as one which should be unalterably wrong. Besides, the assemblies were as much vested with all powers requisite for resistance as the conventions were. If therefore these powers included that of modelling the form of government in the one case, they did so in the other. The assemblies then as well as the conventions may model the government; that is, they may alter the ordinance of government. 2. They urge, that if the convention had meant that this instrument should be alterable, as their other ordinances were, they would have called it an ordinance: but they have called it a *constitution*, which ex vi termini means 'an act above the power of the ordinary legislature.' I answer that *constitutio, constitutum, statutum, lex,* are convertible terms. '*Constitutio* dicitur jus quod a principe conditur.' '*Constitutum,* quod ab imperatoribus rescriptum statutumve est.' '*Statutum,* idem quod lex.' Calvini Lexicon juridicum. *Constitution* and *statute* were originally terms of the *civil law, and from thence introduced by Ecclesiastics into the English law. Thus in the statute 25 Hen. 8 c. 19. §. 1. '*Constitutions* and *ordinances*' are used as synonimous. The term *constitution* has many other significations in physics and in politics; but in Jurisprudence, whenever it is applied to any act of the legislature, it invariably means a statute, law, or ordinance, which is the present case. No inference then of a different meaning can be drawn from the adoption of this title: on the contrary, we might conclude, that, by their affixing to it a term synonimous with ordinance, or statute, they meant it to be an ordinance or statute. But of what consequence is their meaning, where their power is denied? If they meant to do more than they had power to do, did this give them power? It is not the name, but the authority which renders an act obligatory. Lord Coke says, 'an article of the statute II R. 2. c. 5. that no person should attempt to revoke any ordinance then made, is repealed, for that such restraint is against the jurisdiction and power of the parliament.' 4. inst. 42. and again, 'though divers parliaments have attempted to restrain subsequent parliaments, yet could they never effect it; for the latter parliament hath ever power to abrogate, suspend, qualify, explain, or make void the former in the whole or in any part thereof, notwithstanding any words of restraint, prohibition, or penalty, in the former: for it is a maxim in the laws of the parliament, quod leges posteriores priores contrarias abrogant.' 4. inst. 43.— To get rid of the magic supposed to be in the word *constitution*, let us translate it into its definition as given by those who think it above the power of the law; and let us

---

*To *bid*, to *set*, was the antient legislative word of the English. Ll. Hlotharii & Eadrici, Ll. Inae. Ll. Eadwerdi. Ll. Aathelstani.

suppose the convention instead of saying, 'We, the ordinary legislature, establish a *constitution,*' had said, 'We, the ordinary legislature, establish an act *above the power of the ordinary legislature.*' Does not this expose the absurdity of the attempt? 3. But, say they, the people have acquiesced, and this has given it an authority superior to the laws. It is true, that the people did not rebel against it: and was that a time for the people to rise in rebellion? Should a prudent acquiescence, at a critical time, be construed into a confirmation of every illegal thing done during that period? Besides, why should they rebel? At an annual election, they had chosen delegates for the year, to exercise the ordinary powers of legislation, and to manage the great contest in which they were engaged. These delegates thought the contest would be best managed by an organized government. They therefore, among others, passed an ordinance of government. They did not presume to call it perpetual and unalterable. They well knew they had no power to make it so; that our choice of them had been for no such purpose, and at a time when we could have no such purpose in contemplation. Had an unalterable form of government been meditated, perhaps we should have chosen a different set of people. There was no cause then for the people to rise in rebellion. But to what dangerous lengths will this argument lead? Did the acquiescence of the colonies under the various acts of power exercised by Great-Britain in our infant state, confirm these acts, and so far invest them with the authority of the people as to render them unalterable, and our present resistance wrong? On every unauthoritative exercise of power by the legislature, must the people rise in rebellion, or their silence be construed into a surrender of that power to them? If so, how many rebellions should we have had already? One certainly for every session of assembly. The other states in the Union have been of opinion, that to render a form of government unalterable by ordinary acts of assembly, the people must delegate persons with special powers. They have accordingly chosen special conventions to form and fix their governments. The individuals then who maintain the contrary opinion in this country, should have the modesty to suppose it possible that they may be wrong and the rest of America right. But if there be only a possibility of their being wrong, if only a plausible doubt remains of the validity of the ordinance of government, is it not better to remove that doubt, by placing it on a bottom which none will dispute? If they be right, we shall only have the unnecessary trouble of meeting once in convention. If they be wrong, they expose us to the hazard of having no fundamental rights at all. True it is, this is no time for deliberating on forms of government. While an enemy is within our bowels, the first object is to expel him. But when this shall be done, when peace shall be established, and leisure given us for intrenching within good forms, the rights for which we have bled, let no man be found indolent enough to decline a little more trouble for placing them beyond the reach of question. If any thing more be requisite to produce a conviction of the expediency of calling a convention, at a proper season, to fix our form of government, let it be the reflection,

6. That the assembly exercises a power of determining the Quorum of their own body which may legislate for us....

In enumerating the defects of the constitution, it would be wrong to count among them what is only the error of particular persons. In December 1776, our circumstances being much distressed, it was proposed in the house of delegates to create a *dictator*, invested with every power legislative, executive and judiciary, civil and military, of life and of death, over our persons and over our properties: and in June 1781, again under calamity, the same proposition was repeated, and wanted a few votes only of being passed.—One who entered into this contest from a pure love of liberty and a sense of injured rights, who determined to make every sacrifice, and to meet every danger, for the re-establishment of those rights on a firm basis, who did not mean to expend his blood and substance for the wretched purpose of changing this master for that, but to place the powers of governing him in a plurality of hands of his own choice, so that the corrupt will of no one man might in future oppress him, must stand confounded and dismayed when he is told, that a considerable portion of that plurality had meditated the surrender of them into a single hand, and, in lieu of a limited monarch, to deliver him over to a despotic one! How must we find his efforts and sacrifices abused and baffled, if he may still by a single vote be laid prostrate at the feet of one man! In God's name, from whence have they derived this power? Is it from our ancient laws? None such can be produced. Is it from any principle in our new constitution, expressed or implied? Every lineament of that expressed or implied, is in full opposition to it. Its fundamental principle is, that the state shall be governed as a commonwealth. It provides a republican organization, proscribes under the name of *prerogative* the exercise of all powers undefined by the laws; places on this basis the whole system of our laws; and, by consolidating them together, chuses that they shall be left to stand or fall together, never providing for any circumstances, nor admitting that such could arise, wherein either should be suspended, no, not for a moment…. Necessities which dissolve a government, do not convey its authority to an oligarchy or a monarchy. They throw back, into the hands of the people, the powers they had delegated, and leave them as individuals to shift for themselves. A leader may offer, but not impose himself, nor be imposed on them. Much less can their necks be submitted to his sword, their breath be held at his will or caprice. The necessity which should operate these tremendous effects should at least be palpable and irresistible. Yet in both instances, where it was feared, or pretended with us, it was belied by the event….

Education

Another object of the revisal is, to diffuse knowledge more generally through the mass of the people. This bill proposes to lay off every county into small districts of five or six miles square, called hundreds, and in each of them to establish a school for teaching reading, writing, and arithmetic. The tutor to be supported by the hundred, and every person in it entitled to send their children three years gratis, and as much longer as they please, paying for it. These schools to be under a visitor, who is annually to chuse the boy, of best genius in the school, of those whose parents are too poor to give them further education, and to send him forward to one of the grammar schools, of which twenty are proposed to be erected in different parts of the country, for teaching Greek, Latin, geography, and the higher branches of numerical arithmetic. Of the boys thus sent in any one year, trial is to be made at the grammar schools one or two years, and the best genius of the whole selected, and continued six years, and the residue dismissed. By this means twenty of the best geniusses will be raked from the rubbish annually, and be instructed, at the public expence, so far as the grammer schools go. At the end of six years instruction, one half are to be discontinued (from among whom the grammar schools will probably be supplied with future masters); and the other half, who are to be chosen for the superiority of their parts and disposition, are to be sent and continued three years in the study of such sciences as they shall chuse, at William and Mary college, the plan of which is proposed to be enlarged, as will be hereafter explained, and extended to all the useful sciences. The ultimate result of the whole scheme of education would be the teaching all the children of the state reading, writing, and common arithmetic: turning out ten annually of superior genius, well taught in Greek, Latin, geography, and the higher branches of arithmetic: turning out ten others annually, of still superior parts, who, to those branches of learning, shall have added such of the sciences as their genius shall have led them to: the furnishing to the wealthier part of the people convenient schools, at which their children may be educated, at their own expence…. By that part of our plan which prescribes the selection of the youths of genius from among the classes of the poor, we hope to avail the state of those talents which nature has sown as liberally among the poor as the rich, but which perish without use, if not sought for and cultivated.—But of all the views of this law none is more important, none more legitimate, than that of rendering the people the safe, as they are the ultimate, guardians of their own liberty. For this purpose the reading in the first stage, where *they* will receive their whole education, is proposed, as has been said, to be chiefly historical. History by apprising them of the past will enable them to judge of the future; it will avail them of the experience of other times and other nations; it will qualify them as judges of the actions and designs of men; it will enable them to know ambition under every disguise it may assume; and knowing it, to defeat its views. In every government on earth is some trace of human weakness, some germ of corruption and degeneracy, which cunning will discover, and wickedness insensibly open, cultivate, and improve. Every government degenerates when trusted to the rulers of the people alone. The people themselves therefore are its only safe depositories. And to render even them safe their minds must be improved to a certain degree. This indeed is not all that is necessary, though it be essentially necessary. An amendment of our constitution must here come in aid of the public education. The influence over government must be shared among all the people. If every individual which composes their mass participates of the ultimate authority, the government will be safe; because the corrupting the whole mass will exceed any private resources of wealth: and public ones cannot be provided but by levies on the people. In this case every man would have to pay his own price. The government of Great-Britain has been corrupted, because but one man in ten has a right to vote for members of parliament. The sellers of the government therefore get nine-tenths of their price clear. It has been thought that corruption is restrained by confining the right of suffrage to a few of the wealthier of the people: but it would be more effectually restrained by an extension of that right to such numbers as would bid defiance to the means of corruption.

Lastly, it is proposed, by a bill in this revisal, to begin a public library and gallery, by laying out a certain sum annually in books, paintings, and statues.

Religion

… The error seems not sufficiently eradicated, that the operations of the mind, as well as the acts of the body, are subject to the coercion of the laws. But our rulers can have authority over such natural rights only as we have submitted to them. The rights of conscience we never submitted, we could not submit. We are answerable for them to our God. The legitimate powers of government extend to such acts only as are injurious to others. But it does me no injury for my neighbour to say there are twenty gods, or no god. It neither picks my pocket nor breaks my leg. If it be said, his testimony in a court of justice cannot be relied on, reject it then, and be the stigma on him. Constraint may make him worse by making him a hypocrite, but it will never make him a truer man. It may fix him obstinately in his errors, but will not cure them. Reason and free enquiry are the only effectual agents against error. Give a loose to them, they will support the true religion, by bringing every false one to their tribunal to the test of their investigation…. It is error alone which needs the support of government. Truth can stand by itself. Subject opinion to coercion: whom will you make your inquisitors? Fallible men; men governed by bad passions, by private as well as public reasons. And why subject it to coercion? To produce uniformity. But is uniformity of opinion desireable? No more than of face and stature. Introduce the bed of Procrustes then, and as there is danger that the large men may beat the small, make us all of a size, by lopping the former and stretching the latter. Difference of opinion is advantageous in religion. The several sects perform the office of a Censor morum over each other. Is uniformity attainable? Millions of innocent men, women, and children, since the introduction of Christianity, have been burnt, tortured, fined, imprisoned; yet we have not advanced one inch towards uniformity. What has been the effect of coercion? To make one half the world fools, and the other half hypocrites….

Slavery

It is difficult to determine on the standard by which the manners of a nation may be tried, whether *catholic,* or *particular.* It is more difficult for a native to bring to that standard the manners of his own nation, familiarized to him by habit. There must doubtless be an unhappy influence on the manners of our people produced by the existence of slavery among us. The whole commerce between master and slave is a perpetual exercise of the most boisterous passions, the most unremitting despotism on the one part, and degrading submissions on the other. Our children see this, and learn to imitate it; for man is an imitative animal. This quality is the germ of all education in him. From his cradle to his grave he is learning to do what he sees others do. If a parent could find no motive either in his philanthropy or his self-love, for restraining the intemperance of passion towards his slave, it should always be a sufficient one that his child is present. But generally it is not sufficient. The parent storms, the child look on, catches the lineaments of wrath, puts on the same airs in the circle of smaller slaves, gives a loose to his worst of passions, and thus nursed, educated, and daily exercised in tyranny, cannot but be stamped by it with odious peculiarities. The man must be a prodigy who can retain his manners and morals undepraved by such circumstances. And with what execration should the statesman be loaded, who permitting one half the citizens thus to trample on the rights of the other, transforms those into despots, and these into enemies, destroys the morals of the one part, and the amor patriæ of the other. For if a slave can have a country in this world, it must be any other in preference to that in which he is born to live and labour for another: in which he must lock up the faculties of his nature, contribute as far as depends on his individual endeavours to the evanishment of the human race, or entail his own miserable condition on the endless generations proceeding from him. With the morals of the people, their industry also is destroyed. For in a warm climate, no man will labour for himself who can make another labour for him. This is so true, that of the proprietors of slaves a very small proportion indeed are ever seen to labour. And can the liberties of a nation be thought secure when we have removed their only firm basis, a conviction in the minds of the people that these liberties are of the gift of God? That they are not to be violated but with his wrath? Indeed I tremble for my country when I reflect that God is just: that his justice cannot sleep for ever: that considering numbers, nature and natural means only, a revolution of the wheel of fortune, an exchange of situation, is among possible events: that it may become probable by supernatural interference! The Almighty has no attribute which can take side with us in such a contest....

Manufactures

The political œconomists of Europe have established it as a principle that every state should endeavour to manufacture for itself: and this principle, like many others, we transfer to America, without calculating the difference of circumstance which should often produce a difference of result. In Europe the lands are either cultivated, or locked up against the cultivator. Manufacture must therefore be resorted to of necessity not of choice, to support the surplus of their people. But we have an immensity of land courting the industry of the husbandman. Is it best then that all our citizens should be employed in its improvement, or that one half should be called off from that to exercise manufactures and handicraft arts for the other? Those who labour in the earth are the chosen people of God, if ever he had a chosen people, whose breasts he has made his peculiar deposit for substantial and genuine virtue. It is the focus in which he keeps alive that sacred fire, which otherwise might escape from the face of the earth. Corruption of morals in the mass of cultivators is a phænomenon of which no age nor nation has furnished an example. It is the mark set on those, who not looking up to heaven, to their own soil and industry, as does the husbandman, for their subsistance, depend for it on the casualties and caprice of customers. Dependance begets subservience and venality, suffocates the germ of virtue, and prepares fit tools for the designs of ambition. This, the natural progress and consequence of the arts, has sometimes perhaps been retarded by accidental circumstances: but, generally speaking, the proportion which the aggregate of the other classes of citizens bears in any state to that of its husbandmen, is the proportion of its unsound to its healthy parts, and is a good-enough barometer whereby to measure its degree of corruption. While we have land to labour then, let us never wish to see our citizens occupied at a work-bench, or twirling a distaff....

Treaties of Commerce

To James Monroe, June 17, 1785

... I will take the liberty of hazarding to you some thoughts on the policy of entering into treaties with the European nations, and the nature of them. I am not wedded to these ideas, and therefore shall relinquish them chearfully when Congress shall adopt others, and zealously endeavor to carry theirs into effect. First as to the policy of making treaties. Congress, by the Confederation have no original and inherent power over the commerce of the states. But by the 9th article they are authorized to enter into treaties of commerce. The moment these treaties are concluded the jurisdiction of Congress over the commerce of the states springs into existence, and that of the particular states is superseded so far as the articles of the treaty may have taken up the subject. There are two restrictions only on the exercise of the power of treaty by Congress. 1st that they shall not by such treaty restrain the legislatures of the states from imposing such duties on foreigners as their own people are subject to. 2dly nor from prohibiting the exportation or importation of any particular species of goods. Leaving these two points free, Congress may by treaty establish any system of commerce they please. But, as I before observed, it is by treaty alone they can do it. Though they may exercise their other powers by resolution or ordinance, those over commerce can only be exercised by forming a treaty, and this probably by an accidental wording of our Confederation. If therefore it is better for the states that Congress should regulate their commerce, it is proper that they should form treaties with all nations with whom we may possibly trade. You see that my primary object in the formation of treaties is to take the commerce of the states out of the hands of the states, and to place it under the superintendence of Congress, so far as the imperfect provisions of our constitution will admit, and until the states shall by new compact make them more perfect. I would say then to every nation on earth, *by treaty*, your people shall trade freely with us, & ours with you, paying no more than the most favoured nation, in order to put an end to the right of individual states acting by fits and starts to interrupt our commerce or to embroil us with any nation. As to the terms of these treaties, the question becomes more difficult. I will mention three different plans. 1. that no duties shall be laid by either party on the productions of the other. 2. that each may be permitted to equalize their duties to those laid by the other. 3. that each shall pay in the ports of the other such duties only as the most favoured nations pay. 1. Were the nations of Europe as free and unembarrassed of established system as we are, I do verily believe they would concur with us in the first plan. But it is impossible. These establishments are fixed upon them, they are interwoven with the body of their laws & the organization of their government & they make a great part of their revenue; they cannot then get rid of them. 2. The plan of equal imposts presents difficulties insurmountable. For how are the equal imposts to be effected? Is it by laying in the ports of A. an equal percent on the goods of B. with that which B. has laid in his ports on the goods of A.? But how are we to find what is that percent? For this is not the usual form of imposts. They generally pay by the ton, by the measure, by the weight, & not by the value. Besides if A. sends a million's worth of goods to B. & takes back but the half of that, and each pays the same percent, it is evident that A. pays the double of what he recovers in the same way with B. This would be our case with Spain. Shall we endeavour to effect equality then by saying A. may levy so much on the sum of B.'s importations into his ports, as B. does on the sum of A's importations into the ports of B.? But how find out that sum? Will either party lay open their custom house books candidly to evince this sum? Does either keep their books so exactly as to be able to do it? This proposition was started in Congress when our institutions were formed, as you may remember, and the impossibility of executing it occasioned it to be disapproved. Besides who should have a right of deciding when the imposts were equal. A. would say to B. my imposts do not raise so much as yours; I raise them therefore. B. would then say you have made them greater than mine, I will raise mine, and thus a kind of auction would be carried on between them, and a mutual imitation, which would end in anything sooner than equality, and right. 3. I confess then to you that I see no alternative left but that which Congress adopted, of each party placing the other on the footing of the most favoured nation. If the nations of Europe from their actual establishments are not at liberty to say to America that she shall trade in their ports duty free they may say she may trade there paying no higher duties than the most favoured nation. And this is valuable in many of these countries where a very great difference is made between different nations. There is no difficulty in the execution of this contract, because there is not a merchant who does not know, or may not know, the duty paid by every nation on every article. This stipulation leaves each party at liberty to regulate their own commerce by general rules; while it secures the other from partial and oppressive discriminations. The difficulty which arises in our case is, with the nations having American territory. Access to the West Indies is indispensably necessary to us. Yet how to gain it, when it is the established system of these nations to exclude all foreigners from their colonies. The only chance seems to be this, our commerce to the mother countries is valuable to them. We must endeavor then to make this the price of an admission into their West Indies, and to those who refuse the admission we must refuse our commerce or load theirs by odious discriminations in our ports. We have this circumstance in our favour too, that what one grants us in their islands, the others will not find it worth their while to refuse. The misfortune is that with this country we gave this price for their aid in the war, and we have now nothing more to offer. She being withdrawn from the competition leaves Gr. Britain much more at liberty to hold out against us. This is the difficult part of the business of treaty, and I own it does not hold out the most flattering prospect.—I wish you would consider this subject and write me your thoughts on it. Mr. Gherry wrote me on the same subject. Will you give me leave to impose on you the trouble of communicating this to him? It is long, and will save me much labour in copying. I hope he will be so indulgent as to consider it as an answer to that part of his letter, and will give me his further thoughts on it....

AGRICULTURE, COMMERCE, AND SEA POWER
To John Jay, August 23, 1785

DEAR SIR,—I shall sometimes ask your permission to write you letters, not official but private. The present is of this kind, and is occasioned by the question proposed in yours of June 14. "whether it would be useful to us to carry all our own productions, or none?" Were we perfectly free to decide this question, I should reason as follows. We have now lands enough to employ an infinite number of people in their cultivation. Cultivators of the earth are the most valuable citizens. They are the most vigorous, the most independant, the most virtuous, & they are tied to their country & wedded to it's liberty & interests by the most lasting bonds. As long therefore as they can find employment in this line, I would not convert them into mariners, artisans or anything else. But our citizens will find employment in this line till their numbers, & of course their productions, become too great for the demand both internal & foreign. This is not the case as yet, & probably will not be for a considerable time. As soon as it is, the surplus of hands must be turned to something else. I should then perhaps wish to turn them to the sea in preference to manufactures, because comparing the characters of the two classes I find the former the most valuable citizens. I consider the class of artificers as the panders of vice & the instruments by which the liberties of a country are generally overturned. However we are not free to decide this question on principles of theory only. Our people are decided in the opinion that it is necessary for us to take a share in the occupation of the ocean, & their established habits induce them to require that the sea be kept open to them, and that that line of policy be pursued which will render the use of that element as great as possible to them. I think it a duty in those entrusted with the administration of their affairs to conform themselves to the decided choice of their constituents: and that therefore we should in every instance preserve an equality of right to them in the transportation of commodities, in the right of fishing, & in the other uses of the sea. But what will be the consequence? Frequent wars without a doubt. Their property will be violated on the sea, & in foreign ports, their persons will be insulted, imprisoned &c. for pretended debts, contracts, crimes, contraband, &c., &c. These insults must be resented, even if we had no feelings, yet to prevent their eternal repetition, or in other words, our commerce on the ocean & in other countries must be paid for by frequent war. The justest dispositions possible in ourselves will not secure us against it. It would be necessary that all other nations were just also. Justice indeed on our part will save us from those wars which would have been produced by a contrary disposition. But to prevent those produced by the wrongs of other nations? By putting ourselves in a condition to punish them. Weakness provokes insult & injury, while a condition to punish it often prevents it. This reasoning leads to the necessity of some naval force, that being the only weapon with which we can reach an enemy. I think it to our interest to punish the first insult; because an insult unpunished is the parent of many others. We are not at this moment in a condition to do it, but we should put ourselves into it as soon as possible. If a war with england should take place, it seems to me that the first thing necessary would be a resolution to abandon the carrying trade because we cannot protect it. Foreign nations must in that case be invited to bring us what we want & to take our productions in their own bottoms. This alone could prevent the loss of those productions to us & the acquisition of them to our enemy. Our seamen might be employed in depredations on their trade. But how dreadfully we shall suffer on our coasts, if we have no force on the water, former experience has taught us. Indeed I look forward with horror to the very possible case of war with an European power, & think there is no protection against them but from the possession of some force on the sea. Our vicinity to their West India possessions & to the fisheries is a bridle which a small naval force on our part would hold in the mouths of the more powerful of these countries. I hope our land office will rid us of our debts, & that our first attention then will be to the beginning a naval force of some sort. This alone can countenance our people as carriers on the water, & I suppose them to be determined to continue such.] …

I wrote you two public letters on the 14th inst., since which I have received yours of July 13. I shall always be pleased to receive from you in a private way such communications as you might not dhuse to put into a public letter.

"BUT THIS IS THEORY ONLY"
To G. K. van Hogendorp, October 13, 1785

… You ask what I think on the expediency of encouraging our states to be commercial? Were I to indulge in my own theory, I should wish them to practise neither commerce nor navigation, but to stand with respect to Europe precisely on the footing of China. We should thus avoid wars, and all our citizens would be husbandmen. Whenever indeed our numbers should so increase as that our produce would overstock the markets of those nations who should come to seek it, the farmers must either employ the surplus of their time in manufactures, or the surplus of our hands must be employed in manufactures, or in navigation. But that day would, I think be distant, and we should long keep our workmen in Europe, while Europe should be drawing rough materials & even subsistence from America. But this is theory only, & a theory which the servants of America are not at liberty to follow. Our people have a decided taste for navigation & commerce. They take this from their mother country: & their servants are in duty bound to calculate all their measures on this datum: we wish to do it by throwing open all the doors of commerce & knocking off its shackles. But as this cannot be done for others, unless they will do it for us, & there is no great probability that Europe will do this, I suppose we shall be obliged to adopt a system which may shackle them in our ports as they do us in theirs....

PROPERTY AND NATURAL RIGHT
To James Madison, October 28, 1785

... Seven o'clock, and retired to my fireside, I have determined to enter into conversation with you. This is a village of about 15,000 inhabitants [Fontainebleau] when the court is not here, and 20,000 when they are, occupying a valley through which runs a brook and on each side of it a ridge of small mountains, most of which are naked rock. The King comes here, in the fall always, to hunt. His court attend him, as do also the foreign diplomatic corps; but as this is not indispensably required and my finances do not admit the expense of a continued residence here, I propose to come occasionally to attend the King's levees, returning again to Paris, distant forty miles. This being the first trip, I set out yesterday morning to take a view of the place. For this purpose I shaped my course towards the highest of the mountains in sight, to the top of which was about a league.

As soon as I had got clear of the town I fell in with a poor woman walking at the same rate with myself and going the same course. Wishing to know the condition of the laboring poor I entered into conversation with her, which I began by enquiries for the path which would lead me into the mountain: and thence proceeded to enquiries into her vocation, condition and circumstances. She told me she was a day laborer at 8 sous or 4^d sterling the day: that she had two children to maintain, and to pay a rent of 30 livres for her house (which would consume the hire of 75 days), that often she could get no employment and of course was without bread. As we had walked together near a mile and she had so far served me as a guide, I gave her, on parting, 24 sous. She burst into tears of a gratitude which I could perceive was unfeigned because she was unable to utter a word. She had probably never before received so great an aid. This little *attendrissement,* with the solitude of my walk, led me into a train of reflections on that unequal division of property which occasions the numberless instances of wretchedness which I had observed in this country and is to be observed all over Europe.

The property of this country is absolutely concentrated in a very few hands, having revenues of from half a million of guineas a year downwards. These employ the flower of the country as servants, some of them having as many as 200 domestics, not laboring. They employ also a great number of manufacturers and tradesmen, and lastly the class of laboring husbandmen. But after all there comes the most numerous of all classes, that is, the poor who cannot find work. I asked myself what could be the reason so many should be permitted to beg who are willing to work, in a country where there is a very considerable proportion of uncultivated lands? These lands are undisturbed only for the sake of game. It should seem then that it must be because of the enormous wealth of the proprietors which places them above attention to the increase of their revenues by permitting these lands to be labored. I am conscious that an equal division of property is impracticable, but the consequences of this enormous inequality producing so much misery to the bulk of mankind, legislators cannot invent too many devices for subdividing property, only taking care to let their subdivisions go hand in hand with the natural affections of the human mind. The descent of property of every kind therefore to all the children, or to all the brothers and sisters, or other relations in equal degree, is a politic measure and a practicable one. Another means of silently lessening the inequality of property is to exempt all from taxation below a certain point, and to tax the higher portions or property in geometrical progression as they rise. Whenever there are in any country uncultivated lands and unemployed poor, it is clear that the laws of property have been so far extended as to violate natural right. The earth is given as a common stock for man to labor and live on. If for the encouragement of industry we allow it to be appropriated, we must take care that other employment be provided to those excluded from the appropriation. If we do not, the fundamental right to labor the earth returns to the unemployed. It is too soon yet in our country to say that every man who cannot find employment, but who can find uncultivated land, shall be at liberty to cultivate it, paying a moderate rent. But it is not too soon to provide by every possible means that as few as possible shall be without a little portion of land. The small landholders are the most precious part of a state....

🌿

Answers and Observations for Démeunier's Article on the United States for the "Encyclopedie Methodique," 1786
The Confederation

11. The Confederation is a wonderfully perfect instrument, considering the circumstances under which it was formed. There are however some alterations which experience proves to be wanting. These are principally three. 1. To establish a general rule for the admission of new states into the Union. By the Confederation no new state, except Canada, can be permitted to have a vote in Congress without first obtaining the consent of all the thirteen legislatures. It becomes necessary to agree what districts may be established into separate states, and at what period of their population they may come into Congress. The act of Congress of April 23, 1784, has pointed out what ought to be agreed on, to say also what number of votes must concur when the number of voters shall be thus enlarged. 2. The Confederation in it's eighth article, decides that the quota of money to be contributed by the several states shall be proportioned to the value of landed property in the state. Experience has shown it impracticable to come at this value. Congress have therefore recommended to the states to agree that their quotas shall be in proportion to the number of their inhabitants, counting 5 slaves however but as equal to 3 free inhabitants. I believe all the states have agreed to this alteration except Rhode island. 3. The Confederation forbids the states individually to enter into treaties of commerce, or of any other nature, with foreign nations: and it authorizes Congress to establish such treaties, with two reservations however, viz., that they shall agree to no treaty which would 1. restrain the legislatures from imposing such duties on foreigners, as natives are subjected to; or 2. from prohibiting the exportation or importation of any species of commodities. Congress may therefore be said to have a power to regulate commerce, so far as it can be effected by conventions with other nations, & by conventions which do not infringe the two fundamental reservations before mentioned. But this is too imperfect. Because till a

convention be made with any particular nation, the commerce of any one of our states with that nation may be regulated by the State itself, and even when a convention is made, the regulation of the commerce is taken out of the hands of the several states only so far as it is covered or provided for by that convention or treaty. But treaties are made in such general terms, that the greater part of the regulations would still result to the legislatures…. The principal objects in the regulation of our commerce would be: 1. to lay such duties, restrictions, or prohibitions on the goods of any particular nation as might oblige that nation to concur in just & equal arrangements of commerce. 2. To lay such uniform duties on the articles of commerce throughout all the states, as may avail them of that fund for assisting to bear the burthen of public expenses. Now this cannot be done by the states separately; because they will not separately pursue the same plan. New Hampshire cannot lay a given duty on a particular article, unless Massachusetts will do the same; because it will turn the importation of that article from her ports into those of Massachusetts, from whence they will be smuggled into New Hampshire by land. But tho Massachusetts were willing to concur with N Hampshire in laying the same duty, yet she cannot do it, for the same reason, unless Rhode island will also, nor can Rhode island without Connecticut, nor Connecticut without N York, nor N York without N Jersey, & so on quite to Georgia. It is visible therefore that the commerce of the states cannot be regulated to the best advantage but by a single body, and no body so proper as Congress. Many of the states have agreed to add an article to the Confederation for allowing to Congress the regulation of their commerce, only providing that the revenues to be raised on it, shall belong to the state in which they are levied….

21. Broils among the states may happen in the following ways: 1. A state may be embroiled with the other twelve by not complying with the lawful requisitions of Congress. 2. Two states may differ about their boundaries. But the method of settling these is fixed by the Confederation, and most of the states which have any differences of this kind are submitting them to this mode of determination; and there is no danger of opposition to the decree by any state. The individuals interested may complain, but this can produce no difficulty. 3. Other contestations may arise between two states, such as pecuniary demands, affrays among their citizens, & whatever else may arise between any two nations. With respect to these, there are two opinions. One that they

are to be decided according to the 9th article of the Confederation, which says that "Congress shall be the last resort in all differences between two or more states, concerning boundary jurisdiction *or any other cause whatever*"; and prescribes the mode of decision and the weight of reason is undoubtedly in favor of this opinion, yet there are some who question it.

It has been often said that the decisions of Congress are impotent because the Confederation provides no compulsory power. But when two or more nations enter into compact, it is not usual for them to say what shall be done to the party who infringes it. Decency forbids this, and it is unnecessary as indecent, because the right of compulsion naturally results to the party injured by the breach. When any one state in the American Union refuses obedience to the Confederation by which they have bound themselves, the rest have a natural right to compel them to obedience. Congress would probably exercise long patience before they would recur to force; but if the case ultimately required it, they would use that recurrence. Should this case ever arise, they will probably coerce by a naval force, as being more easy, less dangerous to liberty, & less likely to produce much bloodshed.

It has been said too that our governments both federal and particular want energy; that it is difficult to restrain both individuals & states from committing wrong. This is true, & it is an inconvenience. On the other hand that energy which absolute governments derive from an armed force, which is the effect of the bayonet constantly held at the breast of every citizen, and which resembles very much the stillness of the grave, must be admitted also to have it's inconveniences. We weigh the two together, and like best to submit to the former. Compare the number of wrongs committed with impunity by citizens among us, with those committed by the sovereign in other countries, and the last will be found most numerous, most oppressive on the mind, and most degrading of the dignity of man....

Crimes and Punishments

In forming a scale of crimes & punishments, two considerations have principal weight. 1. The atrocity of the crime. 2. The peculiar circumstances of a country which furnish greater temptations to commit it, or greater facilities for escaping detection.

The punishment must be heavier to counterbalance this. Was the first the only consideration, all nations would form the same scale. But as the circumstances of a country have influence on the punishment, and no two countries exist precisely under the same circumstances, no two countries will form the same scale of crimes & punishments. For example in America, the inhabitants let their horses go at large in the uninclosed lands which are so extensive as to maintain them altogether. It is easy therefore to steal them & easy to escape. Therefore the laws are obliged to oppose these temptations with a heavier degree of punishment. For this reason the stealing of a horse in America is punished more severely than stealing the same value in any other form. In Europe where horses are confined so securely that it is impossible to steal them, that species of theft need not be punished more severely than any other. In some countries of Europe, stealing fruit from trees is punished capitally. The reason is that it being impossible to lock fruit trees up in coffers, as we do our money, it is impossible to oppose physical bars to this species of theft. Moral ones are therefore opposed by the laws. This to an unreflecting American, appears the most enormous of all the abuses of power; because he has been used to see fruits hanging in such quantities that if not taken by men they would rot: he has been used to consider it therefore as of no value, as not furnishing materials for the commission of a crime. This must serve as an apology for the arrangements of crimes & punishments in the scale under our consideration. A different one would be formed here; & still different ones in Italy, Turkey, China, &c....

Society of the Cincinnati

Having been in America during the period in which this institution was formed, and being then in a situation which gave me opportunities of seeing it in all it's stages, I may venture to give M. de Meusnier materials for the 1st branch of the preceding distribution of the subject. The 2d and 3d he will best execute himself. I should write it's history in the following form.

When, on the close of that war which established the independance of America, it's army was about to be disbanded, the officers, who during the course of it had gone thro the most trying scenes together, who by mutual aids & good offices had become dear to one another, felt with great oppression of mind the approach of that moment which was to separate them never perhaps to meet again. They were from different states & from distant parts of the same state. Hazard alone could therefore give them but rare & partial occasions of seeing each other. They were of course to abandon altogether the hope of ever meeting again, or to devise some occasion which might bring them together. And why not come together on purpose at stated times? Would not the trouble of such a journey be greatly overpaid by the pleasure of seeing each other again, by the sweetest of all consolations, the talking over the scenes of difficulty & of endearment they had gone through? This too would enable them to know who of them should succeed in the world, who should be unsuccessful, and to open the purses of all to every labouring brother. This idea was too soothing not to be cherished in conversation. It was improved into that of a regular association with an organized administration, with periodical meetings general & particular, fixed contributions for those who should be in distress, & a badge by which not only those who had not had occasion to become personally known should be able to recognize one another, but which should be worn by their descendants to perpetuate among them the friendships which had bound their ancestors together. Genl. Washington was at that moment oppressed with the operation of disbanding an army which was not paid, and the difficulty of this operation was increased by some two or three of the states having expressed sentiments which did not indicate a sufficient attention to their paiment. He was sometimes present when his officers were fashioning in their conversations their newly proposed society. He saw the innocence of it's origin, & foresaw no effects less innocent. He was at that time writing his valedictory letter to the states, which has been so deservedly applauded by the world. Far from thinking it a moment to multiply the causes of irritation, by thwarting a proposition which had absolutely no other basis but of benevolence & friendship, he was rather satisfied to find himself aided in his difficulties by this new incident, which occupied, &, at the same time soothed the minds of the officers. He thought too that this institution would be one instrument the more for strengthening the federal bond, & for promoting federal ideas. The institution was formed. They incorporated into it the officers of the French army & navy by whose sides they had fought, and with whose aid they had finally prevailed, extending it to such grades as they were told might be permitted to enter into it. They sent an officer to France to make the proposition to them & to procure the badges which they had devised for their order. The moment of disbanding the army having come on before they could have a full meeting to appoint their president, the General was prayed to act in that office till their first general meeting which was to be held at Philadelphia in the month of May following. The laws of the society were published. Men who read them in their closets, unwarmed by those sentiments of friendship which had produced them, inattentive to those pains which an approaching separation had excited in the minds of the institutors, Politicians, who see in everything only the dangers with which it threatens civil society, in fine the labouring people, who, shielded by equal laws, had never seen any difference between man and man, but had read of terrible oppressions which people of their description experience in other countries from those who are distinguished by titles & badges, began to be alarmed at this new institution. A remarkable silence however was observed. Their sollicitudes were long confined within the circles of private conversation. At length however, a Mr. Burke, chief justice of South Carolina, broke that silence. He wrote against the new institution; foreboding it's dangers very imperfectly indeed, because he had nothing but his imagination to aid him. An American could do no more: for to detail the real evils of aristocracy they must be seen in Europe. Burke's fears were thought exaggerations in America; while in Europe it is known that even Mirabeau has but faintly sketched the curses of hereditary aristocracy as they are experienced here, and as they would have followed in America had this institution remained. The epigraph of Burke's pamphlet was "Blow ye the trumpet in Zion." It's effect corresponded with it's epigraph. This institution became first the subject of general conversation. Next it was made the subject of deliberation in the legislative assemblies of some of the States. The governor of South Carolina censured it in an address to his Assembly. The assemblies of Massachusetts, Rhode island and Pennsylvania condemned it's principles. No circumstance indeed brought the consideration of it expressly before Congress, yet it had sunk deep into their minds. An offer having been made to them on the part of the Polish order of divine providence to receive some of their distinguished citizens into that order, they made that an occasion to declare that these distinctions were contrary to the principles of their confederation. The uneasiness excited by this institution had very early caught the notice of General Washington. Still recollecting all the purity of the motives which gave it birth, he became sensible that it might produce political evils which the warmth of these motives had masked. Add to this that it was disapproved by the mass of citizens of the Union. This alone was reason strong enough in a country where the will of the majority is the law, & ought to be the law. He saw that the objects of the institution were too light to be opposed to considerations as serious as these; and that it was become necessary to annihilate it absolutely. On this therefore he was decided. The first annual meeting at Philadelphia was now at hand. He went to that, determined to exert all his influence for it's suppression. He proposed it to his fellow officers, and urged it with all his powers. It met an opposition which was observed to cloud his face with an anxiety that the most distressful scenes of the war had scarcely ever produced. It was canvassed for several days, & at length it was no more a doubt what would be it's ultimate fate. The order was on the point of receiving it's annihilation by the vote of a very great majority of it's members. In this moment their envoy arrived from France, charged with letters from the French officers accepting with cordiality the proposed badges of union, with sollicitations from others to be received into the order, & with notice that their respectable sovereign had been pleased to recognize it, & permit his officers to wear it's badges. The prospect now changed. The question assumed a new form. After the offer made by them, & accepted by their friends, in what words could they clothe a proposition to retract it which would not cover themselves with the reproaches of levity & ingratitude? which would not appear an insult to those whom they loved? Federal principles, popular discontent, were considerations whose weight was known & felt by themselves. But would foreigners know & feel them equally? Would they so far acknowledge their cogency as to permit without any indignation the eagle & ribbon to be torn from their breasts by the very hands which had placed them there? The idea revolted the whole society. They found it necessary then to preserve so much of their institution as might continue to support this foreign branch, while they should prune off every other which would give offence to their fellow citizens; thus sacrificing on each hand to their friends & to their country. The society was to retain it's existence, it's name, it's meetings, & it's charitable funds: but these last were to be deposited with their respective legislatures; the order was to be no longer hereditary; a reformation which had been pressed even from this side of the Atlantic; it was to be communicated to no new members; the general meetings instead of annual were to be triennial only. The eagle & ribbon indeed were retained; because they were worn, & they wished them to be worn, by their friends who were in a country where they would not be objects of offence; but themselves never wore them. They laid them up in their bureaus with the medals of American Independance, with those of the trophies they had taken & the battles they had won. But through all the United States no officer is seen to offend the public eye with the display of this badge. These changes have tranquilized the American states. Their citizens do justice to the circumstances which prevented a total annihilation of the order. They feel too much interest in the reputation of their officers, and value too much whatever may serve to recall to the memory of their allies the moments wherein they formed but one people. Tho they are obliged by a prudent foresight to keep out everything from among themselves which might pretend to divide them into orders, and to degrade one description of men below another, yet they hear with pleasure that their allies whom circumstances have already placed under these distinctions, are willing to consider it as one to have aided them in the establishment of their liberties & to wear a badge which may recall to their remembrance; and it would be an extreme affliction to them if the domestic reformation which has been found necessary, if the censures of individual writers, or if any other circumstance should discourage the wearing their badge, or lessen it's reputation.

This short but true history of the order of the Cincinnati, taken from the mouths of persons on the spot who were privy to it's origin & progress, & who knew it's present state, is the best apology which can be made for an institution which appeared to be, & was really, so heterogeneous to the governments in which it was erected....

"A CRUSADE AGAINST IGNORANCE"
To George Wythe, August 13, 1786

... The European papers have announced that the assembly of Virginia were occupied on the revisal of their code of laws. This, with some other similar intelligence, has contributed much to convince the people of Europe, that what the English papers are constantly publishing of our anarchy, is false; as they are sensible that such a work is that of a people only who are in perfect tranquillity. Our act for freedom of religion is extremely applauded. The ambassadors & ministers of the several nations of Europe resident at this court have asked of me copies of it to send to their sovereigns, and it is inserted at full length in several books now in the press; among others, in the new Encyclopedie. I think it will produce considerable good even in these countries where ignorance, superstition, poverty, & oppression of body & mind in every form, are so firmly settled on the mass of the people, that their redemption from them can never be hoped. If the Almighty had begotten a thousand sons, instead of one, they would not have sufficed for this task. If all the sovereigns of Europe were to set themselves to work to emancipate the minds of their subjects from their present ignorance & prejudices, & that as zealously as they now endeavor the contrary, a thousand years would not place them on that high ground on which our common people are now setting out. Ours could not have been so fairly put into the hands of their own common sense had they not been separated from their parent stock & kept from contamination, either from them, or the other people of the old world, by the intervention of so wide an ocean. To know the worth of this, one must see the want of it here. I think by far the most important bill in our whole code is that for the diffusion of knowledge among the people. No other sure foundation can be devised, for the preservation of freedom and happiness. If anybody thinks that kings, nobles, or priests are good conservators of the public happiness send them here. It is the best school in the universe to cure them of that folly. They will see here with their own eyes that these descriptions of men are an abandoned confederacy against the happiness of the mass of the people. The omnipotence of their effect cannot be better proved than in this country particularly, where notwithstanding the finest soil upon earth, the finest climate under heaven, and a people of the most benevolent, the most gay and amiable character of which the human form is susceptible, where such a people I say, surrounded by so many blessings from nature, are yet loaded with misery by kings, nobles and priests, and by them alone. Preach, my dear Sir, a crusade against ignorance; establish & improve the law for educating the common people. Let our countrymen know that the people alone can protect us against these evils, and that the tax which will be paid for this purpose is not more than the thousandth part of what will be paid to kings, priests & nobles who will rise up among us if we leave the people in ignorance....

Shays' Rebellion

To Edward Carrington, January 16, 1787

… The tumults in America, I expected would have produced in Europe an unfavorable opinion of our political state. But it has not. On the contrary, the small effect of these tumults seems to have given more confidence in the firmness of our governments. The interposition of the people themselves on the side of government has had a great effect on the opinion here. I am persuaded myself that the good sense of the people will always be found to be the best army. They may be led astray for a moment, but will soon correct themselves. The people are the only censors of their governors: and even their errors will tend to keep these to the true principles of their institution. To punish these errors too severely would be to suppress the only safeguard of the public liberty. The way to prevent these irregular interpositions of the people is to give them full information of their affairs thro' the channel of the public papers, & to contrive that those papers should penetrate the whole mass of the people. The basis of our governments being the opinion of the people, the very first object should be to keep that right; and were it left to me to decide whether we should have a government without newspapers or newspapers without a government, I should not hesitate a moment to prefer the latter. But I should mean that every man should receive those papers & be capable of reading them. I am convinced that those societies (as the Indians) which live without government enjoy in their general mass an infinitely greater degree of happiness than those who live under the European governments. Among the former, public opinion is in the place of law, & restrains morals as powerfully as laws ever did anywhere. Among the latter, under pretence of governing they have divided their nations into two classes, wolves & sheep. I do not exaggerate. This is a true picture of Europe. Cherish therefore the spirit of our people, and keep alive their attention. Do not be too severe upon their errors, but reclaim them by enlightening them. If once they become inattentive to the public affairs, you & I, & Congress & Assemblies, judges & governors shall all become wolves. It seems to be the law of our general nature, in spite of individual exceptions; and experience declares that man is the only animal which devours his own kind, for I can apply no milder term to the governments of Europe, and to the general prey of the rich on the poor....

❦

"A LITTLE REBELLION NOW AND THEN"
To James Madison, January 30, 1787

... I am impatient to learn your sentiments on the late troubles in the Eastern states. So far as I have yet seen, they do not appear to threaten serious consequences. Those states have suffered by the stoppage of the channels of their commerce, which have not yet found other issues. This must render money scarce, and make the people uneasy. This uneasiness has produced acts absolutely unjustifiable; but I hope they will provoke no severities from their governments. A consciousness of those in power that their administration of the public affairs has been honest, may perhaps produce too great a degree of indignation: and those characters wherein fear predominates over hope may apprehend too much from these instances of irregularity. They may conclude too hastily that nature has formed man insusceptible of any other government but that of force, a conclusion not founded in truth, nor experience. Societies exist under three forms sufficiently distinguishable. 1. Without government, as among our Indians. 2. Under governments wherein the will of every one has a just influence, as is the case in England in a slight degree, and in our states, in a great one. 3. Under governments of force: as is the case in all other monarchies and in most of the other republics. To have an idea of the curse of existence under these last, they must be seen. It is a government of wolves over sheep. It is a problem, not clear in my mind, that the 1st condition is not the best. But I believe it to be inconsistent with any great degree of population. The second state has a great deal of good in it. The mass of mankind under that enjoys a precious degree of liberty & happiness. It has it's evils too: the principal of which is the turbulence to which it is subject. But weigh this against the oppressions of monarchy, and it becomes nothing. *Malo periculosam libertatem quam quietam servitutem.* Even this evil is productive of good. It prevents the degeneracy of government, and nourishes a general attention to the public affairs. I hold it that a little rebellion now and then is a

79

good thing, & as necessary in the political world as storms in the physical. Unsuccessful rebellions indeed generally establish the encroachments on the rights of the people which have produced them. An observation of this truth should render honest republican governors so mild in their punishment of rebellions, as not to discourage them too much. It is a medicine necessary for the sound health of government....

THE NEW CONSTITUTION
To William S. Smith, November 13, 1787

... I do not know whether it is to yourself or Mr. Adams I am to give my thanks for the copy of the new constitution. I beg leave through you to place them where due. It will be yet three weeks before I shall receive them from America. There are very good articles in it: & very bad. I do not know which preponderate. What we have lately read in the history of Holland, in the chapter on the Stadtholder, would have sufficed to set me against a chief magistrate eligible for a long duration, if I had ever been disposed towards one: & what we have always read of the elections of Polish kings should have forever excluded the idea of one continuable for life. Wonderful is the effect of impudent & persevering lying. The British ministry have so long hired their gazetteers to repeat and model into every form lies about our being in anarchy, that the world has at length believed them, the English nation has believed them, the ministers themselves have come to believe them, & what is more wonderful, we have believed them ourselves. Yet where does this anarchy exist? Where did it ever exist, except in the single instance of Massachusetts? And can history produce an instance of rebellion so honourably conducted? I say nothing of it's motives. They were founded in ignorance, not wickedness. God forbid we should ever be 20 years without such a rebellion. The people cannot be all, & always, well informed. The part which is wrong will be discontented in proportion to the importance of the facts they misconceive. If they remain quiet under such misconceptions it is a lethargy, the forerunner of death to the public liberty. We have had 13. states independent 11. years. There has been one rebellion. That comes to one rebellion in a century & a half for each state. What country before ever existed a century & half without a rebellion? & what country can preserve it's liberties if their rulers are not warned from time to time that their people preserve the spirit of resistance? Let them take arms. The remedy is to set them right as to facts, pardon & pacify them. What signify a few lives lost in a century or two? The tree of liberty must be refreshed from time to time with the blood of patriots & tyrants. It is it's natural manure. Our Convention has been too much impressed by the insurrection of Massachusetts: and in the spur of the moment they are setting up a kite to keep the hen-yard in order. I hope in God this article will be rectified before the new constitution is accepted....

❧

MORE ON THE CONSTITUTION
To John Adams, November 13, 1787

... How do you like our new constitution? I confess there are things in it which stagger all my dispositions to subscribe to what such an assembly has proposed. The house of federal representatives will not be adequate to the management of affairs either foreign or federal. Their President seems a bad edition of a Polish king. He may be reelected from 4. years to 4. years for life. Reason and experience prove to us that a chief magistrate, so continuable, is an officer for life. When one or two generations shall have proved that this is an office for life, it becomes on every succession worthy of intrigue, of bribery, of force, and even of foreign interference. It will be of great consequence to France and England to have America governed by a Galloman or Angloman. Once in office, and possessing the military force of the union, without either the aid or check of a council, he would not be easily dethroned, even if the people could be induced to withdraw their votes from him. I wish that at the end of the 4. years they had made him for ever ineligible a second time. Indeed I think all the good of this new constitution might have been couched in three or four new articles to be added to the good, old, and venerable fabrick, which should have been preserved even as a religious relique....

"A BILL OF RIGHTS IS WHAT THE PEOPLE ARE ENTITLED TO"
To James Madison, December 20, 1787

… The season admitting only of operations in the Cabinet, and these being in a great measure secret, I have little to fill a letter. I will therefore make up the deficiency by adding a few words on the Constitution proposed by our Convention. I like much the general idea of framing a government which should go on of itself peaceably, without needing continual recurrence to the state legislatures. I like the organization of the government into Legislative, Judiciary & Executive. I like the power given the Legislature to levy taxes, and for that reason solely approve of the greater house being chosen by the people directly. For tho' I think a house chosen by them will be very illy qualified to legislate for the Union, for foreign nations &c. yet this evil does not weigh against the good of preserving inviolate the fundamental principle that the people are not to be taxed but by representatives chosen immediately by themselves. I am captivated by the compromise of the opposite claims of the great & little states, of the latter to equal, and the former to proportional influence. I am much pleased too with the substitution of the method of voting by persons, instead of that of voting by states: and I like the negative given to the Executive with a third of either house, though I should have liked it better had the Judiciary been associated for that purpose, or invested with a similar and separate power. There are other good things of less moment. I will now add what I do not like. First the omission of a bill of rights providing clearly & without the aid of sophisms for freedom of religion, freedom of the press, protection against standing armies, restriction against monopolies, the eternal & unremitting force of the habeas corpus laws, and trials by jury in all matters of fact triable by the laws of the land & not by the law of nations. To say, as Mr. Wilson does that a bill of rights was not necessary because all is reserved in the case of the general government which is not given, while in the particular ones all is given which is not reserved, might do for the audience to whom it was addressed, but is surely a gratis dictum, opposed by strong inferences from the body of the instrument, as well as from the omission of the clause of our present confederation which had declared that in express terms. It was a hard conclusion to say because there has been no uniformity among the states as to the cases triable by jury, because some have been so incautious as to abandon this mode of trial, therefore the more prudent states shall be reduced to the same level of calamity. It would have been much more just & wise to have concluded the other way that as most of the states had judiciously preserved this palladium, those who had wandered should be brought back to it, and to have established general right instead of general wrong. Let me add that a bill of rights is what the people are entitled to against every government on earth, general or particular, & what no just government should refuse, or rest on inferences. The second feature I dislike, and greatly dislike, is the abandonment in every instance of the necessity of rotation in office, and most particularly in the case of the President. Experience concurs with reason in concluding that the first magistrate will always be re-elected if the Constitution permits it. He is then an officer for life. This once observed, it becomes of so much consequence to certain nations to have a friend or a foe at the head of our affairs that they will interfere with money & with arms. A Galloman or an Angloman will be supported by the nation he befriends. If once elected, and at a second or third election out voted by one or two votes, he will pretend false votes, foul play, hold possession of the reins of government, be supported by the States voting for him, especially if they are the central ones lying in a compact body themselves & separating their opponents: and they will be aided by one nation of Europe, while the majority are aided by another. The election of a President of America some years hence will be much more interesting to certain nations of Europe than ever the election of a king of Poland was. Reflect on all the instances in history antient & modern, of elective monarchies, and say if they do not give foundation for my fears. The Roman emperors, the popes, while they were of any importance, the German emperors till they became hereditary in practice, the kings of Poland, the Deys of the Ottoman dependances. It may be said that if elections are to be attended with these disorders, the seldomer they are renewed the better. But experience shews that the only way to prevent disorder is to render them uninteresting by frequent changes. An incapacity to be elected a second time would have been the only effectual preventative. The power of removing him every fourth year by the vote of the people is a power which will not be exercised. The king of Poland is removeable every day by the Diet, yet he is never removed.—Smaller objections are the Appeal in fact as well as law, and the binding all persons Legislative Executive & Judiciary by oath to maintain that constitution. I do not pretend to decide what would be the best method of procuring the establishment of the manifold good things in this constitution, and of getting rid of the bad. Whether by adopting it in hopes of future amendment, or, after it has been duly weighed & canvassed by the people, after seeing the parts they generally dislike, & those they generally approve, to say to them 'We see now what you wish. Send together your deputies again, let them frame a constitution for you omitting what you have condemned, & establishing the powers you approve. Even these will be a great addition to the energy of your government.'—At all events I hope you will not be discouraged from other trials, if the present one should fail of its full effect.—I have thus told you freely what I like & dislike: merely as a matter of curiosity, for I know your own judgment has been formed on all these points after having heard everything which could be urged on them. I own I am not a friend to a very energetic government. It is always oppressive. The late rebellion in Massachusetts has given more alarm than I think it should have done. Calculate that one rebellion in 13 states in the course of 11 years, is but one for each state in a century & a half. No country should be so long without one. Nor will any degree of power in the hands of government prevent insurrections. France, with all it's despotism, and two or three hundred thousand men always in arms has had three insurrections in the three years I have been here in every one of which greater numbers were engaged than in Massachusetts & a great deal more blood was spilt. In Turkey, which Montesquieu supposes more despotic, insurrections are the events of every day. In England, where the hand of power is lighter than here, but heavier than with us they happen every half dozen years. Compare again the ferocious depredations of their insurgents with the order, the moderation & the almost self extinguishment of ours.—After all, it is my principle that the will of the majority should always prevail. If they approve the proposed Convention in all it's parts, I shall concur in it chearfully, in hopes that they will amend it whenever they shall find it work wrong. I think our governments will remain virtuous for many centuries; as long as they are chiefly agricultural; and this will be as long as there shall be vacant lands in any part of America. When they get piled upon one another in large cities, as in Europe, they will become corrupt as in Europe. Above all things I hope the education of the common people will be attended to; convinced that on their good sense we may rely with the most security for the preservation of a due degree of liberty....

Coming of the French Revolution
To Richard Price, January 8, 1789

… Our new Constitution, of which you speak also, has succeeded beyond what I apprehended it would have done. I did not at first believe that eleven States out of thirteen would have consented to a plan consolidating them as much into one. A change in their dispositions, which had taken place since I left them, had rendered this consolidation necessary, that is to say, had called for a federal government which could walk upon its own legs, without leaning for support on the State legislatures. A sense of necessity, and a submission to it, is to me a new and consolatory proof that, whenever the people are well-informed, they can be trusted with their own government; that, whenever things get so far wrong as to attract their notice, they may be relied on to set them to rights. You say you are not sufficiently informed about the nature and circumstances of the present struggle here. Having been on the spot from its first origin, and watched its movements as an uninterested spectator, with no other bias than a love of mankind, I will give you my ideas of it. Though celebrated writers of this and other countries had already sketched good principles on the subject of government, yet the American war seems first to have awakened the thinking part of this nation in general from the sleep of despotism in which they were sunk. The officers too who had been to America, were mostly young men, less shackled by habit and prejudice, and more ready to assent to the dictates of common sense and common right. They came back impressed with these. The press, notwithstanding its shackles, began to disseminate them; conversation, too, assumed new freedom; politics became the theme of all societies, male and female, and a very extensive and zealous party was formed, which may be called the Patriotic party, who, sensible of the abusive government under which they lived, longed for occasions of reforming it. This party comprehended all the honesty of the kingdom, sufficiently at its leisure to think; the men of letters, the easy bourgeois, the young nobility, partly from reflection, partly from mode; for those sentiments became a matter of mode, and as such united most of the young women to the party. Happily for the nation, it happened that, at the same moment, the dissipations of the court had exhausted the money and credit of the State, and M. de Calonnes found himself obliged to appeal to the nation, and to develop to it the ruin of their finances. He had no idea of supplying the deficit by economies, he saw no means but new taxes. To tempt the nation to consent to these some douceurs were necessary. The Notables were called in 1787. The leading vices of the constitution and administration were ably sketched out, good remedies proposed, and under the splendor of the propositions, a demand for more money was couched. The Notables concurred with the minister in the necessity of reformation, adroitly avoided the demand of money, got him displaced, and one of their leading men placed in his room. The archbishop of Thoulouse, by the aid of the hopes formed of him, was able to borrow some money, and he reformed considerably the expenses of the court. Notwithstanding the prejudices since formed against him, he appeared to me to pursue the reformation of the laws and constitution as steadily as a man could do who had to drag the court after him, and even to conceal from them the consequences of the measures he was leading them into. In his time the criminal laws were reformed, provincial assemblies and States established in most of the provinces, the States General promised, and a solemn acknowledgment made by the King that he could not impose a new tax without the consent of the nation. It is true he was continually goaded forward by the public clamors, excited by the writings and workings of the Patriots, who were able to keep up the public fermentation at the exact point which borders on resistance, without entering on it. They had taken into their alliance the Parliaments also, who were led, by very singular circumstances, to espouse, for the first time, the rights of the nation. They had from old causes had personal hostility against M. de Calonnes. They refused to register his laws or his taxes, and went so far as to acknowledge they had no power to do it. They persisted in this with his successor, who therefore exiled them. Seeing that the nation did not interest themselves much for their recall, they began to fear that the new judicatures proposed in their place would be established and that their own suppression would be perpetual. In short, they found their own strength insufficient to oppose that of the King. They therefore insisted that the States General should be called. Here they became united with and supported by the Patriots, and their joint influence was sufficient to produce the promise of that assembly. I always suspected that the archbishops had no objections to this force under which they laid him. But the Patriots and Parliament insisted it was their efforts which extorted the promise against his will. The re-establishment of the Parliament was the effect of the same coalition between the Patriots and Parliament; but, once re-established, the latter began to see danger in that very power, the States General, which they had called for in a moment of despair, but which they now foresaw might very possibly abridge their powers. They began to prepare grounds for questioning their legality, as a rod over the head of the States, and as a refuge if they should really extend their reformations to them. Mr. Neckar came in at this period and very dexterously disembarrassed the administration of these disputes by calling the notables to advise the form of calling and constituting the States. The court was well disposed towards the people, not from principles of justice or love to them; but they want money. No more can be had from the people. They are squeezed to the last drop. The clergy and nobles, by their privileges and influence, have kept their property in a great measure untaxed hitherto. They then remain to be squeezed, and no agent is powerful enough for this but the people. The court therefore must ally itself with the people. But the Notables, consisting mostly of privileged characters, had proposed a method of composing the States, which would have rendered the voice of the people, or Tiers Etats, in the States General, inefficient for the purpose of the court. It concurred then with the Patriots in intriguing with the Parliament to get them to pass a vote in favor of the rights of the people. This vote, balancing that of the Notables, has placed the court at liberty to follow its own views, and they have determined that the Tiers Etats shall have in the States General as many votes as the clergy and nobles put together. Still a great question remains to be decided, that is, shall the States General vote by orders, or by persons? precedents are both ways. The clergy will move heaven and earth to obtain the suffrage by orders, because that parries the effect of all hitherto done for the people. The people will probably send their deputies expressly instructed to consent to no tax, to no adoption of the public debts, unless the unprivileged part of the nation has a voice equal to that of the privileged; that is to say, unless the voice of the Tiers Etats be equalled to that of the clergy and nobles. They will have the young noblesse in general on their side, and the King and court. Against them will be the ancient nobles and the clergy. So that I hope, upon the whole, that by the time they meet, there will be a majority of the nobles themselves in favor of the Tiers Etats. So far history. We are now to come to prophecy; for you will ask, to what will all this lead? I answer, if the States General do not stumble at the threshold on the question before stated, and which must be decided before they can proceed to business, then they will in their first session easily obtain, 1. Their future periodical convocation of the States. 2. Their exclusive right to raise and appropriate money which includes that of establishing a civil list.

3. A participation in legislation; probably at first, it will only be a transfer to them of the portion of it now exercised by parliament, that is to say, a right to propose amendments and a negative. But it must infallibly end in a right of origination. 4. Perhaps they may make a declaration of rights. It will be attempted at least. Two other objects will be attempted, viz., a habeas corpus law and a free press. But probably they may not obtain these in the first session, or with modifications only, and the nation must be left to ripen itself more for their unlimited adoption. Upon the whole, it has appeared to me that the basis of the present struggle is an illumination of the public mind as to the rights of the nation, aided by fortunate incidents; that they can never retrograde, but from the natural progress of things, must press forward to the establishment of a constitution which shall assure to them a good degree of liberty. They flatter themselves they shall form a better constitution than the English. I think it will be better in some points—worse in others. It will be better in the article of representation, which will be more equal. It will be worse, as their situation obliges them to keep up the dangerous machine of a standing army. I doubt, too, whether they will obtain the trial by jury, because they are not sensible of its value....

"NEITHER FEDERALIST NOR ANTIFEDERALIST"
To Francis Hopkinson, March 13, 1789

... I hope by this time you have ceased to make wry faces about your vinegar, and that you have received it safe & good. You say that I have been dished up to you as an antifederalist, and ask me if it be just. My opinion was never worthy enough of notice to merit citing; but since you ask it I will tell it you. I am not a Federalist, because I never submitted the whole system of my opinions to the creed of any party of men whatever in religion, in philosophy, in politics, or in anything else where I was capable of thinking for myself. Such an addiction is the last degradation of a free and moral agent. If I could not go to heaven but with a party, I would not go there at all. Therefore I protest to you I am not of the party of federalists. But I am much farther from that of the Antifederalists. I approved, from the first moment, of the great mass of what is in the new constitution, the consolidation of the government, the organization into Executive legislative & judiciary, the subdivision of the legislative, the happy compromise of interests between the great & little states by the different manner of voting in the different houses, the voting by persons instead of states, the qualified negative on laws given to the Executive which however I should have liked better if associated with the judiciary also as in New York, and the power of taxation. I thought at first that the latter might have been limited. A little reflection soon convinced me it ought not to be. What I disapproved from the first moment also was the want of a bill of rights to guard liberty against the legislative as well as executive branches of the government, that is to say to secure freedom in religion, freedom of the press, freedom from monopolies, freedom from unlawful imprisonment, freedom from a permanent military, and a trial by jury in all cases determinable by the laws of the land. I disapproved also the perpetual reeligibility of the President. To these points of disapprobation I adhere. My first wish was that the 9. first conventions might accept the constitution, as the means of securing to us the great mass of good it contained, and that the 4. last might reject it, as the means of obtaining amendments. But I was corrected in this wish the moment I saw the much better plan of Massachusetts and which had never occurred to me. With respect to the declaration of rights I suppose the majority of the United states are of my opinion: for I apprehend all the antifederalists, and a very respectable proportion of the federalists think that such a declaration should now be annexed. The enlightened part of Europe have given us the greatest credit for inventing this instrument of security for the rights of the people, and have been not a little surprised to see us so soon give it up. With respect to the reeligibility of the president, I find myself differing from the majority of my countrymen, for I think there are but three states out of the 11. which have desired an alteration of this. And indeed, since the thing is established, I would wish it not to be altered during the life of our great leader, whose executive talents are superior to those I believe of any man in the world, and who alone by the authority of his name and the confidence reposed in his perfect integrity, is fully qualified to put the new government so under way as to secure it against the efforts of opposition. But having derived from our error all the good there was in it I hope we shall correct it the moment we can no longer have the same name at the helm....

More on a Bill of Rights
To James Madison, March 15, 1789

... Your thoughts on the subject of the Declaration of rights in the letter of Oct 17. I have weighed with great satisfaction. Some of them had not occurred to me before, but were acknoleged just in the moment they were presented in my mind. In the arguments in favor of a declaration of rights, you omit one which has great weight with me, the legal check which it puts into the hands of the judiciary. This is a body, which if rendered independent & kept strictly to their own department merits great confidence for their learning & integrity. In fact what degree of confidence would be too much for a body composed of such men as Wythe, Blair & Pendleton? On characters like these the "*civium ardor prava jubentium*" would make no impression. I am happy to find that on the whole you are a friend to this amendment. The Declaration of rights is like all other human blessings alloyed with some inconveniences, and not accomplishing fully it's object. But the good in this instance vastly overweighs the evil. I cannot refrain from making short answers to the objections which your letter states to have been raised. 1. That the rights in question are reserved by the manner in which the federal powers are granted. Answer. A constitutive act may certainly be so formed as to need no declaration of rights. The act itself has the force of a declaration as far as it goes; and if it goes to all material points nothing more is wanting. In the draught of a constitution which I had once a thought of proposing in Virginia, & printed afterwards, I endeavored to reach all the great objects of public liberty, and did not mean to add a declaration of rights. Probably the object was imperfectly executed; but the deficiencies would have been supplied by others, in the course of discussion. But in a constitutive act which leaves some precious articles unnoticed, and raises implications against others, a declaration of rights becomes necessary by way of supplement. This is the case of our new federal constitution. This instrument forms us into one state as to certain objects, and gives us a legislative & executive body for these objects. It should therefore guard us against their abuses of power within the field submitted to them. 2. A positive declaration of some essential rights could not be obtained in the requisite latitude. Answer. Half a loaf is better than no bread. If we cannot secure all our rights, let us secure what we can. 3. The limited powers of the federal government & jealousy of the subordinate governments afford a security which exists in no other instance. Answer. The first member of this seems resolvable into the first objection before stated. The jealousy of the subordinate governments is a precious reliance. But observe that those governments are only agents. They must have principles furnished them whereon to found their opposition. The declaration of rights will be the text whereby they will try all the acts of the federal governments, In this view it is necessary to the federal government also; as by the same text they may try the opposition of the subordinate governments. 4. Experience proves the inefficacy of a bill of rights. True. But tho it is not absolutely efficacious under all circumstances, it is of great potency always, and rarely inefficacious. A brace the more will often keep up the building which would have fallen with that brace the less. There is a remarkable difference between the characters of the Inconveniences which attend a Declaration of rights, & those which attend the want of it. The inconveniences of the Declaration are that it may cramp government in it's useful exertions. But the evil of this is short-lived, trivial & reparable. The inconveniences of the want of a Declaration are permanent, afflicting & irreparable. They are in constant progression from bad to worse. The executive in our governments is not the sole, it is scarcely the principal object of my jealousy. The tyranny of the legislatures is the most formidable dread at present, and will be for long years. That of the executive will come in it's turn, but it will be at a remote period. I know there are some among us who would now establish a monarchy. But they are inconsiderable in number and weight of character. The rising race are all republicans. We were educated in royalism; no wonder if some of us retain that idolatry still. Our young people are educated in republicanism, an apostasy from that to royalism is unprecedented & impossible. I am much pleased with the prospect that a declaration of rights will be added; and hope it will be done in that way which will not endanger the whole frame of the government, or any essential part of it....

A CHARTER FOR FRANCE

To Rabout de St. Etienne, with Draft, June 3, 1789

… After you quitted us yesterday evening, we continued our conversation (Monsr de la Fayette, Mr. Short & myself) on the subject of the difficulties which environ you. The desirable object being to secure the good which the King has offered & to avoid the ill which seems to threaten, an idea was suggested, which appearing to make an impression on Monsr de la Fayette, I was encouraged to pursue it on my return to Paris, to put it into form, & now to send it to you & him. It is this, that the King, in a *seance royale* should come forward with a Charter of Rights in his hand, to be signed by himself & by every member of the three orders. This charter to contain the five great points which the Resultat of December offered on the part of the King, the abolition of pecuniary privileges offered by the privileged orders, & the adoption of the National debt and a grant of the sum of money asked from the nation. This last will be a cheap price for the preceding articles, and let the same act declare your immediate separation till the next anniversary meeting. You will carry back to your constituents more good than ever was effected before without violence, and you will stop exactly at the point where violence would otherwise begin. Time will be gained, the public mind will continue to ripen & to be informed, a basis of support may be prepared with the people themselves, and expedients occur for gaining still something further at your next meeting, & for stopping again at the point of force. I have ventured to send to yourself & Monsieur de la Fayette a sketch of my ideas of what this act might contain without endangering any dispute. But it is offered merely as a canvas for you to work on, if it be fit to work on at all. I know too little of the subject, & you know too much of it to justify me in offering anything but a hint. I have done it too in a hurry: insomuch that since committing it to writing it occurs to me that the 5.th article may give alarm, that it is in a good degree included in the 4.th, and is therefore useless. But after all what excuse can I make, Sir, for this presumption. I have none but an unmeasureable love for your nation and a painful anxiety lest Despotism, after an unaccepted offer to bind it's own hands, should seize you again with tenfold fury. Permit me to add to these very sincere assurances of the sentiments of esteem & respect with which I have the honor to be, Sir, Your most obed.ᵗ & most humble servt.

A Charter of Rights, solemnly established by the King and Nation.

1. The States General shall assemble, uncalled, on the first day of November, annually, and shall remain together so long as they shall see cause. They shall regulate their own elections and proceedings, and until they shall ordain otherwise, their elections shall be in the forms observed in the present year, and shall be triennial.

2. The States General alone shall levy money on the nation, and shall appropriate it.

3. Laws shall be made by the States General only, with the consent of the King.

4. No person shall be restrained of his liberty, but by regular process from a court of justice, authorized by a general law. (Except that a Noble may be imprisoned by order of a court of justice, on the prayer of twelve of his nearest relations.) On complaint of an unlawful imprisonment, to any judge whatever, he shall have the prisoner immediately brought before him, and shall discharge him, if his imprisonment be unlawful. The officer in whose custody the prisoner is, shall obey the orders of the judge; and both judge and officer shall be responsible, civilly and criminally, for a failure of duty herein.

5. The military shall be subordinate to the civil authority.

6. Printers shall be liable to legal prosecution for printing and publishing false facts, injurious to the party prosecuting; but they shall be under no other restraint.

7. All pecuniary privileges and exemptions, enjoyed by any description of persons, are abolished.

8. All debts already contracted by the King, are hereby made the debts of the nation; and the faith thereof is pledged for their payment in due time.

9. Eighty millions of livres are now granted to the King, to be raised by loan, and reimbursed by the nation; and the taxes heretofore paid, shall continue to be paid to the end of the present year, and no longer.

10. The States General shall now separate, and meet again on the 1st day of November next.

Done, on behalf of the whole nation, by the King and their representatives in the States General, at Versailles, this — day of June, 1789.

Signed by the King, and by every member individually, and in his presence....

THE FIRST CHAPTER OF EUROPEAN LIBERTY
To Diodati, August 3, 1789

... I presume that your correspondents here have given you a history of all the events which have happened. The Leyden gazette, tho' it contains several inconsiderable errors, gives on the whole a just enough idea. It is impossible to conceive a greater fermentation than has worked in Paris, nor do I believe that so great a fermentation ever produced so little injury in any other place. I have been thro' it daily, have observed the mobs with my own eyes in order to be satisfied of their objects, and declare to you that I saw so plainly the legitimacy of them, that I have slept in my house as quietly thro' the whole as I ever did in the most peaceable moments. So strongly fortified was the despotism of this government by long possession, by the respect & the fears of the people, by possessing the public force, by the imposing authority of forms and of faste, that had it held itself on the defensive only, the national assembly with all their good sense, would probably have only obtained a considerable improvement of the government, not a total revision of it. But, ill informed of the spirit of their nation, the despots around the throne had recourse to violent measures, the forerunners of force. In this they have been completely overthrown, & the nation has made a total resumption of rights, which they had certainly never before ventured even to think of. The National assembly have now as clean a canvas to work on here as we had in America. Such has been the firmness and wisdom of their proceedings in moments of adversity as well as prosperity, that I have the highest confidence that they will use their power justly. As far as I can collect from conversation with their members, the constitution they will propose will resemble that of England in it's outlines, but not in it's defects. They will certainly leave the king possessed completely of the Executive powers, & particularly of the public force. Their legislature will consist of one order only, & not of two as in England: the representation will be equal & not abominably partial as that of England: it will be guarded against corruption, instead of having a majority sold to the king, & rendering his will absolute: whether it will be in one chamber, or broke into two cannot be foreseen. They will meet at certain epochs & sit as long as they please, instead of meeting only when, & sitting only as long as the king pleases as in England. There is a difference of opinion whether the king shall have an absolute, or only a qualified Negative on their acts. The parliaments will probably be suppressed; & juries provided in criminal cases perhaps even in civil ones. This is what appears probable at present. The Assembly is this day discussing the question whether they will have a declaration of rights. Paris has been led by events to assume the government of itself. It has hitherto worn too much the appearance of conformity to continue thus independently of the will of the nation. Reflection will probably make them sensible that the security of all depends on the dependance of all on the national legislature. I have so much confidence on the good sense of man, and his qualifications for self-government, that I am never afraid of the issue where reason is left free to exert her force; and I will agree to be stoned as a false prophet if all does not end well in this country. Nor will it end with this country. Hers is but the first chapter of the history of European liberty....

"THE EARTH BELONGS TO THE LIVING"
To James Madison, September 6, 1789

... The question Whether one generation of men has a right to bind another, seems never to have been started either on this or our side of the water. Yet it is a question of such consequences as not only to merit decision, but place also, among the fundamental principles of every government. The course of reflection in which we are immersed here on the elementary principles of society has presented this question to my mind; and that no such obligation can be transmitted I think very capable of proof. I set out on this ground which I suppose to be self evident, *"that the earth belongs in usufruct to the living;"* that the dead have neither powers nor rights over it. The portion occupied by an individual ceases to be his when himself ceases to be, and reverts to the society. If the society has formed no rules for the appropriation of its lands in severalty, it will be taken by the first occupants. These will generally be the wife and children of the decedent. If they have formed rules of appropriation, those rules may give it to the wife and children, or to some one of them, or to the legatee of the deceased. So they may give it to his creditor. But the child, the legatee or creditor takes it, not by any natural right, but by a law of the society of which they are members, and to which they are subject. Then no man can by *natural right* oblige the lands he occupied, or the persons who succeed him in that occupation, to the paiment of debts contracted by him. For if he could, he might during his own life, eat up the usufruct of the lands for several generations to come, and then the lands would belong to the dead, and not to the living, which would be reverse of our principle. What is true of every member of the society individually, is true of them all collectively, since the rights of the whole can be no more than the sum of the rights of individuals. To keep our ideas clear when applying them to a multitude, let us suppose a whole generation of men to be born on the same day, to attain mature age on the same day, and to die on the same day, leaving a succeeding generation in the moment of attaining their mature age all together. Let the ripe age be supposed of 21. years, and their period of life 34. years more, that being the average term given by the bills of mortality to persons who have already attained 21. years of age. Each successive generation would, in this way, come on and go off the stage at a fixed moment, as individuals do now. Then I say the earth belongs to each of these generations during it's course, fully, and in their own right. The 2d. generation receives it clear of the debts and incumbrances of the 1st., the 3d. of the 2d. and so on. For if the 1st. could charge it with a debt, then the earth would belong to the dead and not the living generation. Then no generation can contract debts greater than may be paid during the course of it's own existence. At 21. years of age they may bind themselves and their lands for 34. years to come: at 22. for 33: at 23 for 32. and at 54 for one year only; because these are the terms of life which remain to them at those respective epochs. But a material difference must be noted between the succession of an individual and that of a whole generation. Individuals are parts only of a society, subject to the laws of a whole. These laws may appropriate the portion of land occupied by a decedent to his creditor rather than to any other, or to his child, on condition he satisfies his creditor. But when a whole generation, that is, the whole society dies, as in the case we have supposed, and another generation or society succeeds, this forms a whole, and there is no superior who can give their territory to a third society, who may have lent money to their predecessors beyond their faculty of paying.

What is true of a generation all arriving to self-government on the same day, and dying all on the same day, is true of those on a constant course of decay and renewal, with this only difference. A generation coming in and going out entire, as in the first case, would have a right in the 1st year of their self dominion to contract a debt for 33. years, in the 10th. for 24. in the 20th. for 14. in the 30th. for 4. whereas generations changing daily, by daily deaths and births, have one constant term beginning at the date of their contract, and ending when a majority of those of full age at that date shall be dead. The length of that term may be estimated from the tables of mortality, corrected by the circumstances of climate, occupation &c. peculiar to the country of the contractors. Take, for instance, the table of M. de Buffon wherein he states that 23,994 deaths, and the ages at which they happened. Suppose a society in which 23,994 persons are born every year and live to the ages stated in this table. The conditions of that society will be as follows. 1st. it will consist constantly of 617,703 persons of all ages. 2dly. of those living at any one instant of time, one half will be dead in 24. years 8. months. 3dly. 10,675 will arrive every year at the age of 21. years complete. 4thly. it will constantly have 348,417 persons of all ages above 21. years. 5ly. and the half of those of 21. years and upwards living at any one instant of time will be dead in 18. years 8. months, or say 19. years as the nearest integral number. Then 19. years is the term beyond which neither the representatives of a nation, nor even the whole nation itself assembled, can validly extend a debt.

To render this conclusion palpable by example, suppose that Louis XIV. and XV. had contracted debts in the name of the French nation to the amount of 10.000 milliards of livres and that the whole had been contracted in Genoa. The interest of this sum would be 500 milliards, which is said to be the whole rent-roll, or nett proceeds of the territory of France. Must the present generation of men have retired from the territory in which nature produced them, and ceded it to the Genoese creditors? No. They have the same rights over the soil on which they were produced, as the preceding generations had. They derive these rights not from their predecessors, but from nature. They then and their soil are by nature clear of the debts of their predecessors. Again suppose Louis XV. and his contemporary generation had said to the money lenders of Genoa, give us money that we may eat, drink, and be merry in our day; and on condition you will demand no interest till the end of 19. years, you shall then forever after receive an annual interest of * 12.⁵ per cent. The money is lent on these conditions, is divided among the living, eaten, drank, and squandered. Would the present generation be obliged to apply the produce of the earth and of their labour to replace their dissipations? Not at all.

I suppose that the received opinion, that the public debts of one generation devolve on the next, has been suggested by our seeing habitually in private life that he who succeeds to lands is required to pay the debts of his ancestor or testator, without considering that this requisition is municipal only, not moral, flowing from the will of the society which has found it convenient to appropriate the lands become vacant by the death of their occupant on the condition of a paiment of his debts; but that between society and society, or generation and generation there is no municipal obligation, no umpire but the law of nature. We seem not to have perceived that, by the law of nature, one generation is to another as one independant nation to another.

The interest of the national debt of France being in fact but a two thousandth part of it's rent-roll, the paiment of it is practicable enough; and so becomes a question merely of honor or expediency. But with respect to future debts; would it not be wise and just for that nation to declare in the constitution they are forming that neither the legislature, nor the nation itself can validly contract more debt, than they may pay within their own age, or within the term of 19. years? And that all future contracts shall be deemed void as to what shall remain unpaid at the end of 19. years from their date? This would put the lenders, and the borrowers also, on their guard. By reducing too the faculty of borrowing within its natural limits, it would bridle the spirit of war, to which too free a course has been procured by the inattention of money lenders to this law of nature, that succeeding generations are not responsible for the preceding.

On similar ground it may be proved that no society can make a perpetual constitution, or even a perpetual law. The earth belongs always to the living generation. They may manage it then, and what proceeds from it, as they please, during their usufruct.

---

*100£ at a compound interest of 6 per cent makes at the end of 19 years an aggregate of principal and interest of £252.14 the interest of which is a £12⁰⁰ 12." 7.ᵈ which is nearly 12." p.ᶜ cent on the first capital of £100.

They are masters too of their own persons, and consequently may govern them as they please. But persons and property make the sum of the objects of government. The constitution and the laws of their predecessors extinguished them, in their natural course, with those whose will gave them being. This could preserve that being till it ceased to be itself, and no longer. Every constitution, then, and every law, naturally expires at the end of 19. years. If it be enforced longer, it is an act of force and not of right.

It may be said that the succeeding generation exercising in fact the power of repeal, this leaves them as free as if the constitution or law had been expressly limited to 19. years only. In the first place, this objection admits the right, in proposing an equivalent. But the power of repeal is not an equivalent. It might be indeed if every form of government were so perfectly contrived that the will of the majority could always be obtained fairly and without impediment. But this is true of no form. The people cannot assemble themselves; their representation is unequal and vicious. Various checks are opposed to every legislative proposition. Factions get possession of the public councils. Bribery corrupts them. Personal interests lead them astray from the general interests of their constituents; and other impediments arise so as to prove to every practical man that a law of limited duration is much more manageable than one which needs a repeal.

This principle that the earth belongs to the living and not to the dead is of very extensive application and consequences in every country, and most especially in France. It enters into the resolution of the questions Whether the nation may change the descent of lands holden in tail? Whether they may change the appropriation of lands given antiently to the church, to hospitals, colleges, orders of chivalry, and otherwise in perpetuity? whether they may abolish the charges and privileges attached on lands, including the whole catalogue ecclesiastical and feudal? it goes to hereditary offices, authorities and jurisdictions; to hereditary orders, distinctions and appellations; to perpetual monopolies in commerce, the arts or sciences; with a long train of *et ceteras:* and it renders the question of reimbursement a question of generosity and not of right. In all these cases the legislature of the day could authorize such appropriations and establishments for their own time, but no longer; and the present holders, even where they or their ancestors have purchased, are in the case of *bona fide* purchasers of what the seller had no right to convey.

Turn this subject in your mind, my Dear Sir, and particularly as to the power of contracting debts, and develope it with that perspicuity and cogent logic which is so peculiarly yours. Your station in the councils of our country gives you an opportunity of producing it to public consideration, of forcing it into discussion. At first blush it may be rallied as a theoretical speculation; but examination will prove it to be solid and salutary. It would furnish matter for a fine preamble to our first law for appropriating the public revenue; and it will exclude, at the threshold of our new government the contagious and ruinous errors of this quarter of the globe, which have armed despots with means not sanctioned by nature for binding in chains their fellow-men. We have already given, in example one effectual check to the Dog of war, by transferring the power of letting him loose from the executive to the Legislative body, from those who are to spend to those who are to pay. I should be pleased to see this second obstacle held out by us also in the first instance. No nation can make a declaration against the validity of long-contracted debts so disinterestedly as we, since we do not owe a shilling which may not be paid with ease principal and interest, within the time of our own lives. Establish the principle also in the new law to be passed for protecting copy rights and new inventions, by securing the exclusive right for 19. instead of 14. years. Besides familiarizing us to this term, it will be an instance the more of our taking reason for our guide instead of English precedents, the habit of which fetters us, with all the political herecies of a nation, equally remarkable for it's encitement from some errors, as long slumbering under others. I write you no news, because when an occasion occurs I shall write a separate letter for that....

"GREAT EVENTS FROM SMALL CAUSES"
Autobiography, 1821

... Here I discontinue my relation of the French revolution. The minuteness with which I have so far given it's details is disproportioned to the general scale of my narrative. But I have thought it justified by the interest which the whole world must take in this revolution. As yet we are but in the first chapter of it's history. The appeal to the rights of man, which had been made in the U S. was taken up by France, first of the European nations. From her the spirit has spread over those of the South. The tyrants of the North have allied indeed against it, but it is irresistible. Their opposition will only multiply it's millions of human victims; their own satellites will catch it, and the condition of man thro' the civilized world will be finally and greatly ameliorated. This is a wonderful instance of great events from small causes. So inscrutable is the arrangement of causes & consequences in this world that a two-penny duty on tea, unjustly imposed in a sequestered part of it, changes the condition of all it's inhabitants....

REVOLUTION AND HERESY
To George Mason, February 4, 1791

... I look with great anxiety for the firm establishment of the new government in France, being perfectly convinced that if it takes place there, it will spread sooner or later all over Europe. On the contrary a check there would retard the revival of liberty in other countries. I consider the establishment and success of their government as necessary to stay up our own, and to prevent it from falling back to that kind of Half-way house, the English constitution. It cannot be denied that we have among us a sect who believe that to contain whatever is perfect in human institutions; that the members of this sect have, many of them, names & offices which stand high in the estimation of our countrymen. I still rely that the great mass of our community is untainted with these heresies, as is it's head. On this I build my hope that we have not laboured in vain, and that our experiment will still prove that men can be governed by reason. You have excited my curiosity in saying "there is a particular circumstance, little attended to, which is continually sapping the republicanism of the United States." What is it? What is said in our country of the fiscal arrangements now going on? I really fear their effect when I consider the present temper of the Southern states. Whether these measures be right or wrong abstractedly, more attention should be paid to the general opinion. However, all will pass—the excise will pass—the bank will pass. The only corrective of what is corrupt in our present form of government will be the augmentation of the numbers in the lower house, so as to get a more agricultural representation, which may put that interest above that of the stock-jobbers....

Opinion on the Constitutionality of a National Bank

February 15, 1791

… I consider the foundation of the Constitution as laid on this ground: That "all powers not delegated to the United States, by the Constitution, nor prohibited by it to the States, are reserved to the States or to the people." [XIIth amendment.] To take a single step beyond the boundaries thus specially drawn around the powers of Congress, is to take possession of a boundless field of power, no longer susceptible of any definition.

The incorporation of a bank, and the powers assumed by this bill, have not, in my opinion, been delegated to the United States, by the Constitution.

I. They are not among the powers specially enumerated: for these are: 1st. A power to lay taxes for the purpose of paying the debts of the United States; but no debt is paid by this bill, nor any tax laid. Were it a bill to raise money, its origination in the Senate would condemn it by the Constitution.

2d. "To borrow money." But this bill neither borrows money nor ensures the borrowing it. The proprietors of the bank will be just as free as any other money holders, to lend or not to lend their money to the public. The operation proposed in the bill, first, to lend them two millions, and then to borrow them back again, cannot change the nature of the latter act, which will still be a payment, and not a loan, call it by what name you please.

3. To "regulate commerce with foreign nations, and among the States, and with the Indian tribes." To erect a bank, and to regulate commerce, are very different acts. He who erects a bank, creates a subject of commerce in its bills; so does he who makes a bushel of wheat, or digs a dollar out of the mines; yet neither of these persons regulates commerce thereby. To make a thing which may be bought and sold, is not to prescribe regulations for buying and selling. Besides, if this was an exercise of the power of regulating commerce, if would be void, as extending as much to the internal commerce of every State, as to its external. For the power given to Congress by the Constitution does not extend to the internal regulation of the commerce of a State, (that is to

say of the commerce between citizen and citizen,) which remain exclusively with its own legislature; but to its external commerce only, that is to say, its commerce with another State, or with foreign nations, or with the Indian tribes. Accordingly the bill does not propose the measure as a regulation of trade, but as "productive of considerable advantages to trade." Still less are these powers covered by any other of the special enumerations.

II. Nor are they within either of the general phrases, which are the two following:—

1. To lay taxes to provide for the general welfare of the United States, that is to say, "to lay taxes for *the purpose* of providing for the general welfare." For the laying of taxes is the *power,* and the general welfare the *purpose* for which the power is to be exercised. They are not to lay taxes *ad libitum for any purpose they please;* but only *to pay the debts or provide for the welfare of the Union.* In like manner, they are not *to do anything they please* to provide for the general welfare, but only to *lay taxes* for that purpose. To consider the latter phrase, not as describing the purpose of the first, but as giving a distinct and independent power to do any act they please, which might be for the good of the Union, would render all the preceding and subsequent enumerations of power completely useless.

It would reduce the whole instrument to a single phrase, that of instituting a Congress with power to do whatever would be for the good of the United States; and, as they would be the sole judges of the good or evil, it would be also a power to do whatever evil they please.

It is an established rule of construction where a phrase will bear either of two meanings, to give it that which will allow some meaning to the other parts of the instrument, and not that which would render all the others useless. Certainly no such universal power was meant to be given them. It was intended to lace them up straitly within the enumerated powers, and those without which, as means, these powers could not be carried into effect. It is known that the very power now proposed *as a means* was rejected as *an end* by the Convention which formed the Constitution. A proposition was made to them to authorize Congress to open canals, and an amendatory one to empower them to incorporate. But the whole was rejected, and one of the reasons for rejection urged in debate was, that then they would have a power to erect a bank, which would render the great cities, where there were prejudices and jealousies on the subject, adverse to the reception of the Constitution.

2. The second general phrase is, "to make all laws *necessary* and proper for carrying into execution the enumerated powers." But they can all be carried into execution without a bank. A bank therefore is not *necessary,* and consequently not authorized by this phrase.

It has been urged that a bank will give great facility or convenience in the collection of taxes. Suppose this were true: yet the Constitution allows only the means which are "*necessary,*" not those which are merely "convenient" for effecting the enumerated powers. If such a latitude of construction be allowed to this phrase as to give any non-enumerated power, it will go to every one, for there is not one which ingenuity may not torture into a *convenience* in some instance *or other,* to *some one* of so long a list of enumerated powers. It would swallow up all the delegated powers, and reduce the whole to one power, as before observed. Therefore it was that the Constitution restrained them to the *necessary* means, that is to say, to those means without which the grant of power would be nugatory....

Can it be thought that the Constitution intended that for a shade or two of *convenience,* more or less, Congress should be authorised to break down the most ancient and fundamental laws of the several States; such as those against Mortmain, the laws of Alienage, the rules of descent, the acts of distribution, the laws of escheat and forfeiture, the laws of monopoly? Nothing but a necessity invincible by any other means, can justify such a prostitution of laws, which constitute the pillars of our whole system of jurisprudence. Will Congress be too straight-laced to carry the constitution into honest effect, unless they may pass over the foundation-laws of the State government for the slightest convenience of theirs?

The negative of the President is the shield provided by the constitution to protect against the invasions of the legislature: 1. The right of the Executive. 2. Of the Judiciary. 3. Of the States and State legislatures. The present is the case of a right remaining exclusively with the States, and consequently one of those intended by the Constitution to be placed under its protection.

It must be added, however, that unless the President's mind on a view of everything which is urged for and against this bill, is tolerably clear that it is unauthorised by the Constitution; if the pro and the con hang so even as to balance his judgment, a just respect for the wisdom of the legislature would naturally decide the balance in favor of their opinion. It is chiefly for cases where they are clearly misled by error, ambition, or interest, that the Constitution has placed a check in the negative of the President.

STRENGTHENING THE STATE GOVERNMENTS
To Archibald Stuart, December 23, 1791

... I shall hazard my own ideas to you as hastily as my business obliges me. I wish to preserve the line drawn by the federal constitution between the general & particular governments as it stands at present, and to take every prudent means of preventing either from stepping over it. Tho' the experiment has not yet had a long enough course to shew us from which quarter encroachments are most to be feared, yet it is easy to foresee from the nature of things that the encroachments of the state governments will tend to an excess of liberty which will correct itself (as in the late instance) while those of the general government will tend to monarchy, which will fortify itself from day to day, instead of working its own cure, as all experience shews. I would rather be exposed to the inconveniencies attending too much liberty than those attending too small a degree of it. Then it is important to strengthen the state governments: and as this cannot be done by any change in the federal constitution, (for the preservation of that is all we need contend for,) it must be done by the states themselves, erecting such barriers at the constitutional line as cannot be surmounted either by themselves or by the general government. The only barrier in their power is a wise government. A weak one will lose ground in every contest. To obtain a wise & an able government, I consider the following changes as important. Render the legislature a desirable station by lessening the number of representatives (say to 100) and lengthening somewhat their term, and proportion them equally among the electors: adopt also a better mode of appointing Senators. Render the Executive a more desirable post to men of abilities by making it more independant of the legislature. To wit, let him be chosen by other electors, for a longer time, and ineligible for ever after. Responsibility is a tremendous engine in a free government. Let him feel the whole weight of it then by taking away the shelter of his executive council. Experience both ways has already established the superiority of this measure. Render the Judiciary respectable by every possible means, to wit, firm tenure in office, competent salaries, and reduction of their numbers. Men of high learning and abilities are few in every country; & by taking in those who are not so, the able part of the body have their hands tied by the unable. This branch of the government will have the weight of the conflict on their hands, because they will be the last appeal of reason.—These are my general ideas of amendments; but, preserving the ends, I should be flexible & conciliatory as to the means….

"A STEP TO AN ENGLISH CONSTITUTION"
To Lafayette, June 16, 1792

… Behold you, then, my dear friend, at the head of a great army, establishing the liberties of your country against a foreign enemy. May heaven favor your cause, and make you the channel thro' which it may pour it's favors. While you are exterminating the monster aristocracy, & pulling out the teeth & fangs of it's associate monarchy, a contrary tendency is discovered in some here. A sect has shewn itself among us, who declare they espoused our new constitution, not as a good & sufficient thing itself, but only as a step to an English constitution, the only thing good & sufficient in itself, in their eye. It is happy for us that these are preachers without followers, and that our people are firm & constant in their republican purity. You will wonder to be told that it is from the Eastward chiefly that these champions for a king, lords & commons come. They get some important associates from New York, and are puffed off by a tribe of Agioteurs which have been hatched in a bed of corruption made up after the model of their beloved England. Too many of these stock jobbers & king-jobbers have come into our legislature, or rather too many of our legislature have become stock jobbers & king-jobbers. However the voice of the people is beginning to make itself heard, and will probably cleanse their seats at the ensuing election.…

A CONVERSATION WITH PRESIDENT WASHINGTON

The Anas, February 29, 1792*

… I told him that in my opinion there was only a single source of these discontents. Tho' they had indeed appeared to spread themselves over the war department also, yet I considered that as an overflowing only from their real channel which would never have taken place if they had not first been generated in another department, to wit that of the treasury. That a system had there been contrived, for deluging the states with paper money instead of gold & silver, for withdrawing our citizens from the pursuits of commerce, manufactures, buildings, & other branches of useful industry, to occupy themselves & their capitals in a species of gambling, destructive of morality, & which had introduced it's poison into the government itself. That it was a fact, as certainly known as that he & I were then conversing, that particular members of the legislature, while those laws were on the carpet, had feathered their nests with paper, had then voted for the laws, and constantly since lent all the energy of their talents, & instrumentality of their offices to the establishment & enlargement of this system: that they had chained it about our necks for a great length of time, & in order to keep the game in their hands had from time to time aided in making such legislative constructions of the constitution as made it a very different thing from what the people thought they had submitted to; that they had now brought forward a proposition, far beyond every one ever yet advanced, & to which the eyes of many were turned as the decision which was to let us know whether we live under a limited or an unlimited government.—He asked me to what proposition I alluded? I answered to that in the Report on manufactures which, under colour of giving *bounties* for the encouragement of particular manufactures, meant to establish the doctrine that the power given by the Constitution to collect taxes to provide for the *general welfare* of the U.S., permitted Congress to take everything under their management which *they* should deem for the *public welfare*, & which is susceptible of the application of money: consequently that the subsequent enumeration of their powers was not the description to which resort

*Notes and observations, collected in 1818, on political events chiefly in the years 1791–93. Ed.

must be had, & did not at all constitute the limits of their authority: that this was a very different question from that of the bank, which was thought an incident to an enumerated power: that therefore this decision was expected with great anxiety: that indeed I hoped the proposition would be rejected, believing there was a majority in both houses against it, and that if it should be, it would be considered as a proof that things were returning into their true channel; & that at any rate I looked forward to the broad representation which would shortly take place for keeping the general constitution on it's true ground, & that this would remove a great deal of the discontent which had shewn itself. The conversation ended with this last topic. It is here stated nearly as much at length as it really was, the expressions preserved where I could recollect them, and their substance always faithfully stated....

THE QUARREL WITH HAMILTON
To the President of the United States, September 9, 1792

... I now take the liberty of proceeding to that part of your letter wherein you notice the internal dissentions which have taken place within our government, & their disagreeable effect on it's movements. That such dissentions have taken place is certain, & even among those who are nearest to you in the administration. To no one have they given deeper concern than myself: to no one equal mortification at being myself a part of them. Tho' I take to myself no more than my share of the general observations of your letter, yet I am so desirous ever that you should know the whole truth, & believe no more than the truth, that I am glad to seize every occasion of developing to you whatever I do or think relative to the government; & shall therefore ask permission to be more lengthy now than the occasion particularly calls for, or could otherwise perhaps justify.

When I embarked in the government, it was with a determination to intermeddle not at all with the legislature, & as little as possible with my co-departments. The first and only instance of variance from the former part of my resolution, I was duped into by the Secretary of the Treasury and made a tool for forwarding his schemes, not then sufficiently understood by me; and of all the errors of my political life, this has occasioned me the deepest regret. It has ever been my purpose to explain this to you, when, from being actors on the scene, we shall have become uninterested spectators only. The second part of my resolution has been religiously observed with the war department; & as to that of the Treasury, has never been farther swerved from than by the mere enunciation of my sentiments in conversation, and chiefly among those who, expressing the same sentiments, drew mine from me. If it has been supposed that I have ever intrigued among the members of the legislatures to defeat the plans of the Secretary of the Treasury, it is contrary to all truth. As I never had the desire to influence the members, so neither had I any other means than my friendships, which I valued too highly to risk by usurpations on their freedom of judgment, & the conscientious pursuit of their own sense of duty. That I have utterly, in my private conversations, disapproved of the system of the Secretary of the treasury, I acknolege & avow: and this was not merely a speculative difference. His system flowed from principles adverse to liberty, & was calculated to undermine and demolish the republic, by creating an influence of his department over the members of the legislature. I saw this influence actually produced, & it's first fruits to be the establishment of the great outlines of his project by the votes of the very persons who, having swallowed his bait were laying themselves out to profit by his plans: & that had these persons withdrawn, as those interested in a question ever should, the vote of the disinterested majority was clearly the reverse of what they made it. These were no longer the votes then of the representatives of the people, but of deserters from the rights & interests of the people: & it was impossible to consider their decisions, which had nothing in view but to enrich themselves, as the measures of the fair majority, which ought always to be respected.— If what was actually doing begat uneasiness in those who wished for virtuous government, what was further proposed was not less threatening to the friends of the Constitution. For, in a Report on the subject of manufactures (still to be acted on) it was expressly assumed that the general government has a right to exercise all powers which may be for the *general welfare,* that is to say, all the legitimate powers of government: since no government has a legitimate right to do what is not for the welfare of the governed. There was indeed a sham-limitation of the universality of this power *to cases where money is to be employed.* But about what is it that money cannot be employed? Thus the object of these plans taken together is to draw all the powers of government into the hands of the general legislature, to establish means for corrupting a sufficient corps in that legislature to divide the honest votes & preponderate, by their own, the scale which suited, & to have that corps under the command of the Secretary of the Treasury for the purpose of subverting step by step the principles of the constitution, which he has so often declared to be a thing of nothing which must be changed. Such views might have justified something more than mere expressions of dissent, beyond which, nevertheless, I never went.—Has abstinence from the department committed to me been equally observed by him? To say nothing of other interferences equally known, in the case of the two nations with which we have the most intimate connections, France & England, my system was to give some satisfactory distinctions to the former, of little cost to us, in return for the solid advantages yielded us by them; & to have met the English with some restrictions which might induce them to abate their severities against our commerce. I have always supposed this coincided with your sentiments. Yet the Secretary of the treasury, by his cabals with members of the legislature, & by high-toned declamation on other occasions, has forced down his own system, which was exactly the reverse. He undertook, of his own authority, the conferences with the ministers of those two nations, & was, on every consultation, provided with some report of a conversation with the one or the other of them, adapted to his views. These views, thus made to prevail, their execution fell of course to me; & I can safely appeal to you, who have seen all my letters & proceedings, whether I have not carried them into execution as sincerely as if they had been my own, tho' I ever considered them as inconsistent with the honor & interest of our country. That they have been inconsistent with our interest is but too fatally proved by the stab to our navigation given by the French....

"THE WILL OF THE NATION"
To the Minister to France (Gouverneur Morris)
December 30, 1792

... I am apprehensive that your situation must have been difficult during the transition from the late form of government to the re-establishment of some other legitimate authority, and that you may have been at a loss to determine with whom business might be done. Nevertheless when principles are well understood their application is less embarrassing. We surely cannot deny to any nation that right whereon our own government is founded, that every one may govern itself under whatever forms it pleases, and change these forms at it's own will, and that it may transact it's business with foreign nations through whatever organ it thinks proper, whether King, convention, assembly, committee, President, or whatever else it may chuse. The will of the nation is the only thing essential to be regarded....

Paean to the French Revolution
To William Short, January 3, 1793

... The tone of your letters had for some time given me pain, on account of the extreme warmth with which they censured the proceedings of the Jacobins of France. I considered that sect as the same with the Republican patriots, & the Feuillants as the Monarchical patriots, well known in the early part of the revolution, & but little distant in their views, both having in object the establishment of a free constitution, & differing only on the question whether their chief Executive should be hereditary or not. The Jacobins (as since called) yielded to the Feuillants & tried the experiment of retaining their hereditary Executive. The experiment failed completely, and would have brought on the reestablishment of despotism had it been pursued. The Jacobins saw this, and that the expunging that officer was of absolute necessity. And the Nation was with them in opinion, for however they might have been formerly for the constitution framed by the first assembly, they were come over from their hope in it, and were now generally Jacobins. In the struggle which was necessary, many guilty persons fell without the forms of trial, and with them some innocent. These I deplore as much as any body, & shall deplore some of them to the day of my death. But I deplore them as I should have done had they fallen in battle. It was necessary to use the arm of the people, a machine not quite so blind as balls and bombs, but blind to a certain degree. A few of their cordial friends met at their hands the fate of enemies. But time and truth will rescue & embalm their memories, while their posterity will be enjoying that very liberty for which they would never have hesitated to offer up their lives. The liberty of the whole earth was depending on the issue of the contest, and was ever such a prize won with so little innocent blood? My own affections have been deeply wounded by some of the martyrs to this cause, but rather than it should have failed, I would have seen half the earth desolated. Were there but an Adam & Eve left in every country, & left free, it would be better than as it now is. I have expressed to you my sentiments, because they are really those of 99. in an hundred of our citizens. The universal feasts, and rejoicings which have lately been had on account of the successes of the French shewed the genuine effusions of their hearts....

There are in the U.S. some characters of opposite principles; some of them are high in office, others possessing great wealth, and all of them hostile to France and fondly looking to England as the staff of their hope. These I named to you on a former occasion. Their prospects have certainly not brightened. Excepting them, this country is entirely republican, friends to the constitution, anxious to preserve it and to have it administered according to it's own republican principles. The little party above mentioned have espoused it only as a stepping stone to monarchy, and have endeavored to approximate it to that in it's administration in order to render it's final transition more easy. The successes of republicanism in France have given the coup de grace to their prospects, and I hope to their projects....

PEACEABLE COERCION
To James Madison, March 24, 1793

... The idea seems to gain credit that the naval powers combined against France will prohibit supplies even of provisions to that country. Should this be formally notified I should suppose Congress would be called, because it is a justifiable cause of war, & as the Executive cannot decide the question of war on the affirmative side, neither ought it to do so on the negative side, by preventing the competent body from deliberating on the question. But I should hope that war would not be their choice. I think it will furnish us a happy opportunity of setting another example to the world, by shewing that nations may be brought to do justice by appeals to their interests as well as by appeals to arms. I should hope that Congress instead of a denunciation of war, would instantly exclude from our ports all the manufactures, produce, vessels & subjects of the nations committing this aggression, during the continuance of the aggression & till full satisfaction made for it. This would work well in many ways, safely in all, & introduce between nations another umpire than arms. It would relieve us too from the risks & the horrors of cutting throats....

OPINION ON THE FRENCH TREATIES
April 28, 1793

... I consider the people who constitute a society or nation as the source of all authority in that nation, as free to transact their common concerns by any agents they think proper, to change these agents individually, or the organisation of them in form or function whenever they please: that all the acts done by those agents under the authority of the nation, are the acts of the nation, are obligatory on them, & enure to their use, & can in no wise be annulled or affected by any change in the form of the government, or of the persons administering it. Consequently the Treaties between the U S. and France, were not treaties between the U S. & Louis Capet, but between the two nations of America & France, and the nations remaining in existance, tho' both of them have since changed their forms of government, the treaties are not annulled by these changes.

The Law of nations, by which this question is to be determined, is composed of three branches. 1. The Moral law of our nature. 2. The Usages of nations. 3. Their special Conventions. The first of these only, concerns this question, that is to say the Moral law to which Man has been subjected by his creator, & of which his feelings, or Conscience as it is sometimes called, are the evidence with which his creator has furnished him. The Moral duties which exist between individual and individual in a state of nature, accompany them into a state of society & the aggregate of the duties of all the individuals composing the society constitutes the duties of that society towards any other; so that between society & society the same moral duties exist as did between the individuals composing them while in an unassociated state, their maker not having released them from those duties on their forming themselves into a nation. Compacts then between nation & nation are obligatory on them by the same moral law which obliges individuals to observe their compacts. There are circumstances however which sometimes excuse the non-performance of contracts between man & man: so are there also between nation & nation. When performance, for instance, becomes *impossible,* non-performance is not immoral. So if performance becomes *self-destructive* to the party, the law of self-preservation overrules the laws of obligation to others. For the reality of these principles I appeal to the true fountains of evidence, the head & heart of every rational & honest man. It is there Nature has written her moral laws, & where every man may read them for himself. He will never read there the permission to annul his obligations for a time, or for ever, whenever they become 'dangerous, useless, or disagreeable.' Certainly not when merely *useless* or *disagreeable,* as seems to be said in an authority which has been quoted, Vattel. 2. 197, and tho he may under certain degrees of *danger,* yet the danger must be imminent, & the degree great. Of these, it is true, that nations are to be judges for themselves, since no one nation has a right to sit in judgment over another. But the tribunal of our consciences remains, & that also of the opinion of the world. These will revise the sentence we pass in our own case, & as we respect these, we must see that in judging ourselves we have honestly done the part of impartial & vigorous judges….

The doctrine then of Grotius, Puffendorf & Wolf is that 'treaties remain obligatory notwithstanding any change in the form of government, except in the single case where the preservation of that form was the object of treaty.' There the treaty extinguishes, not by the election or declaration of the party remaining in statu quo; but independantly of that, by the evanishment of the object. Vattel lays down, in fact, the same doctrine, that treaties continue obligatory, notwithstanding a change of government by the will of the other party, that to oppose that will would be a wrong, & that the ally remains an ally notwithstanding the change. So far he concurs with all the previous writers. But he then adds what they had not said, nor would say 'but if this change renders the alliance *useless,* dangerous, or *disagreeable* to it, it is free to renounce it.' It was unnecessary for him to have specified the exception of *danger* in this particular case, because that exception exists in all cases & it's extent has been considered. But when he adds that, because a contract is become merely *useless* or *disagreeable,* we are free to renounce it, he is in opposition to Grotius, Puffendorf, & Wolf, who admit no such licence against the obligation of treaties, & he is in opposition to the morality of every honest man, to whom we may safely appeal to decide whether he feels himself free to renounce a contract the moment it becomes merely *useless* or *disagreeable*, to him? We may appeal too to Vattel himself, in those parts of his book where he cannot be misunderstood, & to his known character, as one of the most zealous & constant advocates for the preservation of good faith in all our dealings. Let us hear him on other occasions; & first where he shews what degree of danger or injury will authorize self-liberation from a treaty. 'If simple lezion' (lezion means the loss sustained by selling a thing for less than half value, which degree of loss rendered the sale void by the Roman law), 'if simple lezion, says he, or some degree of disadvantage in a treaty does not suffice to render it invalid, it is not so as to inconveniences which would go to the *ruin* of the nation. As every treaty ought to be made by a sufficient power, a treaty pernicious to the state is null, & not at all obligatory; no governor of a nation having power to engage things capable of *destroying* the state, for the safety of which the empire is trusted to him. The nation itself, bound necessarily to whatever it's preservation & safety require, cannot enter into engagements contrary to it's indispensable obligations.' Here then we find that the degree of injury or danger which he deems sufficient to liberate us from a treaty, is that which would go to the absolute *ruin* or *destruction* of the state; not simply the lezion of the Roman law, not merely the being disadvantageous, or dangerous....

Upon the whole I conclude

That the treaties are still binding, notwithstanding the change of government in France: that no part of them, but the clause of guarantee, holds up *danger,* even at a distance.

And consequently that a liberation from no other part could be proposed in any case: that if that clause may ever bring *danger,* it is neither extreme, nor imminent, nor even probable: that the authority for renouncing a treaty, when *useless* or *disagreeable,* is either misunderstood, or in opposition to itself, to all their writers, & to every moral feeling: that were it not so, these treaties are in fact neither useless nor disagreeable.

That the receiving a Minister from France at this time is an act of no significance with respect to the treaties, amounting neither to an admission nor a denial of them, forasmuch as he comes not under any stipulation in them:

That were it an explicit admission, or were an express declaration of this obligation now to be made, it would not take from us that right which exists at all times of liberating ourselves when an adherence to the treaties would be *ruinous* or *destructive* to the society: and that the not renouncing the treaties now is so far from being a breach of neutrality, that the doing it would be the breach, by giving just cause of war to France....

REPORT ON THE PRIVILEGES AND RESTRICTIONS ON
THE COMMERCE OF THE UNITED STATES IN FOREIGN COUNTRIES
December 16, 1793

... Were the ocean, which is the common property of all, open to the industry of all, so that every person and vessel should be free to take employment wherever it could be found, the United States would certainly not set the example of appropriating to themselves, exclusively, any portion of the common stock of occupation. They would rely on the enterprise and activity of their citizens for a due participation of the benefits of the seafaring business, and for keeping the marine class of citizens equal to their object. But if particular nations grasp at undue shares, and, more especially, if they seize on the means of the United States, to convert them into aliment for their own strength, and withdraw them entirely from the support of those to whom they belong, defensive and protecting measures become necessary on the part of the nation whose marine resources are thus invaded; or it will be disarmed of its defence; its productions will lie at the mercy of the nation which has possessed itself exclusively of the means of carrying them, and its politics may be influenced by those who command its commerce. The carriage of our own commodities, if once established in another channel, cannot be resumed in the moment we may desire. If we lose the seamen and artists whom it now occupies, we lose the present means of marine defence, and time will be requisite to raise up others, when disgrace or losses shall bring home to our feelings the error of having abandoned them. The materials for maintaining our due share of navigation, are ours in abundance. And, as to the mode of using them, we have only to adopt the principles of those who put us on the defensive, or others equivalent and better fitted to our circumstances.

The following principles, being founded in reciprocity, appear perfectly just, and to offer no cause of complaint to any nation:

1. Where a nation imposes high duties on our productions, or prohibits them altogether, it may be proper for us to do the same by theirs; first burdening or excluding those productions which they bring here, in competition with our own of the same kind; selecting next, such manufactures as we take from them in greatest quantity, and which, at the same time, we could the soonest furnish to ourselves, or obtain from other countries; imposing on them duties lighter at first, but heavier and heavier afterwards, as other channels of supply open. Such duties having the effect of indirect encouragement to domestic manufactures of the same kind, may induce the manufacturer to come himself into these States, where cheaper subsistence, equal laws, and a vent of his wares, free of duty, may ensure him the highest profits from his skill and industry. And here, it would be in the power of the State governments to co-operate essentially, by opening the resources of encouragement which are under their control, extending them liberally to artists in those particular branches of manufacture for which their soil, climate, population and other circumstances have matured them, and fostering the precious efforts and progress of *household* manufacture, by some patronage suited to the nature of its objects, guided by the local informations they possess, and guarded against abuse by their presence and attentions. The oppressions on our agriculture, in foreign ports, would thus be made the occasion of relieving it from a dependence on the councils and conduct of others, and of promoting arts, manufactures and population at home.

2. Where a nation refuses permission to our merchants and factors to reside within certain parts of their dominions, we may, if it should be thought expedient, refuse residence to theirs in any and every part of ours, or modify their transactions.

3. Where a nation refuses to receive in our vessels any productions but our own, we may refuse to receive, in theirs, any but their own productions. The first and second clauses of the bill reported by the committee, are well formed to effect this object.

4. Where a nation refuses to consider any vessel as ours which has not been built

within our territories, we should refuse to consider as theirs, any vessel not built within their territories.

5. Where a nation refuses to our vessels the carriage even of our own productions, to certain countries under their domination, we might refuse to theirs of every description, the carriage of the same productions to the same countries. But as justice and good neighborhood would dictate that those who have no part in imposing the restriction on us, should not be the victims of measures adopted to defeat its effect, it may be proper to confine the restrictions to vessels owned or navigated by any subjects of the same dominant power, other than the inhabitants of the country to which the said productions are to be carried. And to prevent all inconvenience to the said inhabitants, and to our own, by too sudden a check on the means of transportation, we may continue to admit the vessels marked for future exclusion, on an advanced tonnage, and for such length of time only, as may be supposed necessary to provide against that inconvenience.

The establishment of some of these principles by Great Britain, alone, has already lost to us in our commerce with that country and its possessions, between eight and nine hundred vessels of near 40,000 tons burden, according to statements from official materials, in which they have confidence. This involves a proportional loss of seamen, shipwrights, and ship-building, and is too serious a loss to admit forbearance of some effectual remedy.

It is true we must expect some inconvenience in practice from the establishment of discriminating duties. But in this, as in so many other cases, we are left to choose between two evils. These inconveniences are nothing when weighed against the loss of wealth and loss of force, which will follow our perseverance in the plan of indiscrimination. When once it shall be perceived that we are either in the system or in the habit of giving equal advantages to those who extinguish our commerce and navigation by duties and prohibitions, as to those who treat both with liberality and justice, liberality and justice will be converted by all into duties and prohibitions. It is not to the moderation and justice of others we are to trust for fair and equal access to market with our productions, or for our due share in the transportation of them; but to our own means of independence, and the firm will to use them. Nor do the inconveniences of discrimination merit consideration. Not one of the nations before mentioned, perhaps not a commercial nation on earth, is without them. In our case one distinction alone will suffice: that is to say, between nations who favor our productions and navigation, and those who do not favor them. One set of moderate duties, say the present duties, for the first, and a fixed advance on these as to some articles, and prohibitions as to others, for the last.

Still, it must be repeated that friendly arrangements are preferable with all who will come into them; and that we should carry into such arrangements all the liberality and spirit of accommodation which the nature of the case will admit....

WHISKEY REBELS AND FUNDAMENTAL LIBERTIES
To James Madison, December 28, 1794

... The denunciation of the democratic societies is one of the extraordinary acts of boldness of which we have seen so many from the fraction of monocrats. It is wonderful indeed, that the President should have permitted himself to be the organ of such an attack on the freedom of discussion, the freedom of writing, printing & publishing. It must be a matter of rare curiosity to get at the modifications of these rights proposed by them, and to see what line their ingenuity would draw between democratical societies, whose avowed object is the nourishment of the republican principles of our constitution, and the society of the Cincinnati, *a self-created* one, carving out for itself hereditary distinctions, lowering over our Constitution eternally, meeting together in all parts of the Union, periodically, with closed doors, accumulating a capital in their separate treasury, corresponding secretly & regularly, & of which society the very persons denouncing the democrats are themselves the fathers, founders, & high officers. Their sight must be perfectly dazzled by the glittering of crowns & coronets, not to see the extravagance of the proposition to suppress the friends of general freedom, while those who wish to confine that freedom to the few, are permitted to go on in their principles & practices. I here put out of sight the persons whose misbehavior has been taken advantage of to slander the friends of popular rights; and I am happy to observe, that as far as the circle of my observation & information extends, everybody has lost sight of them, and views the abstract attempt on their natural & constitutional rights in all it's nakedness. I have never heard, or heard of, a single expression or opinion which did not condemn it as an inexcusable aggression. And with respect to the transactions against the excise law, it appears to me that you are all swept away in the torrent of governmental opinions, or that we do not know what these transactions have been. We know of none which, according to the definitions of the law, have been anything more than riotous. There was indeed a meeting to consult about a separation. But to consult on a question does not amount to a determination of that question in the affirmative, still less to the acting on such a determination; but we shall see, I suppose, what the court lawyers, & courtly judges, & would-be ambassadors will make of it. The excise law is an infernal one. The first error was to admit it by the Constitution; the 2d., to act on that admission; the 3d & last will be, to make it the instrument of dismembering the Union, & setting us all afloat to chuse which part of it we will adhere to. The information of our militia, returned from the Westward, is uniform, that tho the people there let them pass quietly, they were objects of their laughter, not of their fear; that 1000 men could have cut off their whole force in a thousand places of the Alleganey; that their detestation of the excise law is universal, and has now associated to it a detestation of the government; & that separation which perhaps was a very distant & problematical event, is now near, & certain, & determined in the mind of every man....

MONTESQUIEU'S BRILLIANT FALLACIES
To François D'Ivernois, February 6, 1795

... I suspect that the doctrine, that small States alone are fitted to be republics, will be exploded by experience, with some other brilliant fallacies accredited by Montesquieu & other political writers. Perhaps it will be found, that to obtain a just republic (and it is to secure our just rights that we resort to government at all) it must be so extensive as that local egoisms may never reach it's greater part; that on every particular question, a majority may be found in it's councils free from particular interests, and giving, therefore, an uniform prevalence to the principles of justice. The smaller the societies, the more violent & more convulsive their schisms. We have chanced to live in an age which will probably be distinguished in history, for it's experiments in government on a larger scale than has yet taken place. But we shall not live to see the result. The grosser absurdities, such as hereditary magistracies, we shall see exploded in our day, long experience having already pronounced condemnation against them. But what is to be the substitute? This our children or grand children will answer. We may be satisfied with the certain knowledge that none can ever be tried, so stupid, so unrighteous, so oppressive, so destructive of every end for which honest men enter into government, as that which their forefathers had established, & their fathers alone venture to tumble headlong from the stations they have so long abused. It is unfortunate, that the efforts of mankind to recover the freedom of which they have been so long deprived, will be accompanied with violence, with errors, & even with crimes. But while we weep over the means, we must pray for the end....

AN ANGLICAN PARTY
To Philip Mazzei, April 24, 1796

... The aspect of our politics has wonderfully changed since you left us. In place of that noble love of liberty, & republican government which carried us triumphantly thro' the war, an Anglican monarchical, & aristocratical party has sprung up, whose avowed object is to draw over us the substance, as they have already done the forms, of the British government. The main body of our citizens, however, remain true to their republican principles; the whole landed interest is republican, and so is a great mass of talents. Against us are the Executive, the Judiciary, two out of three branches of the legislature, all the officers of the government, all who want to be officers, all timid men who prefer the calm of despotism to the boisterous sea of liberty, British merchants & Americans trading on British capitals, speculators & holders in the banks & public funds, a contrivance invented for the purposes of corruption, & for assimilating us in all things to the rotten as well as the sound parts of the British model. It would give you a fever were I to name to you the apostates who have gone over to these heresies, men who were Samsons in the field & Solomons in the council, but who have had their heads shorn by the harlot England. In short, we are likely to preserve the liberty we have obtained only by unremitting labors & perils. But we shall preserve them; and our mass of weight & wealth on the good side is so great, as to leave no danger that force will ever be attempted against us. We have only to awake and snap the Lilliputian cords with which they have been entangling us during the first sleep which succeeded our labors....

An Entente with Adams
To James Madison, January 1, 1797

... The event of the election has never been a matter of doubt in my mind. I knew that the Eastern states were disciplined in the schools of their town meetings to sacrifice differences of opinion to the great object of operating in phalanx, & that the more free & moral agency practiced in the other states would always make up the supplement of their weight. Indeed the vote comes much nearer an equality than I had expected. I know the difficulty of obtaining belief to one's declarations of a disinclination to honors, & that it is greatest with those who still remain in the world. But no arguments were wanting to reconcile me to a relinquishment of the first office or acquiescence under the second. As to the first it was impossible that a more solid unwillingness settled on full calculation, could have existed in any man's mind, short of the degree of absolute refusal. The only view on which I would have gone into it for awhile was to put our vessel on her republican tack before she should be thrown too much to leeward of her true principles. As to the second, it is the only office in the world about which I am unable to decide in my own mind whether I had rather have it or not have it. Pride does not enter into the estimate; for I think with the Romans that the general of today should be a soldier tomorrow if necessary. I can particularly have no feelings which would revolt at a secondary position to mr. Adams. I am his junior in life, was his junior in Congress, his junior in the diplomatic line, his junior lately in the civil government. Before the receipt of your letter I had written the enclosed one to him. I had intended it some time, but had deferred it from time to time under the discouragement of a despair of making him believe I could be sincere in it. The papers by the last post not rendering it necessary to change anything in the letter I enclose it open for your perusal, not only that you may possess the actual state of dispositions between us, but that if anything should render the delivery of it ineligible in your opinion, you may return it to me. If mr. Adams can be induced to administer the government on it's true principles, & to relinquish his bias to an English constitution, it is to be considered whether it would not be on the whole for the public good to come to a good understanding with him as to his future elections. He is perhaps the only sure barrier against Hamilton's getting in....

Peace and Commerce
To Thomas Pinckney, May 29, 1797

... You have found on your return a higher style of political difference than you had left here. I fear this is inseparable from the different constitutions of the human mind, & that degree of freedom which permits unrestrained expression. Political dissension is doubtless a less evil than the lethargy of despotism, but still it is a great evil, and it would be as worthy the efforts of the patriot as of the philosopher, to exclude it's influence, if possible, from social life. The good are rare enough at best. There is no reason to subdivide them by artificial lines. But whether we shall ever be able so far to perfect the principles of society, as that political opinions shall, in it's intercourse, be as inoffensive as those of philosophy, mechanics, or any other, may well be doubted. Foreign influence is the present & just object of public hue and cry, &, as often happens, the most guilty are foremost & loudest in the cry. If those who are truly independent, can so trim our vessels as to beat through the waves now agitating us, they will merit a glory the greater as it seems less possible. When I contemplate the spirit which is driving us on here, & that beyond the water which will view us as but a mouthful the more, I have little hope of peace. I anticipate the burning of our sea ports, havoc of our frontiers, household insurgency, with a long train of et ceteras, which is enough for a man to have met once in his life. The exchange, which is to give us new neighbors in Louisiana (probably the present French armies when disbanded) has opened us to combinations of enemies on that side where we are most vulnerable. War is not the best engine for us to resort to, nature has given us one *in our commerce*, which, if properly managed, will be a better instrument for obliging the interested nations of Europe to treat us with justice. If the commercial regulations had been adopted which our legislature were at one time proposing, we should at this moment have been standing on such an eminence of safety & respect as ages can never recover. But having wandered from that, our object should now be to get back, with as little loss as possible, & when peace shall be restored to the world, endeavor so to form our *commercial* regulations as that justice from other nations shall be their mechanical result....

PATIENCE AND THE REIGN OF WITCHES
To John Taylor, June 4, 1798

... Mr. New shewed me your letter on the subject of the patent, which gave me an opportunity of observing what you said as to the effect with you of public proceedings, and that it was not unusual now to estimate the separate mass of Virginia and N. Carolina with a view to their separate existence. It is true that we are compleatly under the saddle of Massachusets & Connecticut, and that they ride us very hard, cruelly insulting our feelings as well as exhausting our strength and substance. Their natural friends, the three other eastern States, join them from a sort of family pride, and they have the art to divide certain other parts of the Union so as to make use of them to govern the whole. This is not new. It is the old practice of despots to use a part of the people to keep the rest in order, and those who have once got an ascendency and possessed themselves of all the resources of the nation, their revenues and offices, have immense means for retaining their advantages. But our present situation is not a natural one. The body of our countrymen is substantially republican through every part of the Union. It was the irresistable influence & popularity of Gen¹ Washington, played off by the cunning of Hamilton, which turned the government over to anti-republican hands, or turned the republican members, chosen by the people, into anti-republicans. He delivered it over to his successor in this state, and very untoward events, since improved with great artifice, have produced on the public mind the impression we see; but still, I repeat it, this is not the natural state. Time alone would bring round an order of things more correspondent to the sentiments of our constituents; but are there not events impending which will do it within a few months? The invasion of England, the public and authentic avowal of sentiments hostile to the leading principles of our Constitution, the prospect of a war in which we shall stand alone, land-tax, stamp-tax, increase of public debt, &c. Be this as it may, in every free & deliberating society there must, from the nature of man, be opposite parties & violent dissensions & discords; and one of these, for the most part, must prevail over the other for a longer or shorter time. Perhaps this party division is necessary to induce each to watch & delate to the people the proceedings of the other. But if on a temporary superiority of the one party, the other is to resort to a scission of the Union, no federal government can ever exist. If to rid ourselves of the present rule of Massachusets & Connecticut we break the Union, will the evil stop there? Suppose the N. England States alone cut off, will our natures be changed? are we not men still to the south of that, & with all the passions of men? Immediately we shall see a Pennsylvania & a Virginia party arise in the residuary con-federacy, and the public mind will be distracted with the same party spirit. What a game, too, will the one party have in their hands by eternally threatening the other that unless they do so & so, they will join their Northern neighbors. If we reduce our Union to Virginia & N. Carolina, immediately the conflict will be established between the representatives of these two States, and they will end by breaking into their simple units. Seeing, therefore, that an association of men who will not quarrel with one another is a thing which never yet existed, from the greatest confederacy of nations down to a town meeting or a vestry, seeing that we must have somebody to quarrel with, I had rather keep our New England associates for that purpose than to see our bickerings transferred to others. They are circumscribed within such narrow limits, & their population so full, that their numbers will ever be the minority, and they are marked, like the Jews, with such a peculiarity of character as to constitute from that circumstance the natural division of our parties. A little patience, and we shall see the reign of witches pass over, their spells dissolve, and the people, recovering their true sight, restore their government to it's true principles. It is true that in the mean time we are suffering deeply in spirit, and incurring the horrors of a war & long oppressions of enormous public debt. But who can say what would be the evils of a scission, and when & where they would end? Better keep together as we are, hawl off from Europe as soon as we can, & from all attachments to any portions of it. And if we feel their power just sufficiently to hoop us together, it will be the happiest situation in which we can exist. If the game runs sometimes against us at home we must have patience till luck turns, & then we shall have an opportunity of winning back the *principles* we have lost, for this is a game where principles are the stake. Better luck, therefore, to us all; and health, happiness, & friendly salutations to yourself. Adieu.

Draft of the Kentucky Resolutions (1798)

1. *Resolved,* That the several States composing the United States of America, are not united on the principle of unlimited submission to their General Government; but that, by a compact under the style and title of a Constitution for the United States, and of amendments thereto, they constituted a General Government for special purposes,—delegated to that government certain definite powers, reserving, each State to itself, the residuary mass of right to their own self-government; and that whensoever the General Government assumes undelegated powers, its acts are unauthoritative, void, and of no force; that to this compact each State acceded as a State, and is an integral party, its co-States forming, as to itself, the other party: that the government created by this compact was not made the exclusive or final judge of the extent of the powers delegated to itself; since that would have made its discretion, and not the Constitution, the measure of its powers; but that, as in all other cases of compact among powers having no common judge, each party has an equal right to judge for itself, as well of infractions as the mode and measure of redress.

2. *Resolved,* That the Constitution of the United States, having delegated to Congress a power to punish treason, counterfeiting the securities and current coin of the United States, piracies, and felonies committed on the high seas, and offences against the law of nations, and no other crimes whatsoever; and it being true as a general principle, and one of the amendments to the Constitution having also declared, that "the powers not delegated to the United States by the Constitution, nor prohibited by it to the States, are reserved to the States respectively, or to the people," therefore the act of Congress, passed on the 14th day of July, 1798, and intituled "An Act in addition to the

act intituled An Act for the punishment of certain crimes against the United States," as also the act passed by them on the—day of June, 1798, intituled "An Act to punish frauds committed on the bank of the United States," (and all their other acts which assume to create, define, or punish crimes, other than those so enumerated in the Constitution,) are altogether void, and of no force; and that the power to create, define, and punish such other crimes is reserved, and, of right, appertains solely and exclusively to the respective States, each within its own territory.

3. *Resolved,* That it is true as a general principle, and is also expressly declared by one of the amendments to the Constitution, that "the powers not delegated to the United States by the Constitution, nor prohibited by it to the States, are reserved to the States respectively, or to the people;" and that no power over the freedom of religion, freedom of speech, or freedom of the press being delegated to the United States by the Constitution, nor prohibited by it to the States, all lawful powers respecting the same did of right remain, and were reserved to the States or the people: that thus was manifested their determination to retain to themselves the right of judging how far the licentiousness of speech and of the press may be abridged without lessening their useful freedom, and how far those abuses which cannot be separated from their use should be tolerated, rather than the use be destroyed. And thus also they guarded against all abridgment by the United States of the freedom of religious opinions and exercises, and retained to themselves the right of protecting the same, as this State, by a law passed on the general demand of its citizens, had already protected them from all human restraint or interference. And that in addition to this general principle and express declaration, another and more special provision has been made by one of the amendments to the Constitution, which expressly declares, that "Congress shall make no law respecting an establishment of religion, or prohibiting the free exercise thereof, or abridging the freedom of speech or of the press:" thereby guarding in the same sentence, and under the same words, the freedom of religion, of speech, and of the press: insomuch, that whatever violated either, throws down the sanctuary which covers the others, and that libels, falsehood, and defamation, equally with heresy and false religion, are withheld from the cognizance of federal tribunals. That, therefore, the act of Congress of the United States, passed on the 14th day of July, 1798, intituled "An Act

in addition to the act intituled An Act for the punishment of certain crimes against the United States," which does abridge the freedom of the press, is not law, but is altogether void, and of no force.

4. *Resolved,* That alien friends are under the jurisdiction and protection of the laws of the State wherein they are: that no power over them has been delegated to the United States, nor prohibited to the individual States, distinct from their power over citizens. And it being true as a general principle, and one of the amendments to the Constitution having also declared, that "the powers not delegated to the United States by the Constitution, nor prohibited by it to the States, are reserved to the States respectively, or to the people," the act of the Congress of the United States, passed on the—day of July, 1798, intituled "An Act concerning aliens," which assumes powers over alien friends, not delegated by the Constitution, is not law, but is altogether void, and of no force.

5. *Resolved,* That in addition to the general principle, as well as the express declaration, that powers not delegated are reserved, another and more special provision, inserted in the Constitution from abundant caution, has declared that "the migration or importation of such persons as any of the States now existing shall think proper to admit, shall not be prohibited by the Congress prior to the year 1808;" that this commonwealth does admit the migration of alien friends, described as the subject of the said act concerning aliens: that a provision against prohibiting their migration, is a provision against all acts equivalent thereto, or it would be nugatory: that to remove them when migrated, is equivalent to a prohibition of their migration, and is, therefore, contrary to the said provision of the Constitution, and void.

6. *Resolved,* That the imprisonment of a person under the protection of the laws of this commonwealth, on his failure to obey the simple *order* of the President to depart out of the United States, as is undertaken by said act intituled "An Act concerning aliens," is contrary to the Constitution, one amendment to which has provided that "no person shall be deprived of liberty without due process of law;" and that another having provided that "in all criminal prosecutions the accused shall enjoy the right to public trial by an impartial jury, to be informed of the nature and cause of the accusation, to be confronted with the witnesses against him, to have compulsory process for obtaining witnesses in his favor, and to have the assistance of counsel for his defence,"

the same act, undertaking to authorize the President to remove a person out of the United States, who is under the protection of the law, on his own suspicion, without accusation, without jury, without public trial, without confrontation of the witnesses against him, without hearing witnesses in his favor, without defence, without counsel, is contrary to the provision also of the Constitution, is therefore not law, but utterly void, and of no force: that transferring the power of judging any person, who is under the protection of the laws, from the courts to the President of the United States, as is undertaken by the same act concerning aliens, is against the article of the Constitution which provides that "the judicial power of the United States shall be vested in courts, the judges of which shall hold their offices during good behavior;" and that the said act is void for that reason also. And it is further to be noted, that this transfer of judiciary power is to that magistrate of the General Government who already possesses all the Executive, and a negative on all legislative powers.

7. *Resolved,* That the construction applied by the General Government (as is evidenced by sundry of their proceedings) to those parts of the Constitution of the United States which delegate to Congress a power "to lay and collect taxes, duties, imports, and excises, to pay the debts, and provide for the common defence and general welfare of the United States," and "to make all laws which shall be necessary and proper for carrying into execution the powers vested by the Constitution in the government of the United States, or in any department or officer thereof," goes to the destruction of all limits prescribed to their power by the Constitution: that words meant by the instrument to be subsidiary only to the execution of limited powers, ought not to be so construed as themselves to give unlimited powers, nor a part to be so taken as to destroy the whole residue of that instrument: that the proceedings of the General Government under color of these articles, will be a fit and necessary subject of revisal and correction, at a time of greater tranquillity, while those specified in the preceding resolutions call for immediate redress.

8th. *Resolved,* That a committee of conference and correspondence be appointed, who shall have in charge to communicate the preceding resolutions to the legislatures of the several States; to assure them that this commonwealth continues in the same esteem of their friendship and union which it has manifested from that moment at which a common danger first suggested a common union: that it considers union, for specified national purposes, and particularly to those specified in their late federal compact, to be friendly to the peace, happiness and prosperity of all the States: that faithful to that compact, according to the plain intent and meaning in which it was understood and acceded to by the several parties, it is sincerely anxious for its preservation: that it does also believe, that to take from the States all the powers of self-government and transfer them to a general and consolidated government, without regard to the special delegations and reservations solemnly agreed to in that compact, is not for the peace, happiness or prosperity of these States; and that therefore this commonwealth is determined, as it doubts not its co-States are, to submit to undelegated, and consequently unlimited powers in no man, or body of men on earth: that in cases of an abuse of the delegated powers, the members of the General Government, being chosen by the people, a change by the people would be the constitutional remedy; but, where powers are assumed which have not been delegated, a nullification of the act is the rightful remedy: that every State has a natural right in cases not within the compact, (casus non fœderis,) to nullify of their own authority all assumptions of power by others within their limits: that without this right, they would be under the dominion, absolute and unlimited, of whosoever might exercise this right of judgment for them: that nevertheless, this commonwealth, from motives of regard and respect for its co-States, has wished to communicate with them on the subject: that with them alone it is proper to communicate, they alone being parties to the compact, and solely authorized to judge in the last resort of the powers exercised under it, Congress being not a party, but merely the creature of the compact, and subject as to its assumptions of power to the final judgment of those by whom, and for whose use itself and its powers were all created and modified: that if the acts before specified should stand, these conclusions would flow from them; that the General Government may place any act they think proper on the list of crimes, and punish it themselves whether enumerated or not enumerated by the Constitution as cognizable by them: that they may transfer its cognizance to the President, or any other person, who may himself be the accuser, counsel, judge and jury, whose *suspicions* may be the evidence, his *order* the sentence, his *officer* the executioner, and his breast the sole record of the transaction: that a very numerous and valuable description of the inhabitants of these States being, by this precedent, reduced, as outlaws, to the absolute dominion of one man, and the barrier of the Constitution thus swept away from us all, no rampart now remains against the passions and the powers of a majority in Congress to protect from a like exportation, or other more grievous punishment, the minority of the same body, the legislatures, judges, governors, and counsellors of the States, nor their other peaceable inhabitants, who may venture to reclaim the constitutional rights and liberties of the States and people, or who for other causes, good or bad, may be obnoxious to the views, or marked by the suspicions of the President, or be thought dangerous to his or their election, or other interests, public or personal: that the friendless alien has indeed been selected as the safest subject of a first experiment; but the citizen will soon follow, or rather, has already followed, for already has a sedition act marked him as its prey: that these and successive acts of the same character, unless arrested at the threshold, necessarily drive these States into revolution and blood, and will furnish new calumnies against republican government, and new pretexts for those who wish it to be believed that man cannot be governed but by a rod of iron: that it would be a dangerous delusion were a confidence in the men of our choice to silence our fears for the safety of our rights: that confidence is everywhere the parent of despotism—free government is founded in jealousy, and not in confidence; it is jealousy and not confidence which prescribes limited constitutions, to bind down those whom we are obliged to trust with power: that our Constitution has accordingly fixed the limits to which, and no further, our confidence may go; and let the honest advocate of confidence read the alien and sedition acts, and say if the Constitution has not been wise in fixing limits to the government it created, and whether we should be wise in destroying those limits. Let him say what the government is, if it be not a tyranny, which the men of our choice have conferred on our President, and the President of our choice has assented to, and accepted over the friendly strangers to whom the mild spirit of our country and its laws have pledged hospitality and protection: that the men of our choice have more respected the bare *suspicions* of the President, than the solid right of innocence, the claims of justification, the sacred force of truth, and the forms and substance of law and justice. In questions of power, then, let no more be heard of confidence in man, but bind him down from mischief by the chains of the Constitution. That this commonwealth does therefore call on its co-States for an expression of their sentiments on the acts concerning aliens, and for the punishment of certain crimes herein before specified, plainly declaring whether these acts are or are not authorized by the federal compact. And it doubts not that their sense will be so announced as to prove their attachment unaltered to limited government, whether general or particular. And that the rights and liberties of their co-States will be exposed to no dangers by remaining embarked in a common bottom with their own. That they will concur with this commonwealth in considering the said acts as so palpably against the Constitution as to amount to an undisguised declaration that that compact is not meant to be the measure of the powers of the General Government, but that it will proceed in the exercise over these States, of all powers whatsoever: that they will view this as seizing the rights of the States, and consolidating them in the hands of the General Government, with a power assumed to bind the States, not merely as the cases made federal, (casus fœderis,) but in all cases whatsoever, by laws made, not with their consent, but by others against their consent: that this would be to surrender the form of government we have chosen, and live under one deriving its powers from its own will, and not from our authority; and that the co-States, recurring to their natural right in cases not made federal, will concur in declaring these acts void, and of no force, and will each take measures of its own for providing that neither these acts, nor any others of the General Government not plainly and intentionally authorized by the Constitution, shall be exercised within their respective territories.

9th. *Resolved,* That the said committee be authorized to communicate by writing or personal conferences, at any times or places whatever, with any person or persons who may be appointed by any one or more co-States to correspond or confer with them; and that they lay their proceedings before the next session of Assembly.

A Profession of Political Faith
To Elbridge Gerry, January 26, 1799

… I do then, with sincere zeal, wish an inviolable preservation of our present federal constitution, according to the true sense in which it was adopted by the States, that in which it was advocated by it's friends, & not that which it's enemies apprehended, who therefore became it's enemies; and I am opposed to the monarchising it's features by the forms of it's administration, with a view to conciliate a first transition to a President & Senate for life, & from that to a hereditary tenure of these offices, & thus to worm out the elective principle. I am for preserving to the States the powers not yielded by them to the Union, & to the legislature of the Union it's constitutional share in the division of powers; and I am not for transferring all the powers of the States to the general government, & all those of that government to the Executive branch. I am for a government rigorously frugal & simple, applying all the possible savings of the public revenue to the discharge of the national debt; and not for a multiplication of officers & salaries merely to make partisans, & for increasing by every device, the public debt, on the principle of it's being a public blessing. I am for relying, for internal defence, on our militia solely, till actual invasion, and for such a naval force only as may protect our coasts and harbors from such depredations as we have experienced; and not for a standing army in time of peace, which may overawe the public sentiment; nor for a navy, which, by it's own expenses and the eternal wars in which it will implicate us, will grind us with public burthens, & sink us under them. I am for free commerce with all nations; political connection with none; & little or no diplomatic establishment. And I am not for linking ourselves by new treaties with the quarrels of Europe; entering that field of slaughter to preserve their balance, or joining in the confederacy of kings to war against the principles of liberty. I am for freedom of religion, & against all maneuvres to bring about a legal ascendancy of one sect over another: for freedom of the press, & against all violations of the constitution to silence by force & not by reason the complaints or criticisms, just or unjust, of our citizens against the conduct of their agents. And I am for encouraging the progress of science in all it's branches; and not for raising a hue and cry against the sacred name of philosophy; for awing the human mind by stories of raw-head & bloody bones to a distrust of its own vision, & to repose implicitly on that of others; to go backwards instead of forwards to look for improvement; to believe that government, religion, morality, & every other science were in the highest perfection in ages of the darkest ignorance, and that nothing can ever be devised more perfect than what was established by our forefathers. To these I will add, that I was a sincere well-wisher to the success of the French revolution, and still wish it may end in the establishment of a free & well-ordered republic; but I have not been insensible under the atrocious depredations they have committed on our commerce. The first object of my heart is my own country. In that is embarked my family, my fortune, & my own existence. I have not one farthing of interest, nor one fibre of attachment out of it, nor a single motive of preference of any one nation to another, but in proportion as they are more or less friendly to us. But though deeply feeling the injuries of France, I did not think war the surest means of redressing them. I did believe, that a mission sincerely disposed to preserve peace, would obtain for us a peaceable & honorable settlement & retribution; and I appeal to you to say, whether this might not have been obtained, if either of your colleagues had been of the same sentiment with yourself....

FREEDOM OF MIND
To William Green Munford, June 18, 1799

... I am among those who think well of the human character generally. I consider man as formed for society, and endowed by nature with those dispositions which fit him for society. I believe also, with Condorcet, as mentioned in your letter, that his mind is perfectible to a degree of which we cannot as yet form any conception. It is impossible for a man who takes a survey of what is already known, not to see what an immensity in every branch of science yet remains to be discovered, & that too of articles to which our faculties seem adequate. In geometry & calculation we know a great deal. Yet there are some desiderata. In anatomy great progress has been made; but much is still to be acquired. In natural history we possess knowledge; but we want a great deal. In chemistry we are not yet sure of the first elements. Our natural philosophy is in a very infantine state; perhaps for great advances in it, a further progress in chemistry is necessary. Surgery is well advanced; but prodigiously short of what may be. The state of medecine is worse than that of total ignorance. Could we divest ourselves of every thing we suppose we know in it, we should start from a higher ground & with fairer prospects. From Hippocrates to Brown we have had nothing but a succession of hypothetical systems each having it's day of vogue, like the fashions & fancies of caps & gowns, & yielding in turn to the next caprice. Yet the human frame, which is to be the subject of suffering & torture under these learned modes, does not change. We have a few medecines, as the bark, opium, mercury, which in a few well defined diseases are of unquestionable virtue: but the residuary list of the materia medica, long as it is, contains but the charlataneries of the art; and of the diseases of doubtful form, physicians have ever had a false knowlege, worse than ignorance. Yet surely the list of unequivocal diseases & remedies is capable of enlargement; and it is still more certain that in the other branches of science, great fields are yet to be explored to which our faculties are equal, & that to an extent of which we cannot fix the limits. I join you therefore in branding as cowardly the idea that the human mind is incapable of further advances. This is precisely the doctrine which the present despots of the earth are inculcating, & their friends here re-echoing; & applying especially to religion & politics; 'that it is not probable that any thing better will be discovered than what was known to our fathers.' We are to look backwards then & not forwards for the improvement of science, & to find it amidst feudal barbarisms and the fires of Spital-fields. But thank heaven the American mind is already too much opened, to listen to these impostures; and while the art of printing is left to us, science can never be retrograde; what is once acquired of real knowlege can never be lost. To preserve the freedom of the human mind then & freedom of the press, every spirit should be ready to devote itself to martyrdom; for as long as we may think as we will, & speak as we think, the condition of man will proceed in improvement. The generation which is going off the stage has deserved well of mankind for the struggles it has made, & for having arrested that course of despotism which had overwhelmed the world for thousands & thousands of years. If there seems to be danger that the ground they have gained will be lost again, that danger comes from the generation your cotemporary. But that the enthusiasm which characterises youth should lift its parricide hands against freedom & science, would be such a monstrous phænomenon as I cannot place among possible things in this age & this country....

THE WILL OF THE NATION AND COMMON LAW
To Edmund Randolph, August 18, 1799

... Of all the doctrines which have ever been broached by the federal government, the novel one, of the common law being in force & cognizable as an existing law in their courts, is to me the most formidable. All their other assumptions of un-given powers have been in the detail. The bank law, the treaty doctrine, the sedition act, alien act, the undertaking to change the state laws of evidence in the state courts by certain parts of the stamp act, &c., &c., have been solitary, unconsequential, timid things, in comparison with the audacious, barefaced and sweeping pretension to a system of law for the U S, without the adoption of their legislature, and so infinitively beyond their power to adopt. If this assumption be yielded to, the state courts may be shut up, as there will then be nothing to hinder citizens of the same state suing each other in the federal courts in every case, as on a bond for instance, because the common law obliges payment of it, & the common law they say is their law. I am happy you have taken up the subject; & I have carefully perused & considered the notes you enclosed, and find but a single paragraph which I do not approve. It is that wherein (page 2.) you say, that laws being emanations from the legislative department, &, when once enacted, continuing in force from a presumption that their will so continues, that that presumption fails & the laws of course fall, on the destruction of that legislative department. I do not think this is the true bottom on which laws & the administering them rest. The whole body of the nation is the sovereign legislative, judiciary and executive power for itself. The inconvenience of meeting to exercise these powers in person, and their inaptitude to exercise them, induce them to appoint special organs to declare their legislative will, to judge & to execute it. It is the will of the nation which makes the law obligatory; it is their will which creates or annihilates the organ which is to declare & announce it. They may do it by a single person, as an Emperor of Russia, (constituting his declarations evidence of their will,) or by a few persons, as the Aristocracy of Venice, or by a complication of councils, as in our former regal government, or our present republican one. The law being law because it is the will of the nation, is not changed by their changing the organ through which they chuse to announce their future will; no more than the acts I have done by one attorney lose their obligation by my changing or discontinuing that attorney. This doctrine has been, in a certain degree sanctioned by the federal executive. For it is precisely that on which the continuance of obligation from our treaty with France was established, and the doctrine was particularly developed in a letter to Gouverneur Morris, written with the approbation of President Washington and his cabinet. Mercer once prevailed on the Virginia Assembly to declare a different doctrine in some resolutions. These met universal disapprobation in this, as well as the other States, and if I mistake not, a subsequent Assembly did something to do away the authority of their former unguarded resolutions. In this case, as in all others, the true principle will be quite as effectual to establish the just deductions, for before the revolution, the nation of Virginia had, by the organs they then thought proper to constitute, established a system of laws, which they divided into three denominations of 1, common law; 2, statute law; 3, Chancery: or if you please, into two only, of 1, common law; 2, Chancery. When, by the declaration of Independence, they chose to abolish their former organs of declaring their will, the acts of will already formally & constitutionally declared, remained untouched. For the nation was not dissolved, was not annihilated; it's will, therefore, remained in full vigor; and on the establishing the new organs, first of a convention, & afterwards a more complicated legislature, the old acts of national will continued in force, until the nation should, by its new organs, declare it's will changed. The common law, therefore, which was not in force when we landed here, nor till we had formed ourselves into a nation, and had manifested by the organs we constituted that the common law was to be our law, continued to be our law, because the nation continued in being, & because though it changed the organs for the future declarations of its will, yet it did not change its former declarations that the common law was it's law. Apply these principles to the present case. Before the revolution there existed no such nation as the U S; they then first associated as a nation, but for special purposes only. They had all their laws to make, as Virginia had on her first establishment as a nation. But they did not, as Virginia had done, proceed to adopt a whole system of laws ready made to their hand. As their association as a nation was only for special purposes, to wit, for the management of their concerns with one another & with foreign nations, and the states composing the association chose to give it powers for those purposes & no others, they could not adopt any general system, because it would have embraced objects on which this association had no right to form or declare a will. It was not the organ for declaring a national will in these cases. In the cases confided to them, they were free to declare the will of the nation, the law; but till it was declared there could be no law. So that the common law did not become, ipso facto, law on the new association; it could only become so by a positive adoption, & so far only as they were authorized to adopt....

"FOREIGN CONCERNS ONLY"

To Gideon Granger, August 13, 1800

… Our country is too large to have all its affairs directed by a single government. Public servants at such a distance, & from under the eye of their constituents, must, from the circumstance of distance, be unable to administer & overlook all the details necessary for the good government of the citizens, and the same circumstance, by rendering detection impossible to their constituents, will invite the public agents to corruption, plunder & waste. And I do verily believe, that if the principle were to prevail, of a common law being in force in the U S, (which principle possesses the general government at once of all the powers of the state governments, and reduces us to a single consolidated government,) it would become the most corrupt government on the earth. You have seen the practises by which the public servants have been able to cover their conduct, or, where that could not be done, delusions by which they have varnished it for the eye of their constituents. What an augmentation of the field for jobbing, speculating, plundering, office-building & office-hunting would be produced by an assumption of all the state powers into the hands of the general government. The true theory of our constitution is surely the wisest & best, that the states are independent as to everything within themselves, & united as to everything respecting foreign nations. Let the general government be reduced to foreign concerns only, and let our affairs be disentangled from those of all other nations, except as to commerce, which the merchants will manage the better, the more they are left free to manage for themselves, and our general government may be reduced to a very simple organization, & a very unexpensive one; a few plain duties to be performed by a few servants. But I repeat, that this simple & economical mode of government can never be secured, if the New England States continue to support the contrary system. I rejoice, therefore, in every appearance of their returning to those principles which I had always imagined to be almost innate in them.…

First Inaugural Address (1801)

Friends and Fellow-Citizens,

Called upon to undertake the duties of the first executive office of our country, I avail myself of the presence of that portion of my fellow-citizens which is here assembled to express my grateful thanks for the favor with which they have been pleased to look toward me, to declare a sincere consciousness that the task is above my talents, and that I approach it with those anxious and awful presentiments which the greatness of the charge and the weakness of my powers so justly inspire. A rising nation, spread over a wide and fruitful land, traversing all the seas with the rich productions of their industry, engaged in commerce with nations who feel power and forget right, advancing rapidly to destinies beyond the reach of mortal eye—when I contemplate these transcendent objects, and see the honor, the happiness, and the hopes of this beloved country committed to the issue and the auspices of this day, I shrink from the contemplation, and humble myself before the magnitude of the undertaking. Utterly, indeed, should I despair did not the presence of many whom I here see remind me that in the other high authorities provided by our Constitution I shall find resources of wisdom, of virtue, and of zeal on which to rely under all difficulties. To you, then, gentlemen, who are charged with the sovereign functions of legislation, and to those associated with you, I look with encouragement for that guidance and support which may enable us to steer with safety the vessel in which we are all embarked amidst the conflicting elements of a troubled world.

During the contest of opinion through which we have passed the animation of discussions and of exertions has sometimes worn an aspect which might impose on strangers unused to think freely and to speak and to write what they think; but this being now decided by the voice of the nation, announced according to the rules of the Constitution, all will, of course, arrange themselves under the will of the law, and unite in common efforts for the common good. All, too, will bear in mind this sacred principle, that though the will of the majority is in all cases to prevail, that will to be rightful must be reasonable; that the minority possess their equal rights, which equal law must protect, and to violate would be oppression. Let us, then, fellow-citizens, unite with one heart and one mind. Let us restore to social intercourse that harmony and affection without which liberty and even life itself are but dreary things. And let us reflect that, having banished from our land that religious intolerance under which mankind so long bled and suffered, we have yet gained little if we countenance a political intolerance as despotic, as wicked, and capable of as bitter and bloody persecutions. During the throes and convulsions of the ancient world, during the agonizing spasms of infuriated man, seeking through blood and slaughter his long-lost liberty, it was not wonderful that the agitation of the billows should reach even this distant and peaceful shore; that this should be more felt and feared by some and less by others, and should divide opinions as to measures of safety. But every difference of opinion is not a difference of principle. We have called by different names brethren of the same principle. We are all Republicans, we are all Federalists. If there be any among us who would wish to dissolve this Union or to change its republican form, let them stand undisturbed as monuments of the safety with which error of opinion may be tolerated where reason is left free to combat it. I know, indeed, that some honest men fear that a republican government can not be strong, that this Government is not strong enough; but would the honest patriot, in the full tide of successful experiment, abandon a government which has so far kept us free and firm on the theoretic and visionary fear that this Government, the world's best hope, may by possibility want energy to preserve itself? I trust not. I believe this, on the contrary, the strongest Government on earth. I believe it the only one where every man, at the call of the law, would fly to the standard of the law, and would meet invasions of the public order as his own personal concern. Sometimes it is said that man can not be trusted with the government of himself. Can he, then, be trusted with the government of others? Or have we found angels in the forms of kings to govern him? Let history answer this question.

Let us, then, with courage and confidence pursue our own Federal and Republican principles, our attachment to union and representative government. Kindly separated by nature and a wide ocean from the exterminating havoc of one quarter of the globe; too high-minded to endure the degradations of the others; possessing a chosen country, with room enough for our descendants to the thousandth and thousandth generation; entertaining a due sense of our equal right to the use of our own faculties, to the acquisitions of our own industry, to honor and confidence from our fellow-citizens, resulting not from birth, but from our actions and their sense of them; enlightened by a benign religion, professed, indeed, and practiced in various forms, yet all of them inculcating honesty, truth, temperance, gratitude, and the love of man; acknowledging and adoring an overruling Providence, which by all its dispensations proves that it delights in the happiness of man here and his greater happiness hereafter—with all these blessings, what more is necessary to make us a happy and a prosperous people? Still one thing more, fellow-citizens—a wise and frugal Government, which shall restrain men from injuring one another, shall leave them otherwise free to regulate their own pursuits of industry and improvement, and shall not take from the mouth of labor the bread it has earned. This is the sum of good government, and this is necessary to close the circle of our felicities.

About to enter, fellow-citizens, on the exercise of duties which comprehend everything dear and valuable to you, it is proper you should understand what I deem the essential principles of our Government, and consequently those which ought to shape its Administration. I will compress them within the narrowest compass they will bear, stating the general principle, but not all its limitations. Equal and exact justice to all men, of whatever state or persuasion, religious or political; peace, commerce, and honest friendship with all nations, entangling alliances with none; the support of the State governments in all their rights, as the most competent administrations for our domestic concerns and the surest bulwarks against antirepublican tendencies; the preservation of the General Government in its whole constitutional vigor, as the sheet anchor of our peace at home and safety abroad; a jealous care of the right of election by the people—a mild and safe corrective of abuses which are lopped by the sword of revolution where peaceable remedies are unprovided; absolute acquiescence in the decisions of the majority, the vital principle of republics, from which is no appeal but to force, the vital principle and immediate parent of despotism; a well-disciplined militia, our best reliance in peace and for the first moments of war till regulars may relieve them; the supremacy of the civil over the military authority; economy in the public expense, that labor may be lightly burthened; the honest payment of our debts and sacred preservation of the public faith; encouragement of agriculture, and of commerce as its handmaid; the diffusion of information and arraignment of all abuses at the bar of the public reason; freedom of religion; freedom of the press, and freedom of person under the protection of the habeas corpus, and trial by juries impartially selected. These principles form the bright constellation which has gone before us and guided our steps through an age of revolution and reformation. The wisdom of our sages and blood of our heroes have been devoted to their attainment. They should be the creed of our political faith, the text of civic instruction, the touchstone by which to try the services of those we trust; and should we wander from them in moments of error or of alarm, let us hasten to retrace our steps and to regain the road which alone leads to peace, liberty, and safety.

I repair, then, fellow-citizens, to the post you have assigned me. With experience enough in subordinate offices to have seen the difficulties of this the greatest of all, I have learnt to expect that it will rarely fall to the lot of imperfect man to retire from this station with the reputation and the favor which bring him into it. Without pretensions to that high confidence you reposed in our first and greatest revolutionary character, whose preeminent services had entitled him to the first place in his country's love and destined for him the fairest page in the volume of faithful history, I ask so much confidence only as may give firmness and effect to the legal administration of your affairs. I shall often go wrong through defect of judgment. When right, I shall often be thought wrong by those whose positions will not command a view of the whole ground. I ask your indulgence for my own errors, which will never be intentional, and your support against the errors of others, who may condemn what they would not if seen in all its parts. The approbation implied by your suffrage is a great consolation to me for the past, and my future solicitude will be to retain the good opinion of those who have bestowed it in advance, to conciliate that of others by doing them all the good in my power, and to be instrumental to the happiness and freedom of all.

Relying, then, on the patronage of your good will, I advance with obedience to the work, ready to retire from it whenever you become sensible how much better choice it is in your power to make. And may that Infinite Power which rules the destinies of the universe lead our councils to what is best, and give them a favorable issue for your peace and prosperity.

The Revolution of 1800
To John Dickinson, March 6, 1801

… No pleasure can exceed that which I received from reading your letter of the 21st ult. It was like the joy we expect in the mansions of the blessed, when received with the embraces of our fathers, we shall be welcomed with their blessing as having done our part not unworthily of them. The storm through which we have passed, has been tremendous indeed. The tough sides of our Argosie have been thoroughly tried. Her strength has stood the waves into which she was steered, with a view to sink her. We shall put her on her republican tack, & she will now show by the beauty of her motion the skill of her builders. Figure apart, our fellow citizens have been led hood-winked from their principles, by a most extraordinary combination of circumstances. But the band is removed, and they now see for themselves. I hope to see shortly a perfect consolidation, to effect which, nothing shall be spared on my part, short of the abandonment of the principles of our revolution. A just and solid republican government maintained here, will be a standing monument & example for the aim & imitation of the people of other countries; and I join with you in the hope and belief that they will see, from our example, that a free government is of all others the most energetic; that the inquiry which has been excited among the mass of mankind by our revolution & it's consequences, will ameliorate the condition of man over a great portion of the globe. What a satisfaction have we in the contemplation of the benevolent effects of our efforts, compared with those of the leaders on the other side, who have discountenanced all advances in science as dangerous innovations, have endeavored to render philosophy and republicanism terms of reproach, to persuade us that man cannot be governed but by the rod, &c. I shall have the happiness of living & dying in the contrary hope….

Something New Under the Sun
To Joseph Priestly, March 21, 1801

… What an effort, my dear Sir, of bigotry in Politics & Religion have we gone through!

The barbarians really flattered themselves they should be able to bring back the times of Vandalism, when ignorance put everything into the hands of power & priestcraft. All advances in science were proscribed as innovations. They pretended to praise and encourage education, but it was to be the education of our ancestors. We were to look backwards, not forwards, for improvement; the President himself declaring, in one of his answers to addresses, that we were never to expect to go beyond them in real science. This was the real ground of all the attacks on you. Those who live by mystery & *charlatanerie,* fearing you would render them useless by simplifying the Christian philosophy,—the most sublime & benevolent, but most perverted system that ever shone on man,—endeavored to crush your well-earnt & well-deserved fame. But it was the Lilliputians upon Gulliver. Our countrymen have recovered from the alarm into which art & industry had thrown them; science & honesty are replaced on their high ground; and you, my dear Sir, as their great apostle, are on it's pinnacle. It is with heartfelt satisfaction that, in the first moments of my public action, I can hail you with welcome to our land, tender to you the homage of it's respect & esteem, cover you under the protection of those laws which were made for the wise and good like you, and disdain the legitimacy of that libel on legislation, which under the form of a law, was for some time placed among them.

As the storm is now subsiding, and the horizon becoming serene, it is pleasant to consider the phenomenon with attention. We can no longer say there is nothing new under the sun. For this whole chapter in the history of man is new. The great extent of our Republic is new. Its sparse habitation is new. The mighty wave of public opinion which has rolled over it is new. But the most pleasing novelty is, it's so quickly subsiding over such an extent of surface to it's true level again. The order & good sense displayed in this recovery from delusion, and in the momentous crisis which lately arose, really bespeak a strength of character in our nation which augurs well for the duration of our Republic; & I am much better satisfied now of it's stability than I was before it was tried. I have been, above all things, solaced by the prospect which opened on us, in the event of a non-election of a President; in which case, the federal government would have been in the situation of a clock or watch run down. There was no idea of force, nor of any occasion for it. A convention, invited by the Republican members of Congress, with the virtual President & Vice President, would have been on the ground in 8. weeks, would have repaired the Constitution where it was defective, & wound it up again. This peaceable & legitimate resource, to which we are in the habit of implicit obedience, superseding all appeal to force, and being always within our reach, shows a precious principle of self-preservation in our composition, till a change of circumstances shall take place, which is not within prospect at any definite period….

"A WALL OF SEPARATION"

Reply to the Danbury Baptist Association,
in Connecticut, January 1, 1802

… Believing with you that religion is a matter which lies solely between man and his God, that he owes account to none other for his faith or his worship, that the legislative powers of government reach actions only, and not opinions, I contemplate with sovereign reverence that act of the whole American people which declared that their legislature should "make no law respecting an establishment of religion, or prohibiting the free exercise thereof," thus building a wall of separation between church and State. Adhering to this expression of the supreme will of the nation in behalf of the rights of conscience, I shall see with sincere satisfaction the progress of those sentiments which tend to restore to man all his natural rights, convinced he has no natural right in opposition to his social duties….

LIMITS OF THE PRACTICABLE

To P. S. Dupont de Nemours, January 18, 1802

… When this government was first established, it was possible to have kept it going on true principles, but the contracted, English, half-lettered ideas of Hamilton, destroyed that hope in the bud. We can pay off his debt in 15. years; but we can never get rid of his financial system. It mortifies me to be strengthening principles which I deem radically vicious, but this vice is entailed on us by the first error. In other parts of our government I hope we shall be able by degrees to introduce sound principles and make them habitual. What is practicable must often controul what is pure theory; and the habits of the governed determine in a great degree what is practicable. Hence the same original principles, modified in practice according to the different habits of different nations, present governments of very different aspects. The same principles reduced to forms of practice accommodated to our habits, and put into forms accommodated to the habits of the French nation would present governments very unlike each other. I have no doubt but that a great man, thoroughly knowing the habits of France, might so accommodate to them the principles of free government as to enable them to live free. But in the hands of those who have not this coup d'oeil, many unsuccessful experiments I fear are yet to be tried before they will settle down in freedom and tranquility....

"A NOISELESS COURSE"
To Thomas Cooper, November 29, 1802

... It delights me to find that there are persons who still think that all is not lost in France: that their retrogradation from a limited to an unlimited despotism, is but to give themselves a new impulse. But I see not how or when. The press, the only tocsin of a nation, is compleatly silenced there, and all means of a general effort taken away. However, I am willing to hope, as long as anybody will hope with me; and I am entirely persuaded that the agitations of the public mind advance its powers, and that at every vibration between the points of liberty and despotism, something will be gained for the former. As men become better informed, their rulers must respect them the more. I think you will be sensible that our citizens are fast returning, from the panic into which they were artfully thrown to the dictates of their own reason; and I believe the delusions they have seen themselves hurried into will be useful as a lesson under similar attempts on them in future. The good effects of our late fiscal arrangements will certainly tend to unite them in opinion, and in a confidence as to the views of their public functionaries, legislative & executive. The path we have to pursue is so quiet that we have nothing scarcely to propose to our Legislature. A noiseless course, not meddling with the affairs of others, unattractive of notice, is a mark that society is going on in happiness....

Civilization and the Indians

To Benjamin Hawkins, February 18, 1803

... Altho' you will receive, thro' the official channel of the War Office, every communication necessary to develop to you our views respecting the Indians, and to direct your conduct, yet, supposing it will be satisfactory to you, and to those with whom you are placed, to understand my personal dispositions and opinions in this particular, I shall avail myself of this private letter to state them generally. I consider the business of hunting as already become insufficient to furnish clothing and subsistence to the Indians. The promotion of agriculture, therefore, and household manufacture, are essential in their preservation, and I am disposed to aid and encourage it liberally. This will enable them to live on much smaller portions of land, and indeed will render their vast forests useless but for the range of cattle; for which purpose, also, as they become better farmers, they will be found useless, and even disadvantageous. While they are learning to do better on less land, our increasing numbers will be calling for more land, and thus a coincidence of interests will be produced between those who have lands to spare, and want other necessaries, and those who have such necessaries to spare, and want lands. This commerce, then, will be for the good of both, and those who are friends to both ought to encourage it. You are in the station peculiarly charged with this interchange, and who have it peculiarly in your power to promote among the Indians a sense of the superior value of a little land, well cultivated, over a great deal, unimproved, and to encourage them to make this estimate truly. The wisdom of the animal which amputates & abandons to the hunter the parts for which he is pursued should be theirs, with this difference, that the former sacrifices what is useful, the latter what is not. In truth, the ultimate point of rest & happiness for them is to let our settlements and theirs meet and blend together, to intermix, and become one people. Incorporating themselves with us as citizens of the U.S., this is what the natural progress of things will of course bring on, and it will be better to promote than to retard it. Surely it will be better for them to be identified with us, and preserved in the occupation of their lands, than be exposed to the many casualties which may endanger them while a separate people. I have little doubt but that your reflections must have led you to view the various ways in which their history may terminate, and to see that this is the one most for their happiness. And we have already had an application from a settlement of Indians to become citizens of the U.S. It is possible, perhaps probable, that this idea may be so novel as that it might shock the Indians, were it even hinted to them. Of course, you will keep it for your own reflection; but, convinced of its soundness, I feel it consistent with pure morality to lead them towards it, to familiarize them to the idea that it is for their interest to cede lands at times to the U S, and for us thus to procure gratifications to our citizens, from time to time, by new acquisitions of land….

THE LOUISIANA PURCHASE
To John Breckinridge, August 12, 1803

… Objections are raising to the Eastward against the vast extent of our boundaries, and propositions are made to exchange Louisiana, or a part of it, for the Floridas. But, as I have said, we shall get the Floridas without, and I would not give one inch of the waters of the Mississippi to any nation, because I see in a light very important to our peace the exclusive right to it's navigation, & the admission of no nation into it, but as into the Potomak or Delaware, with our consent & under our police. These federalists see in this acquisition the formation of a new confederacy, embracing all the waters of the Missipi, on both sides of it, and a separation of it's Eastern waters from us. These combinations depend on so many circumstances which we cannot foresee, that I place little reliance on them. We have seldom seen neighborhood produce affection among nations. The reverse is almost the universal truth. Besides, if it should become the great interest of those nations to separate from this, if their happiness should depend on it so strongly as to induce them to go through that convulsion, why should the Atlantic States dread it? But especially why should we, their present inhabitants, take side in such a question? When I view the Atlantic States, procuring for those on the Eastern waters of the Missipi friendly instead of hostile neighbors on it's Western waters, I do not view it as an Englishman would the procuring future blessings for the French nation, with whom he has no relations of blood or affection. The future inhabitants of the Atlantic & Missipi States will be our sons. We leave them in distinct but bordering establishments. We think we see their happiness in their union, & we wish it. Events may prove it otherwise; and if they see their interest in separation, why should we take side with our Atlantic rather than our Missipi descendants? It is the elder and the younger son differing. God bless them both, & keep them in union, if it be for their good, but separate them, if it be better. The inhabited part of Louisiana, from Point Coupée to the sea, will of course be immediately a territorial government, and soon a State. But above that, the best use we can make of the country for some time, will be to give establishments in it to the Indians on the East side of the Missipi, in exchange for their present country, and open land offices in the last, & thus make this acquisition the means of filling up the Eastern side, instead of drawing off it's population. When we shall be full on this side, we may lay off a range of States on the Western bank from the head to the mouth, & so, range after range, advancing compactly as we multiply.

This treaty must of course be laid before both Houses, because both have important functions to exercise respecting it. They, I presume, will see their duty to their country in ratifying & paying for it, so as to secure a good which would otherwise probably be never again in their power. But I suppose they must then appeal to *the nation* for an additional article to the Constitution, approving & confirming an act which the nation had not previously authorized. The constitution has made no provision for our holding foreign territory, still less for incorporating foreign nations into our Union. The Executive in seizing the fugitive occurrence which so much advances the good of their country, have done an act beyond the Constitution. The Legislature in casting behind them metaphysical subtleties, and risking themselves like faithful servants, must ratify & pay for it, and throw themselves on their country for doing for them unauthorized what we know they would have done for themselves had they been in a situation to do it. It is the case of a guardian, investing the money of his ward in purchasing an important adjacent territory; & saying to him when of age, I did this for your good: I pretend to no right to bind you: you may disavow me, and I must get out of the scrape as I can: I thought it my duty to risk myself for you. But we shall not be disavowed by the nation, and their act of indemnity will confirm & not weaken the Constitution, by more strongly marking out its lines....

Third Annual Message (1803)

... We have seen with sincere concern the flames of war lighted up again in Europe, and nations with which we have the most friendly and useful relations engaged in mutual destruction. While we regret the miseries in which we see others involved let us bow with gratitude to that kind Providence which, inspiring with wisdom and moderation our late legislative councils while placed under the urgency of the greatest wrongs, guarded us from hastily entering into the sanguinary contest, and left us only to look on and to pity its ravages. These will be heaviest on those immediately engaged. Yet the nations pursuing peace will not be exempt from all evil. In the course of this conflict, let it be our endeavor, as it is our interest and desire, to cultivate the friendship of the belligerent nations by every act of justice and of incessant kindness; to receive their armed vessels with hospitality from the distresses of the sea, but to administer the means of annoyance to none; to establish in our harbors such a police as may maintain law and order; to restrain our citizens from embarking individually in a war in which their country takes no part; to punish severely those persons, citizen or alien, who shall usurp the cover of our flag for vessels not entitled to it, infecting thereby with suspicion those of real Americans, and committing us into controversies for the redress of wrongs not our own; to exact from every nation the observance, toward our vessels and citizens, of those principles and practices which all civilized people acknowledge; to merit the character of a just nation, and maintain that of an independent one, preferring every consequence to insult and habitual wrong. Congress will consider whether the existing laws enable us efficaciously to maintain this course with our citizens in all places, and with others while within the limits of our jurisdiction, and will give them the new modifications necessary for these objects. Some contraventions of right have already taken place, both within our jurisdictional limits and on the high seas. The friendly disposition of the governments from whose agents they have proceeded, as well as their wisdom and regard for justice, leave us in reasonable expectation that they will be rectified and prevented in future; and that no act will be countenanced by them which threatens to disturb our friendly intercourse. Separated by a wide ocean from the nations of Europe, and from the political interests which entangle them together, with productions and wants which render our commerce and friendship useful to them and theirs to us, it cannot be the interest of any to assail us, nor ours to disturb them. We should be most unwise, indeed, were we to cast away the singular blessings of the position in which nature has placed us, the opportunity she has endowed us with of pursuing, at a distance from foreign contentions, the paths of industry, peace, and happiness; of cultivating general friendship, and of bringing collisions of interest to the umpirage of reason rather than of force. How desirable then must it be, in a government like ours, to see its citizens adopt individually the views, the interests, and the conduct which their country should pursue, divesting themselves of those passions and partialities which tend to lessen useful friendships, and to embarrass and embroil us in the calamitous scenes of Europe....

MALTHUS AND THE NEW WORLD
To Jean Baptise Say, February 1, 1804

... I have to acknowledge the receipt of your obliging letter, and with it, of two very interesting volumes on Political Economy. These found me engaged in giving the leisure moments I rarely find, to the perusal of Malthus' work on population, a work of sound logic, in which some of the opinions of Adam Smith, as well as of the economists, are ably examined. I was pleased, on turning to some chapters where you treat the same questions, to find his opinions corroborated by yours. I shall proceed to the reading of your work with great pleasure. In the meantime, the present conveyance, by a gentleman of my family going to Paris, is too safe to hazard a delay in making my acknowledgments for this mark of attention, and for having afforded to me a satisfaction, which the ordinary course of literary communications could not have given me for a considerable time.

The differences of circumstance between this and the old countries of Europe, furnish differences of fact whereon to reason, in questions of political economy, and will consequently produce sometimes a difference of result. There, for instance, the quantity of food is fixed, or increasing in a slow and only arithmetical ratio, and the proportion is limited by the same ratio. Supernumerary births consequently add only to your mortality. Here the immense extent of uncultivated and fertile lands enables every one who will labor to marry young, and to raise a family of any size. Our food, then, may increase geometrically with our laborers, and our births, however multiplied, become effective. Again, there the best distribution of labor is supposed to be that which places the manufacturing hands alongside the agricultural; so that the one part shall feed both, and the other part furnish both with clothes and other comforts. Would that be best here? Egoism and first appearances say yes. Or would it be better that all our laborers should be employed in agriculture? In this case a double or treble portion of fertile lands would be brought into culture; a double or treble creation of food be produced, and its surplus go to nourish the now perishing births of Europe, who in return would manufacture and send us in exchange our clothes and other comforts. Morality listens to this, and so invariably do the laws of nature create our duties and interests, that when they seem to be at variance, we ought to suspect some fallacy in our reasonings. In solving this question, too, we should allow its just weight to the moral and physical preference of the agricultural, over the manufacturing, man....

Freedom of the Press

To John Tyler, June 28, 1804

... Amidst the direct falsehoods, the misrepresentations of truth, the calumnies and the insults resorted to by a faction to mislead the public mind, and to overwhelm those entrusted with its interests, our support is to be found in the approving voice of our conscience and country, in the testimony of our fellow citizens, that their confidence is not shaken by these artifices. When to the plaudits of the honest multitude, the sober approbation of the sage in his closet is added, it becomes a gratification of an higher order. It is the sanction of wisdom superadded to the voice of affection. The terms, therefore, in which you are so good as to express your satisfaction with the course of the present administration cannot but give me great pleasure. I may err in my measures, but never shall deflect from the intention to fortify the public liberty by every possible means, and to put it out of the power of the few to riot on the labors of the many. No experiment can be more interesting than that we are now trying, and which we trust will end in establishing the fact, that man may be governed by reason and truth. Our first object should therefore be, to leave open to him all the avenues to truth. The most effectual hitherto found, is the freedom of the press. It is therefore, the first shut up by those who fear the investigation of their actions. The firmness with which the people have withstood the late abuses of the press, the discernment they have manifested between truth and falsehood, show that they may safely be trusted to hear everything true and false, and to form a correct judgment between them. As little is it necessary to impose on their senses, or dazzle their minds by pomp, splendor, or forms. Instead of this artificial, how much surer is that real respect, which results from the use of their reason, and the habit of bringing everything to the test of common sense.

I hold it, therefore, certain, that to open the doors of truth, and to fortify the habit of testing everything by reason, are the most effectual manacles we can rivet on the hands of our successors to prevent their manacling the people with their own consent. The panic into which they were artfully thrown in 1798, the frenzy which was excited in them by their enemies against their apparent readiness to abandon all the principles established for their own protection, seemed for awhile to countenance the opinions of those who say they cannot be trusted with their own government. But I never doubted their rallying; and they did rally much sooner than I expected. On the whole, that experiment on their credulity has confirmed my confidence in their ultimate good sense and virtue....

THE TWO-TERM PRECEDENT
To John Taylor, January 6, 1805

... My opinion originally was that the President of the U.S. should have been elected for 7. years, & forever ineligible afterwards. I have since become sensible that 7. years is too long to be irremovable, and that there should be a peaceable way of withdrawing a man in midway who is doing wrong. The service for 8. years with a power to remove at the end of the first four, comes nearly to my principle as corrected by experience. And it is in adherence to that that I determined to withdraw at the end of my second term. The danger is that the indulgence & attachments of the people will keep a man in the chair after he becomes a dotard, that reelection through life shall become habitual, & election for life follow that. Genl. Washington set the example of voluntary retirement after 8. years. I shall follow it, and a few more precedents will oppose the obstacle of habit to anyone after a while who shall endeavor to extend his term. Perhaps it may beget a disposition to establish it by an amendment of the constitution. I believe I am doing right, therefore, in pursuing my principle. I had determined to declare my intention, but I have consented to be silent on the opinion of friends, who think it best not to put a continuance out of my power in defiance of all circumstances. There is, however, but one circumstance which could engage my acquiescence in another election, to wit, such a division about a successor as might bring in a Monarchist....

TO THE CHIEFS OF THE CHEROKEE NATION (1806)

MY FRIENDS AND CHILDREN, CHIEFLY OF THE CHEROKEE NATION,—Having now finished our business and finished it I hope to mutual satisfaction, I cannot take leave of you without expressing the satisfaction I have received from your visit. I see with my own eyes that the endeavors we have been making to encourage and lead you in the way of improving your situation have not been unsuccessful; it has been like grain sown in good ground, producing abundantly. You are becoming farmers, learning the use of the plough and the hoe, enclosing your grounds and employing that labor in their cultivation which you formerly employed in hunting and in war; and I see handsome specimens of cotton cloth raised, spun and wove by yourselves. You are also raising cattle and hogs for your food, and horses to assist your labors. Go on, my children, in the same way and be assured the further you advance in it the happier and more respectable you will be.

Our brethren, whom you have happened to meet here from the West and Northwest, have enabled you to compare your situation now with what it was formerly. They also make the comparison, and they see how far you are ahead of them, and seeing what you are they are encouraged to do as you have done. You will find your next want to be mills to grind your corn, which by relieving your women from the loss of time in beating it into meal, will enable them to spin and weave more. When a man has enclosed and improved his farm, builds a good house on it and raised plentiful stocks of animals, he will wish when he dies that these things shall go to his wife and children, whom he loves more than he does his other relations, and for whom he will work with pleasure during his life. You will, therefore, find it necessary to establish laws for this. When a man has property, earned by his own labor, he will not like to see another come and take it from him because he happens to be stronger, or else to defend it by spilling blood. You will find it necessary then to appoint good men, as judges, to decide contests between man and man, according to reason and to the rules you shall establish. If you wish to be aided by our counsel and experience in these things we shall always be ready to assist you with our advice.

My children, it is unnecessary for me to advise you against spending all your time and labor in warring with and destroying your fellow-men, and wasting your own members. You already see the folly and iniquity of it. Your young men, however, are not yet sufficiently sensible of it. Some of them cross the Mississippi to go and destroy people who have never done them an injury. My children, this is wrong and must not be; if we permit them to cross the Mississippi to war with the Indians on the other side of that river, we must let those Indians cross the river to take revenge on you. I say again, this must not be. The Mississippi now belongs to us. It must not be a river of blood. It is now the water-path along which all our people of Natchez, St. Louis, Indiana, Ohio, Tennessee, Kentucky and the western parts of Pennsylvania and Virginia are constantly passing with their property, to and from New Orleans. Young men going to war are not easily restrained. Finding our people on the river they will rob them, perhaps kill them. This would bring on a war between us and you. It is better to stop this in time by forbidding your young men to go across the river to make war. If they go to visit or to live with the Cherokees on the other side of the river we shall not object to that. That country is ours. We will permit them to live in it.

My children, this is what I wished to say to you. To go on in learning to cultivate the earth and to avoid war. If any of your neighbors injure you, our beloved men whom we place with you will endeavor to obtain justice for you and we will support them in it. If any of your bad people injure your neighbors, be ready to acknowledge it and to do them justice. It is more honorable to repair a wrong than to persist in it. Tell all your chiefs, your men, women and children, that I take them by the hand and hold it fast. That I am their father, wish their happiness and well-being, and am always ready to promote their good.

My children, I thank you for your visit and pray to the Great Spirit who made us all and planted us all in this land to live together like brothers that He will conduct you safely to your homes, and grant you to find your families and your friends in good health.

A National Academy
To Joel Barlow, February 24, 1806

I return you the draft of the bill for the establishment of a National Academy & University at the city of Washington, with such alterations as we talked over the last night. They are chiefly verbal. I have often wished we could have a Philosophical society or academy so organized as that while the central academy should be at the seat of government, it's members dispersed over the states, should constitute filiated academies in each state, publish their communications, from which the central academy should select unpublished what should be most choice. In this way all the members wheresoever dispersed might be brought into action, and an useful emulation might arise between the filiated societies. Perhaps the great societies now existing might incorporate themselves in this way with the National one. But time does not allow me to pursue this idea, nor perhaps had we time at all to get it into the present bill. I procured an Agricultural society to be established (voluntarily) on this plan, but it has done nothing....

History, Hume, and Newspapers
To John Norvell, June 14, 1807

... I think there does not exist a good elementary work on the organization of society into civil government: I mean a work which presents in one full & comprehensive view the system of principles on which such an organization should be founded, according to the rights of nature. For want of a single work of that character, I should recommend Locke on Government, Sidney, Priestley's Essay on the first Principles of Government, Chipman's Principles of Government, & the Federalist. Adding, perhaps, Beccaria on crimes & punishments, because of the demonstrative manner in which he has treated that branch of the subject. If your views of political inquiry go further, to the subjects of money & commerce, Smith's Wealth of Nations is the best book to be read, unless Say's Political Economy can be had, which treats the same subject on the same principles, but in a shorter compass & more lucid manner. But I believe this work has not been translated into our language.

History, in general, only informs us what bad government is. But as we have employed some of the best materials of the British constitution in the construction of our own government, a knolege of British history becomes useful to the American politician. There is, however, no general history of that country which can be recommended. The elegant one of Hume seems intended to disguise & discredit the good principles of the government, and is so plausible & pleasing in it's style & manner, as to instil it's errors & heresies insensibly into the minds of unwary readers. Baxter has performed a good operation on it. He has taken the text of Hume as his ground work, abridging it by the omission of some details of little interest, and wherever he has found him endeavoring to mislead, by either the suppression of a truth or by giving it a false coloring, he has changed the text to what it should be, so that we may properly call it Hume's history republicanised. He has moreover continued the history (but indifferently) from where Hume left it, to the year 1800. The work is not popular in England, because it is republican; and but a few copies have ever reached America. It is a single 4to. volume. Adding to this Ludlow's Memoirs, Mrs. M'Cauley's & Belknap's histories, a sufficient view will be presented of the free principles of the English constitution.

To your request of my opinion of the manner in which a newspaper should be conducted, so as to be most useful, I should answer, 'by restraining it to true facts & sound principles only.' Yet I fear such a paper would find few subscribers. It is a melancholy truth, that a suppression of the press could not more compleatly deprive the nation of it's benefits, than is done by it's abandoned prostitution to falsehood. Nothing can now be believed which is seen in a newspaper. Truth itself becomes suspicious by being put into that polluted vehicle. The real extent of this state of misinformation is known only to those who are in situations to confront facts within their knolege with the lies of the day. I really look with commiseration over the great body of my fellow citizens, who, reading newspapers, live & die in the belief, that they have known something of what has been passing in the world in their time; whereas the accounts they have read in newspapers are just as true a history of any other period of the world as of the present, except that the real names of the day are affixed to their fables. General facts may indeed be collected from them, such as that Europe is now at war, that Bonaparte has been a successful warrior, that he has subjected a great portion of Europe to his will, &c., &c.; but no details can be relied on. I will add, that the man who never looks into a newspaper is better informed than he who reads them; inasmuch as he who knows nothing is nearer to truth than he whose mind is filled with falsehoods & errors. He who reads nothing will still learn the great facts, and the details are all false.

Perhaps an editor might begin a reformation in some such way as this. Divide his paper into 4 chapters, heading the 1st, Truths. 2d, Probabilities. 3d, Possibilities. 4th, Lies. The first chapter would be very short, as it would contain little more than authentic papers, and information from such sources, as the editor would be willing to risk his own reputation for their truth. The 2d would contain what, from a mature consideration of all circumstances, his judgment should conclude to be probably true. This, however, should rather contain too little than too much. The 3d & 4th should be professedly for those readers who would rather have lies for their money than the blank paper they would occupy.

Such an editor too, would have to set his face against the demoralising practice of feeding the public mind habitually on slander, & the depravity of taste which this nauseous aliment induces. Defamation is becoming a necessary of life; insomuch, that a dish of tea in the morning or evening cannot be digested without this stimulant. Even those who do not believe these abominations, still read them with complaisance to their auditors, and instead of the abhorrence & indignation which should fill a virtuous mind, betray a secret pleasure in the possibility that some may believe them, tho they do not themselves. It seems to escape them, that it is not he who prints, but he who pays for printing a slander, who is it's real author....

Religious Freedom

To Rev. Samuel Miller, January 23, 1808

... I consider the government of the U S. as interdicted by the Constitution from intermeddling with religious institutions, their doctrines, discipline, or exercises. This results not only from the provision that no law shall be made respecting the establishment, or free exercise, of religion, but from that also which reserves to the states the powers not delegated to the U.S. Certainly no power to prescribe any religious exercise, or to assume authority in religious discipline, has been delegated to the general government. It must then rest with the states, as far as it can be in any human authority. But it is only proposed that I should *recommend*, not prescribe a day of fasting & prayer. That is, that I should *indirectly* assume to the U.S. an authority over religious exercises which the Constitution has directly precluded them from. It must be meant too that this recommendation is to carry some authority, and to be sanctioned by some penalty on those who disregard it; not indeed of fine and imprisonment, but of some degree of proscription perhaps in public opinion. And does the change in the nature of the penalty make the recommendation the less *a law* of conduct for those to whom it is directed? I do not believe it is for the interest of religion to invite the civil magistrate to direct it's exercises, it's discipline, or it's doctrines; nor of the religious societies that the general government should be invested with the power of effecting any uniformity of time or matter among them. Fasting & prayer are religious exercises. The enjoining them an act of discipline. Every religious society has a right to determine for itself the times for these exercises, & the objects proper for them, according to their own particular tenets; and this right can never be safer than in their own hands, where the constitution has deposited it....

Reason and Peace

To Caesar A. Rodney, February 10, 1810

... It has been peculiarly unfortunate for us, personally, that the portion in the history of mankind, at which we were called to take a share in the direction of their affairs, was such an one as history has never before presented. At any other period, the even-handed justice we have observed towards all nations, the efforts we have made to merit their esteem by every act which candor or liberality could exercise, would have preserved our peace, and secured the unqualified confidence of all other nations in our faith and probity. But the hurricane which is now blasting the world, physical and moral, has prostrated all the mounds of reason as well as right. All those calculations which, at any other period, would have been deemed honorable, of the existence of a moral sense in man, individually or associated, of the connection which the laws of nature have established between his duties and his interests, of a regard for honest fame and the esteem of our fellow men, have been a matter of reproach on us, as evidences of imbecility. As if it could be a folly for an honest man to suppose that others could be honest also, when it is their interest to be so. And when is this state of things to end? The death of Bonaparte would, to be sure, remove the first and chiefest apostle of the desolation of men and morals, and might withdraw the scourge of the land. But what is to restore order and safety on the ocean? The death of George III? Not at all. He is only stupid; and his ministers, however weak and profligate in morals, are ephemeral. But his nation is permanent, and it is that which is the tyrant of the ocean. The principle that force is right, is become the principle of the nation itself. They would not permit an honest minister, were accident to bring such an one into power, to relax their system of lawless piracy. These were the difficulties when I was with you. I know they are not lessened, and I pity you.

It is a blessing, however, that our people are reasonable; that they are kept so well informed of the state of things as to judge for themselves, to see the true sources of their difficulties, and to maintain their confidence undiminished in the wisdom and integrity of their functionaries. *Macte virtute* therefore. Continue to go straight forward, pursuing always that which is right, as the only clue which can lead us out of the labyrinth. Let nothing be spared of either reason or passion, to preserve the public confidence entire, as the only rock of our safety. In times of peace the people look most to their representatives; but in war, to the executive solely. It is visible that their confidence is even now veering in that direction; that they are looking to the executive to give the proper direction to their affairs, with a confidence as auspicious as it is well founded....

"LITTLE REPUBLICS"
To John Tyler, May 26, 1810

... I have long lamented with you the depreciation of law science. The opinion seems to be that Blackstone is to us what the Alcoran is to the Mahometans, that everything which is necessary is in him, and what is not in him is not necessary. I still lend my counsel and books to such young students as will fix themselves in the neighborhood. Coke's institutes and reports are their first, and Blackstone their last book, after an intermediate course of two or three years. It is nothing more than an elegant digest of what they will then have acquired from the real fountains of the law. Now men are born scholars, lawyers, doctors; in our day this was confined to poets. You wish to see me again in the legislature, but this is impossible; my mind is now so dissolved in tranquillity, that it can never again encounter a contentious assembly; the habits of thinking and speaking off-hand, after a disuse of five and twenty years, have given place to the slower process of the pen. I have indeed two great measures at heart, without which no republic can maintain itself in strength. 1. That of general education, to enable every man to judge for himself what will secure or endanger his freedom. 2. To divide every county into hundreds, of such size that all the children of each will be within reach of a central school in it. But this division looks to many other fundamental provisions. Every hundred, besides a school, should have a justice of the peace, a constable and a captain of militia. These officers, or some others within the hundred, should be a corporation to manage all its concerns, to take care of its roads, its poor, and its police by patrols, &c., (as the select men of the Eastern townships.) Every hundred should elect one or two jurors to serve where requisite, and all other elections should be made in the hundreds separately, and the votes of all the hundreds be brought together. Our present Captaincies might be declared hundreds for the present, with a power to the courts to alter them occasionally. These little republics would be the main strength of the great one. We owe to them the vigor given to our revolution in its commencement in the Eastern States, and by them the Eastern States were enabled to repeal the embargo in opposition to the Middle, Southern and Western States, and their large and lubberly division into counties which can never be assembled. General orders are given out from a centre to the foreman of every hundred, as to the sergeants of an army, and the whole nation is thrown into energetic action, in the same direction in one instant and as one man, and becomes absolutely irresistible. Could I once see this I should consider it as the dawn of the salvation of the republic, and say with old Simeon, "nunc dimittas Domine." But our children will be as wise as we are, and will establish in the fulness of time those things not yet ripe for establishment....

A LAW BEYOND THE CONSTITUTION
To John B. Colvin, September 20, 1810

... The question you propose, whether circumstances do not sometimes occur, which make it a duty in officers of high trust, to assume authorities beyond the law, is easy of solution in principle, but sometimes embarrassing in practice. A strict observance of the written laws is doubtless *one* of the high duties of a good citizen, but it is not *the highest.* The laws of necessity, of self-preservation, of saving our country when in danger, are of higher obligation. To lose our country by a scrupulous adherence to written law, would be to lose the law itself, with life, liberty, property and all those who are enjoying them with us; thus absurdly sacrificing the end to the means. When, in the battle of Germantown, General Washington's army was annoyed from Chew's house, he did not hesitate to plant his cannon against it, although the property of a citizen. When he besieged Yorktown, he leveled the suburbs, feeling that the laws of property must be postponed to the safety of the nation. While the army was before York, the Governor of Virginia took horses, carriages, provisions and even men by force, to enable that army to stay together till it could master the public enemy; and he was justified. A ship at sea in distress for provisions, meets another having abundance, yet refusing a supply; the law of self-preservation authorizes the distressed to take a supply by force. In all these cases, the unwritten laws of necessity, of self-preservation, and of the public safety, control the written laws of *meum* and *tuum.* Further to exemplify the principle, I will state an hypothetical case. Suppose it had been made known to the Executive of the Union in the autumn of 1805, that we might have the Floridas for a reasonable sum, that that sum had not indeed been so appropriated by law, but that Congress were to meet within three weeks, and might appropriate it on the first or second day of their session. Ought he, for so great an advantage to his country, to have risked himself by transcending the law and making the purchase? The public advantage offered, in this supposed case, was indeed immense; but a reverence for law, and the probability that the advantage might still be *legally* accomplished by a delay of only three weeks, were powerful reasons against hazarding the act. But suppose it foreseen that a John Randolph would find means to protract the proceeding on it by Congress, until the ensuing spring, by which time new circumstances would change the mind of the other party. Ought the Executive, in that case, and with that foreknowledge, to have secured the good to his country, and to have trusted to their justice for the transgression of the law? I think he ought, and that the act would have been approved. After the affair of the Chesapeake, we thought war a very possible result. Our magazines were illy provided with some necessary articles, nor had any appropriations been made for their purchase. We ventured, however, to provide them, and to place our country in safety; and stating the case to Congress, they sanctioned the act.

To proceed to the conspiracy of Burr, and particularly to General Wilkinson's situation in New Orleans. In judging this case, we are bound to consider the state of the information, correct and incorrect, which he then possessed. He expected Burr and his band from above, a British fleet from below, and he knew there was a formidable conspiracy within the city. Under these circumstances, was he justifiable, 1st, in seizing notorious conspirators? On this there can be but two opinions; one, of the guilty and their accomplices; the other, that of all honest men. 2d. In sending them to the seat of government, when the written law gave them a right to trial in the territory? The danger of their rescue, of their continuing their machinations, the tardiness and weakness of the law, apathy of the judges, active patronage of the whole tribe of lawyers, unknown disposition of the juries, an hourly expectation of the enemy, salvation of the city, and of the Union itself, which would have been convulsed to its centre, had that conspiracy succeeded; all these constituted a law of necessity and self-preservation, and rendered the *salus populi* supreme over the written law. The officer who is called to act on this superior ground, does indeed risk himself on the justice of the controlling powers of the constitution, and his station makes it his duty to incur that risk. But those controlling powers, and his fellow citizens generally, are bound to judge according to the circumstances under which he acted. They are not to transfer the information of this place or moment to the time and place of his action; but to put themselves into his situation. We knew here that there never was danger of a British fleet from below, and that Burr's band was crushed before it reached the Mississippi. But General Wilkinson's information was very different, and he could act on no other.

From these examples and principles you may see what I think on the question proposed. They do not go to the case of persons charged with petty duties, where consequences are trifling, and time allowed for a legal course, nor to authorize them to take such cases out of the written law. In these, the example of overleaping the law is of greater evil than a strict adherence to its imperfect provisions. It is incumbent on those only who accept of great charges, to risk themselves on great occasions, when the safety of the nation, or some of its very high interests are at stake. An officer is bound to obey orders; yet he would be a bad one who should do it in cases for which they were not intended, and which involved the most important consequences. The line of discrimination between cases may be difficult; but the good officer is bound to draw it at his own peril, and throw himself on the justice of his country and the rectitude of his motives....

THE EXECUTIVE OFFICE
To A. L. C. Destutt de Tracy, January 26, 1811

... I had, with the world, deemed Montesquieu's work of much merit; but saw in it, with every thinking man, so much of paradox, of false principle and misapplied fact, as to render its value equivocal on the whole. Williams and others had nibbled only at its errors. A radical correction of them, therefore, was a great desideratum. This want is now supplied, and with a depth of thought, precision of idea, of language and of logic, which will force conviction into every mind. I declare to you, Sir, in the spirit of truth and sincerity, that I consider it the most precious gift the present age has received.

... One of its doctrines, indeed, the preference of a plural over a singular executive, will probably not be assented to here. When our present government was first established, we had many doubts on this question, and many leanings towards a supreme executive council. It happened that at that time the experiment of such an one was commenced in France, while the single executive was under trial here. We watched the motions and effects of these two rival plans, with an interest and anxiety proportioned to the importance of a choice between them. The experiment in France failed after a short course, and not from any circumstance peculiar to the times or nation, but from those internal jealousies and dissensions in the Directory, which will ever arise among men equal in power, without a principal to decide and control their differences. We had tried a similar experiment in 1784, by establishing a committee of the States, composed of a member from every State, then thirteen, to exercise the executive functions during the recess of Congress. They fell immediately into schisms and dissensions, which became at length so inveterate as to render all co-operation among them impracticable: they dissolved themselves, abandoning the helm of government, and it continued without a head, until Congress met the ensuing winter. This was then imputed to the temper of two or three individuals; but the wise ascribed it to the nature of man. The failure of the French Directory, and from the same cause, seems to have authorized a belief that the form of a plurality, however promising in theory, is impracticable with men constituted with the ordinary passions. While the tranquil and steady tenor of our single executive, during a course of twenty-two years of the most tempestuous times the history of the world has ever presented, gives a rational hope that this important problem is at length solved. Aided by the counsels of a cabinet of heads of departments, originally four, but now five, with whom the President consults, either singly or altogether, he has the benefit of their wisdom and information, brings their views to one centre, and produces an unity of action and direction in all the branches of the government. The excellence of this construction of the executive power has already manifested itself here under very opposite circumstances. During the administration of our first President, his cabinet of four members was equally divided by as marked an opposition of principle as monarchism and republicanism could bring into conflict. Had that cabinet been a directory, like positive and negative quantities in algebra, the opposing wills would have balanced each other and produced a state of absolute inaction. But the President heard with calmness the opinions and reasons of each, decided the course to be pursued, and kept the government steadily in it, unaffected by the agitation. The public knew well the dissensions of the cabinet, but never had an uneasy thought on their account, because they knew also they had provided a regulating power which would keep the machine in steady movement. I speak with an intimate knowledge of these scenes, *quorum pars fui;* as I may of others of a character entirely opposite. The third administration, which was of eight years, presented an example of harmony in a cabinet of six persons, to which perhaps history has furnished no parallel. There never arose, during the whole time, an instance of an unpleasant thought or word between the members. We sometimes met under differences of opinion, but scarcely ever failed, by conversing and reasoning, so to modify each other's ideas, as to produce an unanimous result. Yet, able and amicable as these members were, I am not certain this would have been the case, had each possessed equal and independent powers. Ill-defined limits of their respective departments, jealousies, trifling at first, but nourished and strengthened by repetition of occasions, intrigues without doors of designing persons to build an importance to themselves on the divisions of others, might, from small beginnings, have produced persevering oppositions. But the power of decision in the President left no object for internal dissension, and external intrigue was stifled in embryo by the knowledge which incendiaries possessed, that no division they could foment would change the course of the executive power. I am not conscious that my participations in executive authority have produced any bias in favor of the single executive; because the parts I have acted have been in the subordinate, as well as superior stations, and because, if I know myself, what I have felt, and what I have wished, I know that I have never been so well pleased, as when I could shift power from my own, on the shoulders of others; nor have I ever been able to conceive how any rational being could propose happiness to himself from the exercise of power over others.

I am still, however, sensible of the solidity of your principle, that, to insure the safety of the public liberty, its depository should be subject to be changed with the greatest ease possible, and without suspending or disturbing for a moment the movements of the machine of government. You apprehend that a single executive, with eminence of talent, and destitution of principle, equal to the object, might, by usurpation, render his powers hereditary. Yet I think history furnishes as many examples of a single usurper arising out of a government by a plurality, as of temporary trusts of power in a single hand rendered permanent by usurpation. I do not believe, therefore, that this danger is lessened in the hands of a plural executive. Perhaps it is greatly increased, by the state of inefficiency to which they are liable from feuds and divisions among themselves. The conservative body you propose might be so constituted, as, while it would be an admirable sedative in a variety of smaller cases, might also be a valuable sentinel and check on the liberticide views of an ambitious individual. I am friendly to this idea. But the true barriers of our liberty in this country are our State governments; and the wisest conservative power ever contrived by man, is that of which our Revolution and present government found us possessed. Seventeen distinct States, amalgamated into one as to their foreign concerns, but single and independent as to their internal administration, regularly organized with legislature and governor resting on the choice of the people, and enlightened by a free press, can never be so fascinated by the arts of one man, as to submit voluntarily to his usurpation. Nor can they be constrained to it by any force he can possess. While that may paralyze the single State in which it happens to be encamped, sixteen others, spread over a country of two thousand miles diameter, rise up on every side, ready organized for deliberation by a constitutional legislature, and for action by their governor, constitutionally the commander of the militia of the State, that is to say, of every man in it able to bear arms; and that militia, too, regularly formed into regiments and battalions, into infantry, cavalry and artillery, trained under officers general and subordinate, legally appointed, always in readiness, and to whom they are already in habits of obedience. The republican government of France was lost without a struggle, because the party of "*un et indivisible*" had prevailed; no provincial organizations existed to which the people might rally under authority of the laws, the seats of the directory were virtually vacant, and a small force sufficed to turn the legislature out of their chamber, and to salute its leader chief of the nation. But with us, sixteen out of seventeen States rising in mass, under regular organization, and legal commanders, united in object and action by their Congress, or, if that be in *duresse*, by a special convention, present such obstacles to an usurper as forever to stifle ambition in the first conception of that object.

Dangers of another kind might more reasonably be apprehended from this perfect and distinct organization, civil and military, of the States; to wit, that certain States from local and occasional discontents, might attempt to secede from the Union. This is certainly possible; and would be befriended by this regular organization. But it is not probable that local discontents can spread to such an extent, as to be able to face the sound parts of so extensive an Union; and if ever they should reach the majority, they would then become the regular government, acquire the ascendency in Congress, and be able to redress their own grievances by laws peaceably and constitutionally passed. And even the States in which local discontents might engender a commencement of fermentation, would be paralyzed and self-checked by that very division into parties into which we have fallen, into which all States must fall wherein men are at liberty to think, speak, and act freely, according to the diversities of their individual conformations, and which are, perhaps, essential to preserve the purity of the government, by the censorship which these parties habitually exercise over each other….

TYRANTS OF LAND AND SEA
To Madame de Staël, May 24, 1813

I received with great pleasure, my dear Madam and friend, your letter of November the 10th, from Stockholm, and am sincerely gratified by the occasion it gives me of expressing to you the sentiments of high respect and esteem which I entertain for you. It recalls to my remembrance a happy portion of my life, passed in your native city; then the seat of the most amiable and polished society of the world, and of which yourself and your venerable father were such distinguished members. But of what scenes has it since been the theatre, and with what havoc has it overspread the earth! Robespiere met the fate, and his memory the execration, he so justly merited. The rich were his victims, and perished by thousands. It is by millions that Buonaparte destroys the poor, and he is eulogised and deified by the sycophants even of science. These merit more than the mere oblivion to which they will be consigned; and the day will come when a just posterity will give to their hero the only pre-eminence he has earned, that of having been the greatest of the destroyers of the human race. What year of his military life has not consigned a million of human beings to death, to poverty and wretchedness! What field in Europe may not raise a monument of the murders, the burnings, the desolations, the famines and miseries it has witnessed from him! And all this to acquire a reputation, which Cartouche attained with less injury to mankind, of being fearless of God or man.

To complete and universalise the desolation of the globe, it has been the will of Providence to raise up, at the same time, a tyrant as unprincipled and as overwhelming, for the ocean. Not in the poor maniac George, but in his government and nation. Buonaparte will die, and his tyrannies with him. But a nation never dies. The English government and its piratical principles and practices, have no fixed term of duration. Europe feels, and is writhing under the scorpion whips of Buonaparte. We are assailed by those of England. The one continent thus placed under the gripe of England, and the other of Buonaparte, each has to grapple with the enemy immediately pressing on itself. We must extinguish the fire kindled in our own house, and leave to our friends beyond the water that which is consuming theirs. It was not till England had taken one thousand of our ships, and impressed into her service more than six thousand of our citizens; till she had declared, by the proclamation of her Prince Regent, that she would not repeal her aggressive orders *as to us,* until Buonaparte should have repealed his *as to all nations;* till her minister, in formal conference with ours, declared, that no proposition for protecting our seamen from being impressed, under color of taking their own, was practicable or admissible; that, the door to justice and to all amicable arrangement being closed, and negotiation become both desperate and dishonorable, we concluded that the war she had been for years waging against us, might as well become a war on both sides. She takes fewer vessels from us since the declaration of war than before, because they venture more cautiously; and we now make full reprisals where before we made none. England is, in principle, the enemy of all maritime nations, as Buonaparte is of the continental; and I place in the same line of insult to the human understanding, the pretension of conquering the ocean, to establish continental rights, as that of conquering the continent, to restore maritime rights. No, my dear Madam; the object of England is the *permanent dominion of the ocean,* and the *monopoly of the trade of the world.* To secure this, she must keep a larger fleet than her own resources will maintain. The resources of other nations, then, must be impressed to supply the deficiency of her own. This is sufficiently developed and evidenced by her successive strides towards the usurpation of the sea. Mark them, from her first war after William Pitt the little, came into her administration. She first forbade to neutrals all trade with her enemies in time of war, which they had not in time of peace. This deprived them of their trade from port to port of the same nation. Then she forbade them to trade from the port of one nation to that of any other at war with her, although a right fully exercised in time of peace. Next, instead of taking vessels only *entering* a blockaded port, she took them over the whole ocean, if destined to that port, although ignorant of the blockade, and without intention to violate it. Then she took them returning from that port, as if infected by previous infraction of blockade. Then came her paper blockades, by which she might shut up the whole world without sending a ship to sea, except to take all those sailing on it, as they must, of course, be bound to some port. And these were followed by her orders of council, forbidding every nation to go to the port of any other, without coming first to some port of Great Britain, there paying a tribute to her, regulated by the cargo, and taking from her a license to proceed to the port of destination; which operation the vessel was to repeat with the return cargo on its way home. According to these orders, we could not send a vessel from St. Mary's to St. Augustine, distant six hours' sail, on our own coast, without crossing the Atlantic four times, twice with the outward cargo, and twice with the inward. She found this too daring and outrageous for a single step, retracted as to certain articles of commerce, but left it in force as to others which constitute important branches of our exports. And finally, that her views may no longer rest on inference, in a recent debate, her minister declared in open parliament, that the object of the present war is a *monopoly of commerce....*

PUBLIC DEBT AND THE LIVING GENERATION
To John Wayles Eppes, June 24, 1813

... It is a wise rule and should be fundamental in a government disposed to cherish its credit, and at the same time to restrain the use of it within the limits of its faculties, "never to borrow a dollar without laying a tax in the same instant for paying the interest annually, and the principal within a given term; and to consider that tax as pledged to the creditors on the public faith." On such a pledge as this, sacredly observed, a government may always command, on a *reasonable interest*, all the lendable money of their citizens, while the necessity of an equivalent tax is a salutary warning to them and their constituents against oppressions, bankruptcy, and its inevitable consequence, revolution. But the term of redemption must be moderate, and at any rate within the limits of their rightful powers. But what limits, it will be asked, does this prescribe to their powers? What is to hinder them from creating a perpetual debt? The laws of nature, I answer. The earth belongs to the living, not to the dead. The will and the power of man expire with his life, by nature's law. Some societies give it an artificial continuance, for the encouragement of industry; some refuse it, as our aboriginal neighbors, whom we call barbarians. The generations of men may be considered as bodies or corporations. Each generation has the usufruct of the earth during the period of its continuance. When it ceases to exist, the usufruct passes on to the succeeding generation, free and unincumbered, and so on, successively, from one generation to another forever. We may consider each generation as a distinct nation, with a right, by the will of its majority, to bind themselves, but none to bind the succeeding generation, more than the inhabitants of another country. Or the case may be likened to the ordinary one of a tenant for life, who may hypothecate the land for his debts, during the continuance of his usufruct; but at his death, the reversioner (who is also for life only) receives it exonerated from all burthen. The period of a generation, or the term of its life, is determined by the laws of mortality, which, varying a little only in different climates, offer a general average, to be found by observation. I turn, for instance, to Buffon's tables, of twenty-three thousand nine hundred and ninety-four deaths, and the ages at which they happened, and I find that of the numbers of all ages living at one moment, half will be dead in twenty-four years and eight months. But (leaving out minors, who have not the power of self-government) of the adults (of twenty-one years of age) living at one moment, a majority of whom act for the society, one half will be dead in eighteen years and eight months. At nineteen years then from the date of a contract, the majority of the contractors are dead, and their contract with them. Let this general theory be applied to a particular case. Suppose the annual births of the State of New York to be twenty-three thousand nine hundred and ninety-four, the whole number of its inhabitants, according to Buffon, will be six hundred and seventeen thousand seven hundred and three, of all ages. Of these there would constantly be two hundred and sixty-nine thousand two hundred and eighty-six minors, and three hundred and forty-eight thousand four hundred and seventeen adults, of which last, one hundred and seventy-four thousand two hundred and nine will be a majority.

Suppose that majority, on the first day of the year 1794, had borrowed a sum of money equal to the fee-simple value of the State, and to have consumed it in eating, drinking and making merry in their day; or, if your please, in quarrelling and fighting with their unoffending neighbors. Within eighteen years and eight months, one half of the adult citizens were dead. Till then, being the majority, they might rightfully levy the interest of their debt annually on themselves and their fellow-revellers, or fellow-champions. But at that period, say at this moment, a new majority have come into place, in their own right, and not under the rights, the conditions, or laws of their predecessors. Are they bound to acknowledge the debt, to consider the preceding generation as having had a right to eat up the whole soil of their country, in the course of a life, to alienate it from them, (for it would be an alienation to the creditors,) and would they think themselves either legally or morally bound to give up their country and emigrate to another for subsistence? Every one will say no; that the soil is the gift of God to the living, as much as it had been to the deceased generation; and that the laws of nature impose no obligation on them to pay this debt. And although, like some other natural rights, this has not yet entered into any declaration of rights, it is no less a law, and ought to be acted on by honest governments. It is, at the same time, a salutary curb on the spirit of war and indebtment, which, since the modern theory of the perpetuation of debt, has drenched the earth with blood, and crushed its inhabitants under burthens ever accumulating. Had this principle been declared in the British bill of rights, England would have been placed under the happy disability of waging eternal war, and of contracting her thousand millions of public debt. In seeking, then, for an ultimate term for the redemption of our debts, let us rally to this principle, and provide for their payment within the term of nineteen years at the farthest....

THE NATURAL ARISTOCRACY
To John Adams, October 28, 1813

... The passage you quote from Theognis, I think has an Ethical, rather than a political object. The whole piece is a moral *exhortation*, παραίνεσις and this passage particularly seems to be a reproof to man, who, while with his domestic animals he is curious to improve the race by employing always the finest male, pays no attention to the improvement of his own race, but intermarries with the vicious, the ugly, or the old, for considerations of wealth or ambition. It is in conformity with the principle adopted afterwards by the Pythagoreans, and expressed by Ocellus in another form. Περὶ δὲ τῆς ἐκ τῶν ἀλλήλων ἀνθρώπων γενέσεως etc.—οὐχ ἡδονῆς ἕνεκα ἡ μῖξις. Which, as literally as intelligibility will admit, may be thus translated. 'Concerning the interprocreation of men, how, and of whom it shall be, in a perfect manner, and according to the laws of modesty and sanctity, conjointly, this is what I think right. First to lay it down that we do not commix for the sake of pleasure, but of the procreation of children. For the powers, the organs and desires for coition have not been given by god to man for the sake of pleasure, but for the procreation of the race. For as it were incongruous for a mortal born to partake of divine life, the immortality of the race being taken away, god fulfilled the purpose by making the generations uninterrupted and continuous. This therefore we are especially to lay down as a principle, that coition is not for the sake of pleasure.' But Nature, not trusting to this moral and abstract motive, seems to have provided more securely for the perpetuation of the species by making it the effect of the oestrum implanted in the constitution of both sexes. And not only has the commerce of love been indulged on this unhallowed impulse, but made subservient also to wealth and ambition by marriages without regard to the beauty, the healthiness, the understanding, or virtue of the subject from which we are to breed. The selecting the best male for a Haram of well chosen females also, which Theognis seems to recommend from the example of our sheep and asses, would doubtless improve the human, as it does the brute animal, and produce a race of veritable ἄριστοι ["aristocrats"]. For experience proves that the moral and physical qualities of man, whether good or evil, are transmissible in a certain degree from father to son. But I suspect that the equal rights of men will rise up against this privileged Solomon, and oblige us to continue acquiescence under the Ἀμαύρωσις γένεος ἀστῶν ["the degeneration of the race of men"] which Theognis complains of, and to content ourselves with the accidental aristoi produced by the fortuitous concourse of breeders. For I agree with you that there is a natural aristocracy among men. The grounds of this are virtue and talents. Formerly bodily powers gave place among the aristoi. But since the invention of gunpowder has armed the weak as well as the strong with missile death, bodily strength, like beauty, good humor, politeness and other accomplishments, has become but an auxiliary ground of distinction. There is also an artificial aristocracy founded on wealth and birth, without either virtue or talents; for with these it would belong to the first class. The natural aristocracy I consider as the most precious gift of nature for the instruction, the trusts, and government of society. And indeed it would have been inconsistent in creation to have formed man for the social state, and not to have provided virtue and wisdom enough to manage the concerns of the society. May we not even say that that form of government is the best which provides the most effectually for a pure selection of these natural aristoi into the offices of government? The artificial aristocracy is a mischievous ingredient in government, and provision should be made to prevent it's ascendancy. On the question, What is the best provision, you and I differ; but we differ as rational friends, using the free exercise of our own reason, and mutually indulging it's errors. *You* think it best to put the Pseudo-aristoi into a separate chamber of legislation where they may be hindered from doing mischief by their coordinate branches, and where also they may be a protection to wealth against the Agrarian and plundering enterprises of the Majority of the people. I think that to give them power in order to prevent them from doing mischief, is arming them for it, and increasing instead of remedying the evil. For if the coordinate branches can arrest their action, so may they that of the coordinates. Mischief may be done negatively as well as positively. Of this a cabal in the Senate of the U.S. has furnished many proofs. Nor do I believe them necessary to protect the wealthy; because enough of these will find their way into every branch of the legislation to protect themselves. From 15. to 20. legislatures of our own, in action for 30. years past, have proved that no fears of an equalisation of property are to be apprehended from them.

I think the best remedy is exactly that provided by all our constitutions, to leave to the citizens the free election and separation of the aristoi from the pseudo-aristoi, of the wheat from the chaff. In general they will elect the real good and wise. In some instances, wealth may corrupt, and birth blind them; but not in sufficient degree to endanger the society....

The Moral Sense

To Thomas Law, June 13, 1814

… The copy of your Second Thoughts on Instinctive Impulses, with the letter accompanying it, was received just as I was setting out on a journey to this place [Poplar Forest], two or three days' distant from Monticello. I brought it with me and read it with great satisfaction, and with the more as it contained exactly my own creed on the foundation of morality in man. It is really curious that on a question so fundamental, such a variety of opinions should have prevailed among men, and those, too, of the most exemplary virtue and first order of understanding. It shows how necessary was the care of the Creator in making the moral principle so much a part of our constitution as that no errors of reasoning or of speculation might lead us astray from its observance in practice. Of all the theories on this question, the most whimsical seems to have been that of Wollaston, who considers *truth* as the foundation of morality. The thief who steals your guinea does wrong only inasmuch as he acts a lie in using your guinea as if it were his own. Truth is certainly a branch of morality, and a very important one to society. But presented as its foundation, it is as if a tree taken up by the roots, had its stem reversed in the air, and one of its branches planted in the ground. Some have made the *love of God* the foundation of morality. This, too, is but a branch of our moral duties, which are generally divided into duties to God and duties to man. If we did a good act merely from the love of God and a belief that it is pleasing to Him, whence arises the morality of the Atheist? It is idle to say, as some do, that no such being exists. We have the same evidence of the fact as of most of those we act on, to-wit: their own affirmations, and their reasonings in support of them. I have observed, indeed, generally, that while in protestant countries the defections from the Platonic Christianity of the priests is to Deism, in catholic countries they are to Atheism. Diderot, D'Alembert, D'Holbach, Condorcet, are known to have been among the most virtuous of men. Their virtue, then, must have had some other foundation than the love of God.

The Το χυλον of others is founded in a different faculty, that of taste, which is not even a branch of morality. We have indeed an innate sense of what we call beautiful, but that is exercised chiefly on subjects addressed to the fancy, whether through the eye in visible forms, as landscape, animal figure, dress, drapery, architecture, the composition of colors, &c., or to the imagination directly, as imagery, style, or measure in prose or poetry, or whatever else constitutes the domain of criticism or taste, a faculty entirely distinct from the moral one. Self-interest, or rather self-love, or *egoism,* has been more plausibly substituted as the basis of morality. But I consider our relations with others as constituting the boundaries of morality. With ourselves we stand on the ground of identity, not of relation, which last, requiring two subjects, excludes self-love confined to a single one. To ourselves, in strict language, we can owe no duties, obligation requiring also two parties. Self-love, therefore, is no part of morality. Indeed it is exactly its counterpart. It is the sole antagonist of virtue, leading us constantly by our propensities to self-gratification in violation of our moral duties to others. Accordingly, it is against this enemy that are erected the batteries of moralists and religionists, as the only obstacle to the practice of morality. Take from man his selfish propensities, and he can have nothing to seduce him from the practice of virtue. Or subdue those propensities by education, instruction or restraint, and virtue remains without a competitor. Egoism, in a broader sense, has been thus presented as the source of moral action. It has been said that we feed the hungry, clothe the naked, bind up the wounds of the man beaten by thieves, pour oil and wine into them, set him on our own beast and bring him to the inn, because we receive ourselves pleasure from these acts. So Helvetius, one of the best men on earth, and the most ingenious advocate of this principle, after defining "interest" to mean not merely that which is pecuniary, but whatever may procure us pleasure or withdraw us from pain, [*de l'esprit* 2, 1,] says, [ib. 2, 2,] "the humane man is he to whom the sight of misfortune is insupportable, and who to rescue himself from this spectacle, is forced to succor the unfortunate object." This indeed is true. But it is one step short of the ultimate question. These good acts give us pleasure, but how happens it that they give us pleasure? Because nature hath implanted in our breasts a love of others, a sense of duty to them, a moral instinct, in short, which prompts us irresistibly to feel and to succor their distresses, and protests against the language of Helvetius, [ib. 2, 5,] "what other motive than self-interest could determine a man to generous actions? It is as impossible for him to love what is good for the sake of good, as to love evil for the sake of evil." The Creator would indeed have been a bungling artist, had he intended man for a social animal, without planting in him social dispositions. It is true they are not planted in every man, because there is no rule without exceptions; but it is false reasoning which converts exceptions into the general rule. Some men are born without the organs of sight, or of hearing, or without hands. Yet it would be wrong to say that man is born without these faculties, and sight, hearing, and hands may with truth enter into the general definition of man. The want or imperfection of the moral sense in some men, like the want or imperfection of the senses of sight and hearing in others, is no proof that it is a general characteristic of the species. When it is wanting, we endeavor to supply the defect by education, by appeals to reason and calculation, by presenting to the being so unhappily conformed, other motives to do good and to eschew evil, such as the love, or the hatred, or rejection of those among whom he lives, and whose society is necessary to his happiness and even existence; demonstrations by sound calculation that honesty promotes interest in the long run; the rewards and penalties established by the laws; and ultimately the prospects of a future state of retribution for the evil as well as the good done while here. These are the correctives which are supplied by education, and which exercise the functions of the moralist, the preacher, and legislator; and they lead into a course of correct action all those whose disparity is not too profound to be eradicated. Some have argued against the existence of a moral sense, by saying that if nature had given us such a sense, impelling us to virtuous actions, and warning us against those which are vicious, then nature would also have designated, by some particular ear-marks, the two sets of actions which are, in themselves, the one virtuous and the other vicious. Whereas, we find, in fact, that the same actions are deemed virtuous in one country and vicious in another. The answer is that nature has constituted *utility* to man the standard and best of virtue. Men living in different countries, under different circumstances, different habits and regimens, may have different utilities; the same act, therefore, may be useful, and consequently virtuous in one country which is injurious and vicious in another differently circumstanced. I sincerely, then, believe with you in the general existence of a moral instinct. I think it the brightest gem with which the human character is studded, and the want of it as more degrading than the most hideous of the bodily deformities. I am happy in reviewing the roll of associates in this principle which you present in your second letter, some of which I had not before met with. To these might be added Lord Kaims, one of the ablest of our advocates, who goes so far as to say, in his Principles of Natural Religion, that a man owes no duty to which he is not urged by some impulsive feeling. This is correct, if referred to the standard of general feeling in the given case, and not to the feeling of a single individual. Perhaps I may misquote him, it being fifty years since I read his book....

MANUFACTURES

To Benjamin Austin, January 9, 1816

... You tell me I am quoted by those who wish to continue our dependence on England for manufactures. There was a time when I might have been so quoted with more candor, but within the thirty years which have since elapsed, how are circumstances changed! We were then in peace. Our independent place among nations was acknowledged. A commerce which offered the raw material in exchange for the same material after receiving the last touch of industry, was worthy of welcome to all nations. It was expected that those especially to whom manufacturing industry was important, would cherish the friendship of such customers by every favor, by every inducement, and particularly cultivate their peace by every act of justice and friendship. Under this prospect the question seemed legitimate, whether, with such an immensity of unimproved land, courting the hand of husbandry, the industry of agriculture, or that of manufactures, would add most to the national wealth? And the doubt was entertained on this consideration chiefly, that to the labor of the husbandman a vast addition is made by the spontaneous energies of the earth on which it is employed: for one grain of wheat committed to the earth, she renders twenty, thirty, and even fifty fold, whereas to the labor of the manufacturer nothing is added. Pounds of flax, in his hands, yield, on the contrary, but pennyweights of lace. This exchange, too, laborious as it might seem, what a field did it promise for the occupations of the ocean; what a nursery for that class of citizens who were to exercise and maintain our equal rights on that element? This was the state of things in 1785, when the "Notes on Virginia" were first printed; when, the ocean being open to all nations, and their common right in it acknowledged and exercised under regulations sanctioned by the assent and usage of all, it was thought that the doubt might claim some consideration. But who in 1785 could foresee the rapid depravity which was to render the close of that century the disgrace of the history of man? Who could have imagined that the two most distinguished in the rank of nations, for science and civilization, would have suddenly descended from that honorable eminence, and setting at defiance all those moral laws established by the Author of nature between nation and nation, as between man and man, would cover earth and sea with robberies and piracies, merely because strong enough to do it with temporal impunity; and that under this disbandment of nations from social order, we should have been despoiled of a thousand ships, and have thousands of our citizens reduced to Algerine slavery. Yet all this has taken place. One of these nations interdicted to our vessels all harbors of the globe without having first proceeded to some one of hers, there paid a tribute proportioned to the cargo, and obtained her license to proceed to the port of destination. The other declared them to be lawful prize if they had touched at the port, or been visited by a ship of the enemy nation. Thus were we completely excluded from the ocean. Compare this state of things with that of '85, and say whether an opinion founded in the circumstances of that day can be fairly applied to those of the present. We have experienced what we did not then believe, that there exists both profligacy and power enough to exclude us from the field of interchange with other nations: that to be independent for the comforts of life we must fabricate them ourselves. We must now place the manufacturer by the side of the agriculturist. The former question is suppressed, or rather assumes a new form. Shall we make our own comforts, or go without them, at the will of a foreign nation? He, therefore, who is now against domestic manufacture, must be for reducing us either to dependence on that foreign nation, or to be clothed in skins, and to live like wild beasts in dens and caverns. I am not one of these; experience has taught me that manufactures are now as necessary to our independence as to our comfort; and if those who quote me as of a different opinion, will keep pace with me in purchasing nothing foreign where an equivalent of domestic fabric can be obtained, without regard to difference of price, it will not be our fault if we do not soon have a supply at home equal to our demand, and wrest that weapon of distress from the hand which has wielded it. If it shall be proposed to go beyond our own supply, the question of '85 will then recur, will our *surplus* labor be then most beneficially employed in the culture of the earth, or in the fabrications of art? We have time yet for consideration, before that question will press upon us; and the maxim to be applied will depend on the circumstances which shall then exist; for in so complicated a science as political economy, no one axiom can be laid down as wise and expedient for all times and circumstances, and for their contraries. Inattention to this is what has called for this explanation, which reflection would have rendered unnecessary with the candid, while nothing will do it with those who use the former opinion only as a stalking horse, to cover their disloyal propensities to keep us in eternal vassalage to a foreign and unfriendly people....

EDUCATION, FREEDOM, AND CIVILIZATION
To Colonel Charles Yancey, January 6, 1816

... I am a great friend to the improvements of roads, canals, and schools. But I wish I could see some provision for the former as solid as that of the latter,—something better than fog. The literary fund is a solid provision, unless lost in the impending bankruptcy. If the legislature would add to that a perpetual tax of a cent a head on the population of the State, it would set agoing at once, and forever maintain, a system of primary or ward schools, and an university where might be taught, in its highest degree, every branch of science useful in our time and country; and it would rescue us from the tax of toryism, fanaticism, and indifferentism to their own State, which we now send our youth to bring from those of New England. If a nation expects to be ignorant and free, in a state of civilization, it expects what never was and never will be. The functionaries of every government have propensities to command at will the liberty and property of their constituents. There is no safe deposit for these but with the people themselves; nor can they be safe with them without information. Where the press is free, and every man able to read, all is safe. The frankness of this communication will, I am sure, suggest to you a discreet use of it. I wish to avoid all collisions of opinion with all mankind. Show it to Mr. Maury, with expressions of my great esteem. It pretends to convey no more than the opinions of one of your thousand constituents, and to claim no more attention than every other of that thousand....

YOUR PROPHECY AND MINE

To John Adams, January 11, 1816

... I agree with you in all it's eulogies on the 18th. century. It certainly witnessed the sciences and arts, manners and morals, advanced to a higher degree than the world had ever before seen. And might we not go back to the aera of the Borgias, by which time the barbarous ages had reduced national morality to it's lowest point of depravity, and observe that the arts and sciences, rising from that point, advanced gradually thro' all the 16th. 17th. and 18th. centuries, softening and correcting the manners and morals of man? I think too we may add, to the great honor of science and the arts, that their natural effect is, by illuminating public opinion, to erect it into a Censor, before which the most exalted tremble for their future, as well as present fame. With some exceptions only, through the 17th. and 18th. centuries morality occupied an honorable chapter in the political code of nations. You must have observed while in Europe, as I thought I did, that those who administered the governments of the greater powers at least, had a respect to faith, and considered the dignity of their government as involved in it's integrity. A wound indeed was inflicted on this character of honor in the 18th. century by the partition of Poland. But this was the atrocity of a barbarous government chiefly, in conjunction with a smaller one still scrambling to become great, while one only of those already great, and having character to lose, descended to the baseness of an accomplice in the crime. France, England, Spain shared in it only inasmuch as they stood aloof and permitted it's perpetration. How then has it happened that these nations, France especially and England, so great, so dignified, so distinguished by science and the arts, plunged at once into all the depths of human enormity, threw off suddenly and openly all the restraints of morality, all sensation to character, and unblushingly avowed and acted on the principle that power was right? Can this sudden apostacy from national rectitude be accounted for? The treaty of Pilnitz seems to have begun it, suggested perhaps by the baneful precedent of Poland. Was it from the terror of monarchs, alarmed at the light returning on them from the West, and kindling a Volcano under their thrones? Was it a combination to extinguish that light, and to bring back, as their best auxiliaries, those enumerated by you, the Sorbonne, the Inquisition, the

Index expurgatorius, and the knights of Loyola? Whatever it was, the close of the century saw the moral world thrown back again to the age of the Borgias, to the point from which it had departed 300. years before. France, after crushing and punishing the conspiracy of Pilnitz, went herself deeper and deeper into the crimes she had been chastising. I say France, and not Bonaparte; for altho' he was the head and mouth, the nation furnished the hands which executed his enormities. England, altho' in opposition, kept full pace with France, not indeed by the manly force of her own arms, but by oppressing the weak, and bribing the strong. At length the whole choir joined and divided the weaker nations among them. Your prophecies to Dr. Price proved truer than mine; and yet fell short of the fact, for instead of a million, the destruction of 8. or 10. millions of human beings has probably been the effect of these convulsions. I did not, in 89. believe they would have lasted so long, nor have cost so much blood. But altho' your prophecy has proved true so far, I hope it does not preclude a better final result. That same light from our West seems to have spread and illuminated the very engines employed to extinguish it. It has given them a glimmering of their rights and their power. The idea of representative government has taken root and growth among them. Their masters feel it, and are saving themselves by timely offers of this modification of their own powers. Belgium, Prussia, Poland, Lombardy etc. are now offered a representative organization: illusive probably at first, but it will grow into power in the end. Opinion is power, and that opinion will come. Even France will yet attain representative government. You observe it makes the basis of every constitution which has been demanded or offered: of that demanded by their Senate; of that offered by Bonaparte; and of that granted by Louis XVIII. The idea then is rooted, and will be established, altho' rivers of blood may yet flow between them and their object. The allied armies now couching upon them are first to be destroyed, and destroyed they will surely be. A nation united can never be conquered. We have seen what the ignorant bigotted and unarmed Spaniards could do against the disciplined veterans of their invaders. What then may we not expect from the power and character of the French nation? The oppressors may cut off heads after heads, but like those of the Hydra, they multiply at every stroke. The recruits within a nation's own limits are prompt and without number; while those of their invaders from a distance are slow, limited, and must come to an end. I think too we percieve that all these allies do not see the same interest in the annihilation of the power of France. There are certainly some symptoms of foresight in Alexander that France might produce a salutary diversion of force were Austria and Prussia to become her enemies. France too is the natural ally of the Turk, as having no interfering interests, and might be useful in neutralizing and perhaps turning that power on Austria. That a re-acting jealousy too exists with Austria and Prussia I think their late strict alliance indicates; and I should not wonder if Spain should discover a sympathy with them. Italy is so divided as to be nothing. Here then we see new coalitions in embrio which after France shall in turn have suffered a just punishment for her crimes, will not only raise her from the earth on which she is prostrate, but give her an opportunity to establish a government of as much liberty as she can bear, enough to ensure her happiness and prosperity. When insurrection begins, be it where it will, all the partitioned countries will rush to arms, and Europe again become an Arena of gladiators. And what is the definite object they will propose? A restoration certainly of the status quo prius, of the state of possession of 89. I see no other principle on which Europe can ever again settle down in lasting peace. I hope your prophecies will go thus far, as my wishes do, and that they, like the former, will prove to have been the sober dictates of a superior understanding, and a sound calculation of effects from causes well understood....

The Ward System
To Joseph C. Cabell, February 2, 1816

... My letter of the 24th ult. conveyed to you the grounds of the two articles objected to the College bill. Your last presents one of them in a new point of view, that of the commencement of the ward schools as likely to render the law unpopular to the country. It must be a very inconsiderate and rough process of execution that would do this. My idea of the mode of carrying it into execution would be this: Declare the county *ipso facto* divided into wards for the present, by the boundaries of the militia captaincies; somebody attend the ordinary muster of each company, having first desired the captain to call together a full one. There explain the object of the law to the people of the company, put to their vote whether they will have a school established, and the most central and convenient place for it; get them to meet and build a log school-house; have a roll taken of the children who would attend it, and of those of them able to pay. These would probably be sufficient to support a common teacher, instructing gratis the few unable to pay. If there should be a deficiency, it would require too trifling a contribution from the county to be complained of; and especially as the whole county would participate, where necessary, in the same resource. Should the company, by its vote, decide that it would have no school, let them remain without one. The advantages of this proceeding would be that it would become the duty of the alderman elected by the county, to take an active part in pressing the introduction of schools, and to look out for tutors. If, however, it is intended that the State government shall take this business into its own hands, and provide schools for every county, then by all means strike out this provision of our bill. I would never wish that it should be placed on a worse footing than the rest of the State. But if it is believed that these elementary schools will be better managed by the governor and council, the commissioners of the literary fund, or any other general authority of the government, than by the parents within each ward, it is a belief against all experience. Try the principle one step further, and amend the bill so as to commit to the governor and council the management of all our farms, our mills, and merchants' stores. No, my friend, the way to have good and safe government, is not to trust it all to one, but to divide it among the many, distributing to every one exactly the functions he is competent to. Let the national government be entrusted with the defence of the nation, and its foreign and federal relations; the State governments with the civil rights, laws, police, and administration of what concerns the State generally; the counties with the local concerns of the counties, and each ward direct the interests within itself. It is by dividing and subdividing these republics from the great national one down through all its subordinations, until it ends in the administration of every man's farm by himself; by placing under every one what his own eye may superintend, that all will be done for the best. What has destroyed liberty and the rights of man in every government which has ever existed under the sun? The generalizing and concentrating all cares and powers into one body, no matter whether of the autocrats of Russia or France, or of the aristocrats of a Venetian senate. And I do believe that if the Almighty has not decreed that man shall never be free, (and it is a blasphemy to believe it,) that the secret will be found to be in the making himself the depository of the powers respecting himself, so far as he is competent to them, and delegating only what is beyond his competence by a synthetical process, to higher and higher orders of functionaries, so as to trust fewer and fewer powers in proportion as the trustees become more and more oligarchical. The elementary republics of the wards, the county republics, the States republics, and the republic of the Union, would form a gradation of authorities, standing each on the basis of law, holding every one its delegated share of powers, and constituting truly a system of fundamental balances and checks for the government. Where every man is a sharer in the direction of his ward-republic, or of some of the higher ones, and feels that he is a participator in the government of affairs, not merely at an election one day in the year, but every day; when there shall not be a man in the State who will not be a member of some one of its councils, great or small, he will let the heart be torn out of his body sooner than his power be wrested from him by a Cæsar or a Bonaparte. How powerfully did we feel the energy of this organization in the case of embargo? I felt the foundations of the government shaken under my feet by the New England townships. There was not an individual in their States whose body was not thrown with all its momentum into action; and although the whole of the other States were known to be in favor of the measure, yet the organization of this little selfish minority enabled it to overrule the Union. What would the unwieldy counties of the middle, the south, and the west do? Call a county meeting, and the drunken loungers at and about the court houses would have collected, the distances being too great for the good people and the industrious generally to attend. The character of those who really met would have been the measure of the weight they would have had in the scale of public opinion. As Cato, then, concluded every speech with the words, "*Carthago delenda est,*" so do I every opinion, with the injunction, "divide the counties into wards"....

"CONSTITUTIONALLY AND CONSCIENTIOUSLY DEMOCRATS"
To P. S. Dupont de Nemours, April 24, 1816

... We of the United States, you know, are constitutionally and conscientiously democrats. We consider society as one of the natural wants with which man has been created; that he has been endowed with faculties and qualities to effect its satisfaction by concurrence of others having the same want; that when, by the exercise of these faculties, he has procured a state of society, it is one of his acquisitions which he has a right to regulate and control, jointly indeed with all those who have concurred in the procurement, whom he cannot exclude from its use or direction more than they him. We think experience has proved it safer, for the mass of individuals composing the society, to reserve to themselves personally the exercise of all rightful powers to which they are competent, and to delegate those to which they are not competent to deputies named, and removable for unfaithful conduct, by themselves immediately. Hence, with us, the people (by which is meant the mass of individuals composing the society) being competent to judge of the facts occurring in ordinary life, they have retained the functions of judges of facts, under the name of jurors; but being unqualified for the management of affairs requiring intelligence above the common level, yet competent judges of human character, they chose, for their management, representatives, some by themselves immediately, others by electors chosen by themselves. Thus our President is chosen by ourselves, directly in *practice*, for we vote for A as elector only on the condition he will vote for B, our representatives by ourselves immediately, our Senate and judges of law through electors chosen by ourselves. And we believe that this proximate choice and power of removal is the best security which experience has sanctioned for ensuring an honest conduct in the functionaries of society. Your three or four alembications have indeed a seducing appearance. We should conceive *primâ facie,* that the last extract would be the pure alcohol of the substance, three or four times rectified. But in proportion as they are more and more sublimated, they are also farther and farther removed from the control of the society; and the human character, we believe, requires in general constant and immediate control, to prevent its being biased from right by the seductions of self-love. Your process produces therefore a structure of government from which the fundamental principle of ours is excluded. You first set down as zeros all individuals not having lands, which are the greater number in every society of long standing. Those holding lands are permitted to manage in person the small affairs of their commune or corporation, and to elect a deputy for the canton; in which election, too, every one's vote is to be an unit, a plurality, or a fraction, in proportion to his landed possessions. The assemblies of cantons, then, elect for the districts; those of districts for circles; and those of circles for the national assemblies.

Some of these highest councils, too, are in a considerable degree self-elected, the regency partially, the judiciary entirely, and some are for life. Whenever, therefore, an *esprit de corps*, or of party, gets possession of them, which experience shows to be inevitable, there are no means of breaking it up, for they will never elect but those of their own spirit. Juries are allowed in criminal cases only. I acknowledge myself strong in affection to our own form, yet both of us act and think from the same motive, we both consider the people as our children, and love them with parental affection. But you love them as infants whom you are afraid to trust without nurses; and I as adults whom I freely leave to self-government. And you are right in the case referred to you; my criticism being built on a state of society not under your contemplation. It is, in fact, like a critic on Homer by the laws of the Drama.

But when we come to the moral principles on which the government is to be administered, we come to what is proper for all conditions of society. I meet you there in all the benevolence and rectitude of your native character; and I love myself always most where I concur most with you. Liberty, truth, probity, honor, are declared to be the four cardinal principles of your society. I believe with you that morality, compassion, generosity, are innate elements of the human constitution; that there exists a right independent of force; that a right to property is founded in our natural wants, in the means with which we are endowed to satisfy these wants, and the right to what we acquire by those means without violating the similar rights of other sensible beings; that no one has a right to obstruct another, exercising his faculties innocently for the relief of sensibilities made a part of his nature; that justice is the fundamental law of society; that the majority, oppressing an individual, is guilty of a crime, abuses its strength, and by acting on the law of the strongest breaks up the foundations of society; that action by the citizens in person, in affairs within their reach and competence, and in all others by representatives, chosen immediately, and removable by themselves, constitutes the essence of a republic; that all governments are more or less republican in proportion as this principle enters more or less into their composition; and that a government by representation is capable of extension over a greater surface of country that one of any other form. These, my friend, are the essentials in which you and I agree; however, in our zeal for their maintenance, we may be perplexed and divaricate, as to the structure of society most likely to secure them.

In the constitution of Spain, as proposed by the late Cortes, there was a principle entirely new to me, and not noticed in yours, that no person, born after that day, should ever acquire the rights of citizenship until he could read and write. It is impossible sufficiently to estimate the wisdom of this provision. Of all those which have been thought of for securing fidelity in the administration of the government, constant ralliance to the principles of the constitution, and progressive amendments with the progressive advances of the human mind, or changes in human affairs, it is the most effectual. Enlighten the people generally, and tyranny and oppressions of body and mind will vanish like evil spirits at the dawn of day. Although I do not, with some enthusiasts, believe that the human condition will ever advance to such a state of perfection as that there shall no longer be pain or vice in the world, yet I believe it susceptible of much improvement, and most of all, in matters of government and religion; and that the diffusion of knowledge among the people is to be the instrument by which it is to be effected. The constitution of the Cortes had defects enough; but when I saw in it this amendatory provision, I was satisfied all would come right in time, under its salutary operation. No people have more need of a similar provision than those for whom you have felt so much interest. No mortal wishes them more success than I do. But if what I have heard of the ignorance and bigotry of the mass be true, I doubt their capacity to understand and to support a free government; and fear that their emancipation from the foreign tyranny of Spain, will result in a military despotism at home. Palacios may be great; others may be great; but it is the multitude which possess force: and wisdom must yield to that. For such a condition of society, the constitution you have devised is probably the best imaginable. It is certainly calculated to elicit the best talents; although perhaps not well guarded against the egoism of its functionaries. But that egoism will be light in comparison with the pressure of a military despot, and his army of Janissaries. Like Solon to the Athenians, you have given to your Columbians, not the best possible government, but the best they can bear. By-the-bye, I wish you had called them the Columbian republics, to distinguish them from our American republics. Theirs would be the most honorable name, and they best entitled to it; for Columbus discovered their continent, but never saw ours....

Reform of the Virginia Constitution
To Samuel Kercheval, July 12, 1816

... I duly received your favor of June the 13th, with the copy of the letters on the calling a convention, on which you are pleased to ask my opinion. I have not been in the habit of mysterious reserve on any subject, nor of buttoning up my opinions within my own doublet. On the contrary, while in public service especially, I thought the public entitled to frankness, and intimately to know whom they employed. But I am now retired: I resign myself, as a passenger, with confidence to those at present at the helm, and ask but for rest, peace and good will. The question you propose, on equal representation, has become a party one, in which I wish to take no public share. Yet, if it be asked for your own satisfaction only, and not to be quoted before the public, I have no motive to withhold it, and the less from you, as it coincides with your own. At the birth of our republic, I committed that opinion to the world, in the draught of a constitution annexed to the "Notes on Virginia," in which a provision was inserted for a representation permanently equal. The infancy of the subject at that moment, and our inexperience of self-government, occasioned gross departures in that draught from genuine republican canons. In truth, the abuses of monarchy had so much filled all the space of political contemplation, that we imagined everything republican which was not monarchy. We had not yet penetrated to the mother principle, that "governments are republican only in proportion as they embody the will of their people, and execute it." Hence, our first constitutions had really no leading principles in them. But experience and reflection have but more and more confirmed me in the particular importance of the equal representation then proposed. On that point, then, I am entirely in sentiment with your letters; and only lament that a copy-right of your pamphlet prevents their appearance in the newspapers, where alone they would be generally read, and produce general effect. The present vacancy too, of other matter, would give them place in every paper, and bring the question home to every man's conscience.

But inequality of representation in both Houses of our legislature, is not the only republican heresy in this first essay of our revolutionary patriots at forming a constitution. For let it be agreed that a government is republican in proportion as every member composing it has his equal voice in the direction of its concerns (not indeed in person, which would be impracticable beyond the limits of a city, or small township, but) by representatives chosen by himself, and responsible to him at short periods, and let us bring to the test of this canon every branch of our constitution.

In the legislature, the House of Representatives is chosen by less than half the people, and not at all in proportion to those who do choose. The Senate are still more disproportionate, and for long terms of irresponsibility. In the Executive, the Governor is entirely independent of the choice of the people, and of their control; his Council equally so, and at best but a fifth wheel to a wagon. In the Judiciary, the judges of the highest courts are dependent on none but themselves. In England, where judges were named and removable at the will of an hereditary executive, from which branch most misrule was feared, and has flowed, it was a great point gained, by fixing them for life, to make them independent of that executive. But in a government founded on the public will, this principle operates in an opposite direction, and against that will. There, too, they were still removable on a concurrence of the executive and legislative branches. But we have made them independent of the nation itself. They are irremovable, but by their own body, for any depravities of conduct, and even by their own body for the imbecilities of dotage. The justices of the inferior courts are self-chosen, are for life, and perpetuate their own body in succession forever, so that a faction once possessing themselves of the bench of a county, can never be broken up, but hold their county in chains, forever indissoluble. Yet these justices are the real executive as well as judiciary, in all our minor and most ordinary concerns. They tax us at will; fill the office of sheriff, the most important of all the executive officers of the county; name nearly all our military leaders, which leaders, once named, are removable but by themselves. The juries, our judges of all fact, and of law when they choose it, are not selected by the people, nor amenable to them. They are chosen by an officer named by the court and executive. Chosen, did I say? Picked up by the sheriff from the loungings of the court yard, after everything respectable has retired from it. Where then is our republicanism to be found? Not in our constitution certainly, but merely in the spirit of our people. That would oblige even a despot to govern us republicanly. Owing to this spirit, and to nothing in the form of our constitution, all things have gone well. But this fact, so triumphantly misquoted by the enemies of reformation, is not the fruit of our constitution, but has prevailed in spite of it. Our functionaries have done well, because generally honest men. If any were not so, they feared to show it.

But it will be said, it is easier to find faults than to amend them. I do not think their amendment so difficult as is pretended. Only lay down true principles, and adhere to them inflexibly. Do not be frightened into their surrender by the alarms of the timid, or the croakings of wealth against the ascendency of the people. If experience be called for, appeal to that of our fifteen or twenty governments for forty years, and show me where the people have done half the mischief in these forty years, that a single despot would have done in a single year; or show half the riots and rebellions, the crimes and the punishments, which have taken place in any single nation, under kingly government, during the same period. The true foundation of republican government is the equal right of every citizen, in his person and property, and in their management. Try by this, as a tally, every provision of our constitution, and see if it hangs directly on the will of the people. Reduce your legislature to a convenient number for full, but orderly discussion. Let every man who fights or pays, exercise his just and equal right in their election. Submit them to approbation or rejection at short intervals. Let the executive be chosen in the same way, and for the same term, by those whose agent he is to be; and leave no screen of a council behind which to skulk from responsibility. It has been thought that the people are not competent electors of judges *learned in the law.* But I do not know that this is true, and, if doubtful, we should follow principle. In this, as in many other elections, they would be guided by reputation, which would not err oftener, perhaps, than the present mode of appointment. In one State of the Union, at least, it has long been tried, and with the most satisfactory success. The judges of Connecticut have been chosen by the people every six months, for nearly two centuries, and I believe there has hardly ever been an instance of change; so powerful is the curb of incessant responsibility. If prejudice, however, derived from a monarchical institution, is still to prevail against the vital elective principle of our own, and if the existing example among ourselves of periodical election of judges by the people be still mistrusted, let us at least not adopt the evil, and reject the good, of the English precedent; let us retain amovability on the concurrence of the executive and legislative branches, and nomination by the executive alone. Nomination to office is an executive function. To give it to the legislature, as we do, is a violation of the principle of the separation of powers. It swerves the members from correctness, by temptations to intrigue for office themselves, and to a corrupt barter of votes; and destroys responsibility by dividing it among a multitude. By leaving nomination in its proper place, among executive functions, the principle of the distribution of power is preserved, and responsibility weighs with its heaviest force on a single head.

The organization of our county administrations may be thought more difficult. But follow principle, and the knot unties itself. Divide the counties into wards of such size as that every citizen can attend, when called on, and act in person. Ascribe to them the government of their wards in all things relating to themselves exclusively. A justice, chosen by themselves, in each, a constable, a military company, a patrol, a school, the care of their own poor, their own portion of the public roads, the choice of one or more jurors to serve in some court, and the delivery, within their own wards, of their own votes for all elective officers of higher sphere, will relieve the county administration of nearly all its business, will have it better done, and by making every citizen an acting member of the government, and in the offices nearest and most interesting to him, will attach him by his strongest feelings to the independence of his country, and its republican constitution. The justices thus chosen by every ward, would constitute the county court, would do its judiciary business, direct roads and bridges, levy county and poor rates, and administer all the matters of common interest to the whole country. These wards, called townships in New England, are the vital principle of their governments, and have proved themselves the wisest invention ever devised by the wit of man for the perfect exercise of self-government, and for its preservation. We should thus marshal our government into, 1, the general federal republic, for all concerns foreign and federal; 2, that of the State, for what relates to our own citizens exclusively; 3, the county republics, for the duties and concerns of the county; and 4, the ward republics, for the small, and yet numerous and interesting concerns of the neighborhood; and in government, as well as in every other business of life, it is by division and subdivision of duties alone, that all matters, great and small, can be managed to perfection. And the whole is cemented by giving to every citizen, personally, a part in the administration of the public affairs.

The sum of these amendments is, 1. General Suffrage. 2. Equal representation in the legislature. 3. An executive chosen by the people. 4. Judges elective or amovable.

5. Justices, jurors, and sheriffs elective. 6. Ward divisions. And 7. Periodical amendments of the constitution.

I have thrown out these as loose heads of amendment, for consideration and correction; and their object is to secure self-government by the republicanism of our constitution, as well as by the spirit of the people; and to nourish and perpetuate that spirit. I am not among those who fear the people. They, and not the rich, are our dependence for continued freedom. And to preserve their independence, we must not let our rulers load us with perpetual debt. We must make our election between *economy and liberty,* or *profusion and servitude.* If we run into such debts, as that we must be taxed in our meat and in our drink, in our necessaries and our comforts, in our labors and our amusements, for our callings and our creeds, as the people of England are, our people, like them, must come to labor sixteen hours in the twenty-four, give the earnings of fifteen of these to the government for their debts and daily expenses; and the sixteenth being insufficient to afford us bread, we must live, as they now do, on oatmeal and potatoes; have no time to think, no means of calling the mismanagers to account; but be glad to obtain subsistence by hiring ourselves to rivet their chains on the necks of our fellow-sufferers. Our landholders, too, like theirs, retaining indeed the title and stewardship of estates called theirs, but held really in trust for the treasury, must wander, like theirs, in foreign countries, and be contented with penury, obscurity, exile, and the glory of the nation. This example reads to us the salutary lesson, that private fortunes are destroyed by public as well as by private extravagance. And this is the tendency of all human governments. A departure from principle in one instance becomes a precedent for a second; that second for a third; and so on, till the bulk of the society is reduced to be mere automatons of misery, and to have no sensibilities left but for sinning and suffering. Then begins, indeed, the *bellum omnium in omnia,* which some philosophers observing to be so general in this world, have mistaken it for the natural, instead of the abusive state of man. And the fore horse of this frightful team is public debt. Taxation follows that, and in its train wretchedness and oppression.

Some men look at constitutions with sanctimonious reverence, and deem them like the arc of the covenant, too sacred to be touched. They ascribe to the men of the preceding age a wisdom more than human, and suppose what they did to be beyond amendment. I knew that age well; I belonged to it, and labored with it. It deserved well of its country. It was very like the present, but without the experience of the present; and forty years of experience in government is worth a century of book-reading; and this they would say themselves, were they to rise from the dead. I am certainly not an advocate for frequent and untried changes in laws and constitutions. I think moderate imperfections had better be borne with; because, when once known, we accommodate ourselves to them, and find practical means of correcting their ill effects. But I know also, that laws and institutions must go hand in hand with the progress of the human mind. As that becomes more developed, more enlightened, as new discoveries are made, new truths disclosed, and manners and opinions change with the change of circumstances, institutions must advance also, and keep pace with the times. We might as well require a man to wear still the coat which fitted him when a boy, as civilized society to remain ever under the regimen of their barbarous ancestors. It is this preposterous idea which has lately deluged Europe in blood. Their monarchs, instead of wisely yielding to the gradual change of circumstances, of favoring progressive accommodation to progressive improvement, have clung to old abuses, entrenched themselves behind steady habits, and obliged their subjects to seek through blood and violence rash and ruinous innovations, which, had they been referred to the peaceful deliberations and collected wisdom of the nation, would have been put into acceptable and salutary forms. Let us follow no such examples, nor weakly believe that one generation is not as capable as another of taking care of itself, and of ordering its own affairs. Let us, as our sister States have done, avail ourselves of our reason and experience, to correct the crude essays of our first and unexperienced, although wise, virtuous, and well-meaning councils. And lastly, let us provide in our constitution for its revision at stated periods. What these periods should be, nature herself indicates. By the European tables of mortality, of the adults living at any one moment of time, a majority will be dead in about nineteen years. At the end of that period, then, a new majority is come into place; or, in other words, a new generation. Each generation is as independent as the one preceding, as that was of all which had gone before. It has then, like them, a right to choose for itself the form of government it believes most promotive of its own happiness; consequently, to accommodate to the circumstances in which it finds itself, that received from its predecessors; and it is for the peace and good of mankind, that a solemn opportunity of doing this every nineteen or twenty years, should be provided by the constitution; so that it may be handed on, with periodical repairs, from generation to generation, to the end of time, if anything human can so long endure. It is now forty years since the constitution of Virginia was formed. The same tables inform us, that, within that period, two-thirds of the adults then living are now dead. Have then the remaining third, even if they had the wish, the right to hold in obedience to their will, and to laws heretofore made by them, the other two-thirds, who, with themselves, compose the present mass of adults? If they have not, who has? The dead? But the dead have no rights. They are nothing; and nothing cannot own something. Where there is no substance, there can be no accident. This corporeal globe, and everything upon it, belong to its present corporeal inhabitants, during their generation. They alone have a right to direct what is the concern of themselves alone, and to declare the law of that direction; and this declaration can only be made by their majority. That majority, then, has a right to depute representatives to a convention, and to make the constitution what they think will be the best for themselves. But how collect their voice? This is the real difficulty. If invited by private authority, or county or district meetings, these divisions are so large that few will attend; and their voice will be imperfectly, or falsely pronounced. Here, then, would be one of the advantages of the ward divisions I have proposed. The mayor of every ward, on a question like the present, would call his ward together, take the simple yea or nay of its members, convey these to the county court, who would hand on those of all its wards to the proper general authority; and the voice of the whole people would be thus fairly, fully, and peaceably expressed, discussed, and decided by the common reason of the society. If this avenue be shut to the call of sufferance, it will make itself heard through that of force, and we shall go on, as other nations are doing, in the endless circle of oppression, rebellion, reformation; and oppression, rebellion, reformation, again; and so on forever....

ARISTOTLE'S "POLITICS"

To Isaac H. Tiffany, August 26, 1816

... In answer to your inquiry as to the merits of Gillies' translation of the Politics of Aristotle, I can only say that it has the reputation of being preferable to Ellis', the only rival translation into English. I have never seen it myself, and therefore do not speak of it from my own knowledge. But so different was the style of society then, and with those people, from what it is now and with us, that I think little edification can be obtained from their writings on the subject of government. They had just ideas of the value of personal liberty, but none at all of the structure of government best calculated to preserve it. They knew no medium between a democracy (the only pure republic, but impracticable beyond the limits of a town) and an abandonment of themselves to an aristocracy, or a tyranny independent of the people. It seems not to have occurred that where the citizens cannot meet to transact their business in person, they alone have the right to choose the agents who shall transact it; and that in this way a republican, or popular government, of the second grade of purity, may be exercised over any extent of country. The full experiment of a government democratical, but representative, was and is still reserved for us. The idea (taken, indeed, from the little specimen formerly existing in the English constitution, but now lost) has been carried by us, more or less, into all our legislative and executive departments; but it has not yet, by any of us, been pushed into all the ramifications of the system, so far as to leave no authority existing not responsible to the people; whose rights, however, to the exercise and fruits of their own industry, can never be protected against the selfishness of rulers not subject to their control at short periods. The introduction of this new principle of representative democracy has rendered useless almost everything written before on the structure of government; and, in a great measure, relieves our regret, if the political writings of Aristotle, or of any other ancient, have been lost, or are unfaithfully rendered or explained to us. My most earnest wish is to see the republican element of popular control pushed to the maximum of its practicable exercise. I shall then believe that our government may be pure and perpetual. Accept my respectful salutations.

EDUCATION AND PROGRESS

Report of the Commissioners for the University of Virginia, August 4, 1818

… Education generates habits of application, of order, and the love of virtue; and controls, by the force of habit, any innate obliquities in our moral organization. We should be far, too, from the discouraging persuasion that man is fixed, by the law of his nature, at a given point; that his improvement is a chimera, and the hope delusive of rendering ourselves wiser, happier or better than our forefathers were. As well might it be urged that the wild and uncultivated tree, hitherto yielding sour and bitter fruit only, can never be made to yield better; yet we know that the grafting art implants a new tree on the savage stock, producing what is most estimable both in kind and degree. Education, in like manner, engrafts a new man on the native stock, and improves what in his nature was vicious and perverse into qualities of virtue and social worth. And it cannot be but that each generation succeeding to the knowledge acquired by all those who preceded it, adding to it their own acquisitions and discoveries, and handing the mass down for successive and constant accumulation, must advance the knowledge and well-being of mankind, not *infinitely*, as some have said, but *indefinitely*, and to a term which no one can fix and foresee. Indeed, we need look back half a century, to times which many now living remember well, and see the wonderful advances in the sciences and arts which have been made within that period. Some of these have rendered the elements themselves subservient to the purposes of man, have harnessed them to the yoke of his labors, and effected the great blessings of moderating his own, of accomplishing what was beyond his feeble force, and extending the comforts of life to a much enlarged circle, to those who had before known its necessaries only. That these are not the vain dreams of sanguine hope, we have before our eyes real and living examples. What, but education, has advanced us beyond the condition of our indigenous neighbors? And what chains them to their present state of barbarism and wretchedness, but a bigotted veneration for the supposed superlative wisdom of their fathers, and the preposterous idea that they are to look backward for better things, and not forward, longing, as it should seem, to return to the days of eating acorns and roots, rather than indulge in the degeneracies of civilization? And how much more encouraging to the achievements of science and improvement is this, than the desponding view that the condition of man cannot be ameliorated, that what has been must ever be, and that to secure ourselves where we are, we must tread with awful reverence in the footsteps of our fathers. This doctrine is the genuine fruit of the alliance between Church and State; the tenants of which, finding themselves but too well in their present condition, oppose all advances which might unmask their usurpations, and monopolies of honors, wealth, and power, and fear every change, as endangering the comforts they now hold. Nor must we omit to mention, among the benefits of education, the incalculable advantage of training up able counsellors to administer the affairs of our country in all its departments, legislative, executive and judiciary, and to bear their proper share in the councils of our national government; nothing more than education advancing the prosperity, the power, and the happiness of a nation....

❦

The Federal Judiciary
Autobiography (1821)

... But there was another amendment [to the Constitution] of which none of us thought at the time and in the omission of which lurks the germ that is to destroy this happy combination of National powers in the General government for matters of National concern, and independent powers in the states for what concerns the states severally. In England it was a great point gained at the Revolution, that the commissions of the judges, which had hitherto been during pleasure, should thenceforth be made during good behavior. A Judiciary dependent on the will of the King had proved itself the most oppressive of all tools in the hands of that Magistrate. Nothing then could be more salutary than a change there to the tenure of good behavior; and the question of good behavior left to the vote of a simple majority in the two houses of parliament. Before the revolution we were all good English Whigs, cordial in their free principles, and in their jealousies of their executive Magistrate. These jealousies are very apparent in all our state constitutions; and, in the general government in this instance, we have gone even beyond the English caution, by requiring a vote of two thirds in one of the Houses for removing a judge; a vote so impossible where* any defence is made, before men of ordinary prejudices & passions, that our judges are effectually independent of the nation. But this ought not to be. I would not indeed make them dependant on the Executive authority, as they formerly were in England;

---

*In the impeachment of judge Pickering of New Hampshire, a habitual & maniac drunkard, no defence was made. Had there been, the party vote of more than one third of the Senate would have acquitted him.

but I deem it indispensable to the continuance of this government that they should be submitted to some practical & impartial controul: and that this, to be imparted, must be compounded of a mixture of state and federal authorities. It is not enough that honest men are appointed judges. All know the influence of interest on the mind of man, and how unconsciously his judgment is warped by that influence. To this bias add that of the esprit de corps, of their peculiar maxim and creed that "it is the office of a good judge to enlarge his jurisdiction," and the absence of responsibility, and how can we expect impartial decision between the General government, of which they are themselves so eminent a part, and an individual state from which they have nothing to hope or fear. We have seen too that, contrary to all correct example, they are in the habit of going out of the question before them, to throw an anchor ahead and grapple further hold for future advances of power. They are then in fact the corps of sappers & miners, steadily working to undermine the independant rights of the States, & to consolidate all power in the hands of that government in which they have so important a freehold estate. But it is not by the consolidation, or concentration of powers, but by their distribution, that good government is effected. Were not this great country already divided into states, that division must be made, that each might do for itself what concerns itself directly, and what it can so much better do than a distant authority. Every state again is divided into counties, each to take care of what lies within it's local bounds; each county again into townships or wards, to manage minuter details; and every ward into farms, to be governed each by it's individual proprietor. Were we directed from Washington when to sow, & when to reap, we should soon want bread. It is by this partition of cares, descending in gradation from general to particular, that the mass of human affairs may be best managed for the good and prosperity of all. I repeat that I do not charge the judges with wilful and ill-intentioned error; but honest error must be arrested where it's toleration leads to public ruin. As, for the safety of society, we commit honest maniacs to Bedlam, so judges should be withdrawn from their bench, whose erroneous biases are leading us to dissolution. It may indeed injure them in fame or in fortune; but it saves the republic, which is the first and supreme law....

THE SUPREME COURT

To Justice William Johnson, October 27, 1822

... There is a subject respecting the practice of the court of which you are a member, which has long weighed on my mind, on which I have long thought I would write to you, and which I will take this opportunity of doing. It is in truth a delicate undertaking, & yet such is my opinion of your candor and devotedness to the Constitution, in it's true spirit, that I am sure I shall meet your approbation in unbosoming myself to you. The subject of my uneasiness is the habitual mode of making up and delivering the opinions of the supreme court of the US.

You know that from the earliest ages of the English law, from the date of the year-books, at least, to the end of the IId George, the judges of England, in all but self-evident cases, delivered their opinions seriatim, with the reasons and authorities which governed their decisions. If they sometimes consulted together, and gave a general opinion, it was so rarely as not to excite either alarm or notice. Besides the light which their separate arguments threw on the subject, and the instruction communicated by their several modes of reasoning, it shewed whether the judges were unanimous or divided, and gave accordingly more or less weight to the judgment as a precedent. It sometimes happened too that when there were three opinions against one, the reasoning of the one was so much the most cogent as to become afterwards the law of the land. When Ld. Mansfield came to the bench he introduced the habit of caucusing opinions. The judges met at their chambers, or elsewhere, secluded from the presence of the public, and made up what was to be delivered as the opinion of the court. On the retirement of Mansfield, Ld. Kenyon put an end to the practice, and the judges returned to that of seriatim opinions, and practice it habitually to this day, I believe. I am not acquainted with the late reporters, do not possess them, and state the fact from the information of others. To come now to ourselves I know nothing of what is done in other states, but in this our great and good Mr. Pendleton was, after the revolution, placed at the head of the court of Appeals. He adored Ld. Mansfield, & considered him as the greatest luminary of law that any age had ever produced, and he introduced into the court over which he presided, Mansfield's practice of making up opinions in secret & delivering them as the Oracles of the court, in mass. Judge Roane, when he came to that bench, broke up the practice, refused to hatch judgments, in Conclave, or to let others deliver opinions for him. At what time the seriatim opinions ceased in the supreme Court of the US., I am not informed. They continued I know to the end of the 3d Dallas in 1800. Later than which I have no Reporter of that court. About that time the present C.J. came to the bench. Whether he carried the practice of Mr. Pendleton to it, or who, or when I do not know; but I understand from others it is now the habit of the court, & I suppose it true from the cases sometimes reported in the newspapers, and others which I casually see, wherein I observe that the opinions were uniformly prepared in private. Some of these cases too have been of such importance, of such difficulty, and the decisions so grating to a portion of the public as to have merited the fullest explanation from every judge seriatim, of the reasons which had produced such convictions on his mind. It was interesting to the public to know whether these decisions were really unanimous, or might not perhaps be of 4. against 3. and consequently prevailing by the preponderance of one voice only. The Judges holding their offices for life are under two responsibilities only. 1. Impeachment. 2. Individual reputation. But this practice compleatly withdraws them from both. For nobody knows what opinion any individual member gave in any case, nor even that he who delivers the opinion, concurred in it himself. Be the opinion therefore ever so impeachable, having been done in the dark it can be proved on no one. As to the 2d guarantee, personal reputation, it is shielded compleatly. The practice is certainly convenient for the lazy, the modest & the incompetent. It saves them the trouble of developing their opinion methodically and even of making up an opinion at all. That of seriatim argument shews whether every judge has taken the trouble of understanding the case, of investigating it minutely, and of forming an opinion for himself, instead of pinning it on another's sleeve. It would certainly be right to abandon this practice in order to give to our citizens one and all, that confidence in their judges which must be so desirable to the judges themselves, and so important to the cement of the union. During the administration of Genl. Washington, and while E. Randolph was Attorney General, he was required by Congress to digest the judiciary laws into a single one, with such amendments as might be thought proper. He prepared a section requiring the Judges to give their opinions seriatim, in writing, to be recorded in a distinct volume. Other business prevented this bill from being taken up, and it passed off, but such a volume would have been the best possible book of reports, and the better, as unincumbered with the hired sophisms and perversions of Counsel.

What do you think of the state of parties at this time? An opinion prevails that there is no longer any distinction, that the republicans & Federalists are compleatly amalgamated but it is not so. The amalgamation is of name only, not of principle. All indeed call themselves by the name of Republicans, because that of Federalists was extinguished in the battle of New Orleans. But the truth is that finding that monarchy is a desperate wish in this country, they rally to the point which they think next best, a consolidated government. Their aim is now therefore to break down the rights reserved by the constitution to the states as a bulwark against that consolidation, the fear of which produced the whole of the opposition to the constitution at it's birth. Hence new Republicans in Congress, preaching the doctrines of the old Federalists, and the new nick-names of Ultras and Radicals. But I trust they will fail under the new, as the old name, and that the friends of the real constitution and union will prevail against consolidation, as they have done against monarchism. I scarcely know myself which is most to be deprecated, a consolidation, or dissolution of the states. The horrors of both are beyond the reach of human foresight....

THE MONROE DOCTRINE
To James Monroe, October 24, 1823

... The question presented by the letters you have sent me, is the most momentous which has ever been offered to my contemplation since that of Independence. That made us a nation, this sets our compass and points the course which we are to steer through the ocean of time opening on us. And never could we embark on it under circumstances more auspicious. Our first and fundamental maxim should be, never to entangle ourselves in the broils of Europe. Our second, never to suffer Europe to intermeddle with cis-Atlantic affairs. America, North and South, has a set of interests distinct from those of Europe, and peculiarly her own. She should therefore have a system of her own, separate and apart from that of Europe. While the last is laboring to become the domicil of despotism, our endeavor should surely be, to make our hemisphere that of freedom. One nation, most of all, could disturb us in this pursuit; she now offers to lead, aid, and accompany us in it. By acceding to her proposition, we detach her from the bands, bring her mighty weight into the scale of free government, and emancipate a continent at one stroke, which might otherwise linger long in doubt and difficulty. Great Britain is the nation which can do us the most harm of any one, or all on earth; and with her on our side we need not fear the whole world. With her then, we should most sedulously cherish a cordial friendship; and nothing would tend more to knit our affections than to be fighting once more, side by side, in the same cause. Not that I would purchase even her amity at the price of taking part in her wars. But the war in which the present proposition might engage us, should that be its consequence, is not her war, but ours. Its object is to introduce and establish the American system, of keeping out of our land all foreign powers, of never permitting those of Europe to intermeddle with the affairs of our nations. It is to maintain our own principle, not to depart from it. And if, to facilitate this, we can effect a division in the body of the European powers, and draw over to our side its most powerful member, surely we should do it. But I am clearly of Mr. Canning's opinion, that it will prevent instead of provoking war. With Great Britain withdrawn from their scale and shifted into that of our two continents, all Europe combined would not undertake such a war. For how would they propose to get at either enemy without superior fleets? Nor is the occasion to be slighted which this proposition offers, of declaring our protest against the atrocious violations of the rights of nations, by the interference of any one in the internal affairs of another, so flagitiously begun by Bonaparte, and now continued by the equally lawless Alliance, calling itself Holy.

But we have first to ask ourselves a question. Do we wish to acquire to our own confederacy any one or more of the Spanish provinces? I candidly confess, that I have ever looked on Cuba as the most interesting addition which could ever be made to our system of States. The control which, with Florida Point, this island would give us over the Gulf of Mexico, and the countries and isthmus bordering on it, as well as all those whose waters flow into it, would fill up the measure of our political well-being. Yet, as I am sensible that this can never be obtained, even with her own consent, but by war; and its independence, which is our second interest, (and especially its independence of

England,) can be secured without it, I have no hesitation in abandoning my first wish to future chances, and accepting its independence, with peace and the friendship of England, rather than its association, at the expense of war and her enmity.

I could honestly, therefore, join in the declaration proposed, that we aim not at the acquisition of any of those possessions, that we will not stand in the way of any amicable arrangement between them and the mother country; but that we will oppose, with all our means, the forcible interposition of any other power, as auxiliary, stipendiary, or under any other form or pretext, and most especially, their transfer to any power by conquest, cession, or acquisition in any other way. I should think it, therefore, advisable, that the Executive should encourage the British government to a continuance in the dispositions expressed in these letters, by an assurance of his concurrence with them as far as his authority goes; and that as it may lead to war, the declaration of which requires an act of Congress, the case shall be laid before them for consideration at their first meeting, and under the reasonable aspect in which it is seen by himself....

SLAVERY, EMANCIPATION, AND COLONIZATION
To Jared Sparks, February 4, 1824

... The article on the African colonization of the people of color, to which you invite my attention, I have read with great consideration. It is, indeed, a fine one, and will do much good. I learn from it more, too, than I had before known, of the degree of success and promise of that colony.

In the disposition of these unfortunate people, there are two rational objects to be distinctly kept in view. First. The establishment of a colony on the coast of Africa, which may introduce among the aborigines the arts of cultivated life, and the blessings of civilization and science. By doing this, we may make to them some retribution for the long course of injuries we have been committing on their population. And considering that these blessings will descend to the "*nati natorum, et qui nascentur ab illis,*" we shall in the long run have rendered them perhaps more good than evil. To fulfil this object, the colony of Sierra Leone promises well, and that of Mesurado adds to our prospect of success. Under this view, the colonization society is to be considered as a missionary society, having in view, however, objects more humane, more justifiable, and less aggressive on the peace of other nations, than the others of that appellation.

The subject object, and the most interesting to us, as coming home to our physical and moral characters, to our happiness and safety, is to provide an asylum to which we can, by degrees, send the whole of that population from among us, and establish them under our patronage and protection, as a separate, free and independent people, in some country and climate friendly to human life and happiness. That any place on the coast of Africa should answer the latter purpose, I have ever deemed entirely impossible. And without repeating the other arguments which have been urged by others, I will appeal to figures only, which admit no controversy. I shall speak in round numbers, not absolutely accurate, yet not so wide from truth as to vary the result materially. There are in the United States a million and a half of people of color in slavery. To send off the whole of these at once, nobody conceives to be practicable for us, or expedient for them. Let us take twenty-five years for its accomplishment, within which time they will be doubled. Their estimated value as property, in the first place, (for actual property has been lawfully vested in that form, and who can lawfully take it from the possessors?) at an average of two hundred dollars each, young and old, would amount to six hundred millions of dollars, which must be paid or lost by somebody. To this, add the cost of their transportation by land and sea to Mesurado, a year's provision of food and clothing, implements of husbandry and of their trades, which will amount to three hundred millions more, making thirty-six millions of dollars a year for twenty-five years, with insurance of peace all that time, and it is impossible to look at the question a second time. I am aware that at the end of about sixteen years, a gradual detraction from this sum will commence, from the gradual diminution of breeders, and go on during the remaining nine years. Calculate this deduction, and it is still impossible to look at the enterprise a second time. I do not say this to induce an inference that the getting rid of them is forever impossible. For that is neither my opinion nor my hope. But only that it cannot be done in this way. There is, I think, a way in which it can be done; that is, by emancipating the after-born, leaving them, on due compensation, with their mothers, until their services are worth their maintenance, and then putting them to industrious occupations, until a proper age for deportation. This was the result of my reflections on the subject five and forty years ago, and I have never yet been able to conceive any other practicable plan. It was sketched in the Notes on Virginia, under the fourteenth query. The estimated value of the new-born infant is so low, (say twelve dollars and fifty cents,) that it would probably be yielded by the owner gratis, and would thus reduce the six hundred millions of dollars, the first head of expense, to thirty-seven millions and a half; leaving only the expense of nourishment while with the mother, and of transportation. And from what fund are these expenses to be furnished? Why not from that of the lands which have been ceded by the very States now needing this relief? And ceded on no consideration, for the most part, but that of the general good of the whole. These cessions already constitute one fourth of the States of the Union. It may be said that these lands have been sold; are now the property of the citizens composing those States; and the money long ago received and expended. But an equivalent of lands in the territories since acquired, may be appropriated to that object, or so much, at least, as may be sufficient; and the object, although more important to the slave States, is highly so to the others also, if they were serious in their arguments on the Missouri question. The slave States, too, if more interested, would also contribute more by their gratuitous liberation, thus taking on themselves alone the first and heaviest item of expense.

In the plan sketched in the Notes on Virginia, no particular place of asylum was specified; because it was thought possible, that in the revolutionary state of America, then commenced, events might open to us some one within practicable distance. This has now happened. St. Domingo has become independent, and with a population of that color only; and if the public papers are to be credited, their Chief offers to pay their passage, to receive them as free citizens, and to provide them employment. This leaves, then, for the general confederacy, no expense but of nurture with the mother a few years, and would call, of course, for a very moderate appropriation of the vacant lands. Suppose the whole annual increase to be of sixty thousand effective births, fifty vessels, of four hundred tons burthen each, constantly employed in that short run, would carry off the increase of every year, and the old stock would die off in the ordinary course of nature, lessening from the commencement until its final disappearance. In this way no violation of private right is proposed. Voluntary surrenders would probably come in as fast as the means to be provided for their care would be competent to it. Looking at my own State only, and I presume not to speak for the others, I verily believe that this surrender of property would not amount to more, annually, than half our present direct taxes, to be continued fully about twenty or twenty-five years, and then gradually diminishing for as many more until their final extinction; and even this half tax would not be paid in cash, but by the delivery of an object which they have never yet known or counted as part of their property; and those not possessing the object will be called on for nothing. I do not go into all the details of the burthens and benefits of this operation. And who could estimate its blessed effects? I leave this to those who will live to see their accomplishment, and to enjoy a beatitude forbidden to my age. But I leave it with this admonition, to rise and be doing. A million and a half are within their control; but six millions, (which a majority of those now living will see them attain,) and one million of these fighting men, will say, "we will not go."

I am aware that this subject involves some constitutional scruples. But a liberal construction, justified by the object, may go far, and an amendment of the constitution, the whole length necessary. The separation of infants from their mothers, too, would produce some scruples of humanity. But this would be straining at a gnat, and swallowing a camel....

CONSTITUTIONS AND CHANGE
To Major John Cartwright, June 5, 1824

... I am much indebted for your kind letter of February the 29th, and for your valuable volume on the English constitution. I have read this with pleasure and much approbation, and think it has deduced the constitution of the English nation from its rightful root, the Anglo-Saxon. It is really wonderful, that so many able and learned men should have failed in their attempts to define it with correctness. No wonder then, that Paine, who thought more than he read, should have credited the great authorities who have declared, that the will of parliament is the constitution of England. So Marbois, before the French revolution, observed to me, that the Almanac Royal was the constitution of France. Your derivation of it from the Anglo-Saxons, seems to be made on legitimate principles. Having driven out the former inhabitants of that part of the island called England, they became aborigines as to you, and your lineal ancestors. They doubtless had a constitution; and although they have not left it in a written formula, to the precise text of which you may always appeal, yet they have left fragments of their history and laws, from which it may be inferred with considerable certainty. Whatever their history and laws shew to have been practised with approbation, we may presume was permitted by their constitution; whatever was not so practised, was not permitted. And although this constitution was violated and set at naught by Norman force, yet force cannot change right. A perpetual claim was kept up by the nation, by their perpetual demand of a restoration of their Saxon laws; which shews they were never relinquished by the will of the nation. In the pullings and haulings for these antient rights, between the nation, and its kings of the races of Plantagenets, Tudors and Stuarts, there was sometimes gain, and sometimes loss, until the final re-conquest of their rights from the Stuarts. The destitution and expulsion of this race broke the thread of pretended inheritance, extinguished all regal usurpations, and the nation re-entered into all its rights; and although in their bill of rights they specifically reclaimed some only, yet the omission of the others was no renunciation of the right to assume their exercise also, whenever occasion should occur. The new King received no rights or powers, but those expressly granted to him. It has ever appeared to me, that the difference between the whig and the tory of England is, that the whig deduces his rights from the Anglo-Saxon source, and the tory from the Norman. And Hume, the great apostle of toryism, says, in so many words, note AA to chapter 42, that, in the reign of the Stuarts, 'it was the people who encroached upon the sovereign, not the sovereign who attempted, as is pretended, to usurp upon the people.' This supposes the Norman usurpations to be rights in his successors. And again, C, 159, 'the commons established a principle, which is noble in itself, and seems specious, but is belied by all history and experience, *that the people are the origin of all just power.*' And where else will this degenerate son of science, this traitor to his fellow men, find the origin of just powers, if not in the majority of the society? Will it be in the minority? Or in an individual of that minority?

Our Revolution commenced on more favorable ground. It presented us an album on which we were free to write what we pleased. We had no occasion to search into musty records, to hunt up royal parchments, or to investigate the laws and institutions of a semi-barbarous ancestry. We appealed to those of nature, and found them engraved on our hearts. Yet we did not avail ourselves of all the advantages of our position. We had never been permitted to exercise self-government. When forced to assume it, we were novices in its science. Its principles and forms had entered little into our former education. We established however some, although not all its important principles. The constitutions of most of our States assert, that all power is inherent in the people; that they may exercise it by themselves, in all cases to which they think themselves competent, (as in electing their functionaries executive and legislative, and deciding by a jury of themselves, in all judiciary cases in which any fact is involved,) or they may act by representatives, freely and equally chosen; that it is their right and duty to be at all times armed; that they are entitled to freedom of person, freedom of religion, freedom of property, and freedom of the press. In the structure of our legislatures, we think experience has proved the benefit of subjecting questions to two separate bodies of deliberants; but in constituting these, natural right has been mistaken, some making one of these bodies, and some both, the representatives of property instead of persons; whereas the double deliberation might be as well obtained without any violation of true principle, either by requiring a greater age in one of the bodies, or by electing a proper number of representatives of persons, dividing them by lots into two chambers, and renewing the division at frequent intervals, in order to break up all cabals. Virginia, of which I am myself a native and resident, was not only the first of the States, but, I believe I may say, the first of the nations of the earth, which assembled its wise men peaceably together to form a fundamental constitution, to commit it to writing, and place it among their archives, where every one should be free to appeal to its text. But this act was very imperfect. The other States, as they proceeded successively to the same work, made successive improvements; and several of them, still further corrected by experience, have, by conventions, still further amended their first forms. My own State has gone on so far with its *premiere ebauche;* but it is now proposing to call a convention for amendment. Among other improvements, I hope they will adopt the subdivision of our counties into wards. The former may be estimated at an average of twenty-four miles square; the latter should be about six miles square each, and would answer to the hundreds of your Saxon Alfred. In each of these might be, 1. An elementary school. 2. A company of militia, with its officers. 3. A justice of the peace and constable. 4. Each ward should take care of their own poor. 5. Their own roads. 6. Their own police. 7. Elect within themselves one or more jurors to attend the courts of justice. And 8. Give in at their Folk-house, their votes for all functionaries reserved to their election. Each ward would thus be a small republic within itself, and every man in the State would thus become an acting member of the common government, transacting in person a great portion of its rights and duties, subordinate indeed, yet important, and entirely within his competence. The wit of man cannot devise a more solid basis for a free, durable and well administered republic.

With respect to our State and federal governments, I do not think their relations correctly understood by foreigners. They generally suppose the former subordinate to the latter. But this is not the case. They are co-ordinate departments of one simple and integral whole. To the State governments are reserved all legislation and administration, in affairs which concern their own citizens only, and to the federal government is given whatever concerns foreigners, or the citizens of other States; these functions alone being made federal. The one is the domestic, the other the foreign branch of the same government; neither having control over the other, but within its own department. There are one or two exceptions only to this partition of power. But, you may ask, if the two departments should claim each the same subject of power, where is the common umpire to decide ultimately between them? In cases of little importance or urgency, the prudence of both parties will keep them aloof from the questionable ground: but if it can neither be avoided nor compromised, a convention of the States must be called, to ascribe the doubtful power to that department which they may think best. You will perceive by these details, that we have not yet so far perfected our constitutions as to venture to make them unchangeable. But still, in their present state, we consider them not otherwise changeable than by the authority of the people, on a special election of representatives for that purpose expressly: they are until then the *lex legum.*

But can they be made unchangeable? Can one generation bind another, and all others, in succession forever? I think not. The Creator has made the earth for the living, not the dead. Rights and powers can only belong to persons, not to things, not to mere matter, unendowed with will. The dead are not even things. The particles of matter which composed their bodies, make part now of the bodies of other animals, vegetables, or minerals, of a thousand forms. To what then are attached the rights and powers they held while in the form of men? A generation may bind itself as long as its majority continues in life; when that has disappeared, another majority is in place, holds all the rights and powers their predecessors once held, and may change their laws and institutions to suit themselves. Nothing then is unchangeable but the inherent and unalienable rights of man....

❧

THE ADVANCE OF CIVILIZATION
To William Ludlow, September 6, 1824

... The idea which you present in your letter of July 30th, of the progress of society from its rudest state to that it has now attained, seems conformable to what may be probably conjectured. Indeed, we have under our eyes tolerable proofs of it. Let a philosophic observer commence a journey from the savages of the Rocky Mountains, eastwardly towards our sea-coast. These he would observe in the earliest stage of association living under no law but that of nature, subscribing and covering themselves with the flesh and skins of wild beasts. He would next find those on our frontiers in the pastoral state, raising domestic animals to supply the defects of hunting. Then succeed our own semi-barbarous citizens, the pioneers of the advance of civilization, and so in his progress he would meet the gradual shades of improving man until he would reach his, as yet, most improved state in our seaport towns. This, in fact, is equivalent to a survey, in time, of the progress of man from the infancy of creation to the present day. I am eighty-one years of age, born where I now live, in the first range of mountains in the interior of our country. And I have observed this march of civilization advancing from the sea coast, passing over us like a cloud of light, increasing our knowledge and improving our condition, insomuch as that we are at this time more advanced in civilization here than the seaports were when I was a boy. And where this progress will stop no one can say....

A Government Curriculum

Minutes of the Board of Visitors, University of Virginia, March 4, 1825

... A resolution was moved and agreed to in the following words:

Whereas, it is the duty of this Board to the government under which it lives, and especially to that of which this University is the immediate creation, to pay especial attention to the principles of government which shall be inculcated therein, and to provide that none shall be inculcated which are incompatible with those on which the Constitutions of this State, and of the United States were genuinely based, in the common opinion; and for this purpose it may be necessary to point out specially where these principles are to be found legitimately developed:

Resolved, that it is the opinion of this Board that as to the general principles of liberty and the rights of man, in nature and in society, the doctrines of Locke, in his "Essay concerning the true original extent and end of civil government," and of Sidney in his "Discourses on government," may be considered as those generally approved by our fellow citizens of this, and the United States, and that on the distinctive principles of the government of our State, and of that of the United States, the best guides are to be found in, 1. The Declaration of Independence, as the fundamental act of union of these States. 2. The book known by the title of "The Federalist," being an authority to which appeal is habitually made by all, and rarely declined or denied by any as evidence of the general opinion of those who framed, and of those who accepted the Constitution of the United States, on questions as to its genuine meaning. 3. The Resolutions of the General Assembly of Virginia in 1799 on the subject of the alien and sedition laws, which appeared to accord with the predominant sense of the people of the United States. 4. The valedictory address of President Washington, as conveying political lessons of peculiar value. And that in the branch of the school of law, which is to treat on the subject of civil polity, these shall be used as the text and documents of the school....

Last Letter: Apotheosis of Liberty
To Roger C. Weightman, June 24, 1826

... The kind invitation I receive from you, on the part of the citizens of the city of Washington, to be present with them at their celebration on the fiftieth anniversary of American Independence, as one of the surviving signers of an instrument pregnant with our own, and the fate of the world, is most flattering to myself, and heightened by the honorable accompaniment proposed for the comfort of such a journey. It adds sensibly to the sufferings of sickness, to be deprived by it of a personal participation in the rejoicings of that day. But acquiescence is a duty, under circumstances not placed among those we are permitted to control. I should, indeed, with peculiar delight, have met and exchanged there congratulations personally with the small band, the remnant of that host of worthies, who joined with us on that day, in the bold and doubtful election we were to make for our country, between submission or the sword; and to have enjoyed with them the consolatory fact, that our fellow citizens, after half a century of experience and prosperity, continue to approve the choice we made. May it be to the world, what I believe it will be, (to some parts sooner, to others later, but finally to all,) the signal of arousing men to burst the chains under which monkish ignorance and superstition had persuaded them to bind themselves, and to assume the blessings and security of self-government. That form which we have substituted, restores the free right to the unbounded exercise of reason and freedom of opinion. All eyes are opened, or opening, to the rights of man. The general spread of the light of science has already laid open to every view the palpable truth, that the mass of mankind has not been born with saddles on their backs, nor a favored few booted and spurred, ready to ride them legitimately, by the grace of God. These are grounds of hope for others. For ourselves, let the annual return of this day forever refresh our recollections of these rights, and an undiminished devotion to them....